Utopia and Terror in The 20th Century
Part II

Professor Vejas Gabriel Liulevicius

THE TEACHING COMPANY ®

PUBLISHED BY:

THE TEACHING COMPANY
4151 Lafayette Center Drive, Suite 100
Chantilly, Virginia 20151-1232
1-800-TEACH-12
Fax—703-378-3819
www.teach12.com

ISBN 1-56585-687-2

Vejas Gabriel Liulevicius, Ph.D.

Associate Professor of History, University of Tennessee

Vejas Gabriel Liulevicius was born in Chicago, Illinois. He grew up on Chicago's Southside in a Lithuanian-American neighborhood and spent some years attending school in Aarhus, Denmark, and Bonn, Germany. He received his B.A. from the University of Chicago. In 1989, he spent the summer in Moscow and Leningrad (today St. Petersburg) in intensive language study in Russian. He earned his Ph.D. from the University of Pennsylvania in European history in 1994, specializing in modern German history.

After receiving his doctorate, Professor Liulevicius spent a year as a postdoctoral research fellow at the Hoover Institution on War, Peace, and Revolution at Stanford University in Palo Alto, California. Since 1995, he has been a history professor at the University of Tennessee in Knoxville. He teaches courses on modern German history, Western civilization, Nazi Germany, World War I, war and culture, 20th-century Europe, nationalism, and utopian thought. In 2003, he received the University of Tennessee's Excellence in Teaching award.

Professor Liulevicius's research focuses on German relations with Eastern Europe in the modern period. His other interests include the utopian tradition and its impact on modern politics, images of the United States abroad, and the history of Lithuania and the Baltic region. He has published numerous articles and his first book, *War Land on the Eastern Front: Culture, National Identity and German Occupation in the First World War* (2000), published by Cambridge University Press, also appeared in German translation in 2002. His next project is a larger study of German stereotypes of Eastern Europeans and ideas of a special German cultural mission in the East over the last two centuries.

Professor Liulevicius lives in Knoxville, Tennessee, with his wife, Kathleen.

Table of Contents

Utopia and Terror in the 20th Century
Part II

Utopia and Terror in the 20th Century

Scope:

Our course examines a fundamental question of our times: Why was the 20th century so violent? This terrible century saw bloodletting on an unprecedented scale. Scholars estimate that around the globe, wars cost more than 40 million lives, while government-sponsored persecutions, mass murder, and genocide accounted for 170 million victims.

Viewing the past century as a whole, this course examines the ideologies that promised utopias and total solutions to social problems (Fascism, Nazism, Communism, and others), and relates the terrible human toll of attempts to realize these blueprints. Such ideologies functioned as political religions, commanding faith and fanatical adherence and promising salvation. At the same time, the ideological regimes were an emphatically modern phenomenon, using new technology, the capabilities of the modern state, and sophisticated methods of control. The four elements making up such a regime were masses, machines, mobsters, and master plans. Masses of people to organize and the machinery of social control were the means by which a movement came to prominence. Within the regime, a mobster elite of political criminals functioned as leaders, following a master plan laying out an ideological blueprint for the future. Terror would be used to shape the intractable human material to fit the ambitions of the ideological movement.

Our course discusses how these elements came together, taking different forms and variations over the course of the 20th century. To begin with, the revolutionary legacies of the 18th and 19th centuries are examined, showing the utopian hopes vested in technological and social progress. At the same time, political philosophies that saw conflict as the motor of progress are noted. World War I had a massive brutalizing effect, inaugurating the phenomenon of *total war* and militarizing and mobilizing entire societies. Civilians were increasingly the targets of this war, most cruelly in the first modern genocide, the Armenian massacres of 1915. Total war also led to total revolution, as radical Socialists directed by Lenin took power in Russia in 1917 and established a new Soviet regime, championing a global revolution. In the aftermath of World War I, aftershocks of the war continued in an unsettled political landscape. Millions of refugees were uprooted, civil wars raged in many countries, and the fortunes of democracy were battered.

In the Soviet Union, an elaborate Communist dictatorship emerged, built up by Josef Stalin, the "Man of Steel," at a massive cost in lives, as in the Gulag state camp system. The utopian outlines of the new Soviet civilization are examined. In Italy, Fascists came to power under Benito Mussolini, proclaiming slogans of order, unity, and absolute state power. The decade of the 1930s saw gathering storm clouds in international politics, with the Japanese rampage in China, the Italian invasion of Ethiopia, the Spanish Civil War, and a growing pessimism in culture and thought. In Germany, the Nazi Party, led by Adolf Hitler, promised a racial utopia, reordering German society with brutal means and the persecution of a minority group, German Jews. Unleashed by Hitler with help from Stalin, World War II brought a further escalation of total war and violence directed against civilians. The Nazis' program of racial murder of the Jews, the murderously efficient "final solution," unfolded against the background of ambitious future plans for domination.

No sooner had World War II ended than a new global ideological confrontation emerged, the Cold War. In China, Chairman Mao's Communists came to power and, over the next decades, launched campaigns to reconstruct Chinese society fundamentally, no matter the cost. An even more radical project was put into effect in nearby Cambodia, where the Khmer Rouge revolutionaries, under the elusive Pol Pot, abolished cities, eliminated perceived enemies among the ordinary people, and caused the death of a quarter of the population. During the Cold War, Communist regimes took differing forms; the cases of isolated North Korea, seemingly efficient East Germany, and the formidable Soviet Union are examined.

At the end of the 20th century, even with democratic revolutions taking place in Eastern Europe and Russia, darker trends also emerged. In Yugoslavia, Slobodan Milosevic pressed "ethnic cleansing" as a way to achieve his goal of a "Greater Serbia." In Africa, a renewed genocide occurred in Rwanda, as the Hutu government masterminded a carefully planned slaughter of the Tutsi minority. In the Middle East, Saddam Hussein's regime championed the ideological precepts of Ba'athism and sought and used weapons of mass destruction, including chemical arms used against Iraq's Kurdish minority.

At its conclusion, the course poses the question of the future of terror, assessing the role of terrorism in the world at present and what lessons have been learned by the hard experience of this past century. Throughout the narrative of these tragedies, the lectures also point out individuals who resisted these inhuman trends, acting as remarkable witnesses to the century, dissenting from its violent course, often at great personal cost. Their examples represent a hopeful conclusion.

Lecture Thirteen
Nazism

Scope:

This lecture surveys the origins of the Nazi movement, its ideological roots, and its rise to power in Germany. All of these were linked to the brutalizing legacies of World War I. In many ways, the mobilization for total war would be a model the Nazis strove to recreate on coming to power in 1933. The brown-shirted gangsters gathered into the SA storm-troop units saw themselves as "political soldiers," and they were led by a former soldier, Adolf Hitler. This lecture examines the Nazi worldview and its promises for fundamentally reordering German society along racial lines after 1933, fusing terror with modernizing programs for superhighways, superweapons, and supermen.

Outline

I. Origins of Nazism.

    A. Effects of World War I.

        1. The war's destructive impact laid the groundwork for the emergence of the Nazi movement in Germany and informed its ideology.

        2. Defeat in 1918 left many ordinary Germans embittered, unable to accept the fact of failure.

        3. Faith in the democratic Weimar Republic was undermined by its association with defeat; the Versailles Treaty, universally condemned in German society; and economic hardship. In spite of a period of stability from 1924–1929, German democracy remained fragile.

        4. Nationalists propagated the "stab-in-the-back legend."

        5. In the postwar turmoil, a small new party, the German Workers' Party (DAP), was established in Munich in January 1919 by Nationalists who had also been active earlier in the Fatherland Party, one among hundreds of such groups in Germany.

        6. In September 1919, a DAP meeting was visited by a soldier, Adolf Hitler, who soon became a member and, by 1921, became chairman. At his urging, the party renamed itself the National Socialist German Workers' Party (NSDAP).

B. Hitler as an "unknown soldier" of the Great War.
1. The obscure Hitler presented himself as the embodiment of unknown trench soldiers. Hitler aimed to be a "drummer" summoning a new political coalition to do away with democracy.
2. Because of his skills in oratory, as well as organization and propaganda, Hitler himself became ever more crucial to the Nazis, often called the "Hitler movement." Followers called him *Führer*, "leader."
3. In urban legend, Hitler's oratorical skills were ascribed to his being gassed in the trenches.

C. SA: Nazi storm troopers.
1. Nazi organization and ritual were permeated with influences of World War I, most clearly in the case of the SA (*Sturmabteilung*), storm troopers organized in 1921 as a police arm of the party. These brown-shirted thugs also drew inspiration from Italian Fascist Blackshirts.
2. The SA grew out of a wider milieu of thugs in Germany. More than a million men belonged to paramilitary organizations in Germany in 1919–1920.
3. The leadership prided itself on a gangster style. Ernst Röhm, a former *Freikorps* captain, led the SA.

D. The Beer Hall *putsch*.
1. In imitation of Mussolini's March on Rome, on November 8, 1923, Hitler launched a march on Berlin.
2. The revolt ended in failure and a treason trial, which Hitler exploited to win a media victory, crucial to relaunching the party in 1925 on his release from prison.

II. Nazi ideology.
A. Ideological core.
1. The core ideas were racism and anti-Semitism. Hitler's Social Darwinist worldview saw constant race war and struggle for *Lebensraum* ("living space").
2. Conscious application of racial strategies and embrace of natural conflict was presented as the key to history.
3. Nazism posited a superior "Aryan" race, embodying creativity and health, juxtaposed with demonized stereotypes of Jews, depicted as parasites, contaminating

influences, and eternal enemies. Germans were supposedly the purest remnants of original Aryans.

B. Nazis promised creation of a true racial unity, *Volksgemeinschaft*, or "people's community." This racial utopia would be achieved by purification and consolidation of Germany within, elimination of Jews, and aggressive expansion.

C. Other elements of Nazism included opposition to democracy, Marxism (though Nazis claimed to represent true German Socialism), pacifism, individualism, capitalism, rationality, and intellectuals. Influenced by World War I, the Nazis valued a strong state, military mobilization, and war.

III. The rise to power.

  A. Organizational work.

    1. In prison, Hitler dictated his manifesto, *Mein Kampf* (*"My Struggle"*), presenting a "legal route to power," creating a mass party, and discussing remarkably innovative ideas on the use of manipulative propaganda.

    2. Nazis outdid other parties in organization and intensive activity. They set up a nationwide party network in imitation of Communist Party cells.

    3. Yet Nazis gained less than three percent of the vote in the 1928 parliamentary elections.

    4. The Great Depression sped their way to power. The Weimar democracy was already moribund even before 1933.

    5. In the 1930 breakthrough election, the Nazis became the second largest party, a mass movement.

    6. In the July 1932 elections, they became the largest party in Germany.

  B. Propaganda.

    1. Nazi mass meetings generated excitement and an image of dynamism. In 1932, the Nazis organized up to 3000 meetings every day nationwide.

    2. They used modern technology, including airplanes, to orchestrate their campaigns.

    3. The image of the youthfulness of Nazi Party members and activists was another important feature of their self-image.

4. Coordinated marching masses were to have an exhilarating effect.

C. Polarization.

  1. Marxist parties, the Social Democrats, and the German Communist Party did not cooperate against Nazism.

  2. The Comintern, following Stalin's orders, directed German Communists to denounce Social Democrats as "Social Fascists." In the coming struggle, Communists were confident of being able to pick up the pieces after the collapse of the Nazis and their Social Democratic rivals, as reflected in the slogan, "After Hitler—Us."

  3. By contrast, Nazis presented themselves to Germans as the only alternative to Communism, now that democracy had failed.

  4. Curiously, a reciprocal antagonistic relationship emerged between the Nazis and Communists in this crisis.

D. Coming to power.

  1. Ironically, in spite of Hitler's ambitions to come to power through the ballot box, the Nazis came to power in January 1933 through backroom intrigue.

  2. In the November 1932 elections, the Nazis were stunned to see their vote dip, suggesting ebbing support.

  3. Nonetheless, on January 30, 1933, Hitler became chancellor, in coalition with conservative Nationalists who planned to manipulate him.

IV. The worldview in power.

A. Nazification: *Gleichschaltung*.

  1. Once in power, Hitler outflanked his conservative Nationalist allies by securing control of police forces and, after the Reichstag fire on February 27, passage of an Enabling Act on March 23, 1933, which gave Hitler control of legal authority.

  2. In the six months following their seizure of power, Nazis pursued the policy of *Gleichschaltung*, or "coordination to consolidate control." They purged the civil service, outlawed other political parties, shut down labor unions, and terrorized political opponents.

B. The promise of *Volksgemeinschaft*.

1. The Nazis vowed to create a national community of solidarity in which "the common good comes before individual good."
2. Their striving for total power was presented as a transcendence of earlier divisions.
3. In the August 1934 plebiscite, 85 percent of voters approved the Nazi regime.

C. The use of terror.
1. The Nazis made open use of terror in quelling resistance or challenges. In 1934, the SA consisted of four million men.
2. Concentration camps were established openly, not hidden, supposedly for "reeducation" and "protective custody." A "model camp" was established in March 1933 in Dachau, which was later imitated widely.
3. In spite of their brutality, these camps were not yet places of mass murder, but they prefigured the later horror of the death camps.

D. Building the future.
1. The Nazis announced the rebuilding of Germany with vast public works projects, including *Autobahn* superhighways. The *Volkswagen*, "people's car," was planned for the future, while rearmament began.
2. In 1936, the Four-Year Plan was announced, in imitation of Stalin's industrialization drives.
3. By 1939, the regime boasted full employment.

E. Nazifying society.
1. Nazi propaganda urged an idealized utopia of a united *Volk*, with images of shared meals of communal stew (*Eintopf*) or winter relief campaigns.
2. To shape opinion, in March 1933, the Ministry of Popular Enlightenment and Propaganda was established, led by Josef Goebbels (1897–1945), a propaganda mastermind, exemplified by his earlier "Ten Commandments for National Socialists."
3. The regime subsidized production of millions of *Volkssender*, "people's radios," and set up thousands of loudspeaker pillars in public places throughout Germany.

4. The regime intervened in the family. Women's chief role was to be breeders of new soldiers, and medals were awarded for large numbers of children, as in the Soviet Union.

5. Special attention was given to young people. Ritual burning of books showed the downgrading of traditional humanistic education, replaced with induction of boys into the Hitler Youth for military training and girls into the League of German Maidens.

F. Nazi German language.

1. German-Jewish philologist Victor Klemperer, famed for his diaries, made a study of Nazi perversion of the German language.

2. A witness to these times, he observed with horror the transvaluation of such terms as *fanaticism* into highest praise.

G. Racial persecution.

1. In the racial utopia promised by the Nazis, solidarity was also defined against those labeled as outsiders (German Jews, gypsies, Slavs, homosexuals, and other minorities).

2. The Nazi state attacked these groups with growing radicalism.

Essential Reading:

Michael Burleigh and Wolfgang Wippermann, *The Racial State: Germany 1933–1945*.

Peter Fritzsche, *Germans into Nazis*.

George L. Mosse, *The Crisis of German Ideology: Intellectual Origins of the Third Reich*.

Supplementary Reading:

Victor Klemperer, *The Language of the Third Reich: lti—Lingua Tertii Imperii: A Philologist's Notebook.*

Questions to Consider:

1. Which Nazi promises were most appealing to ordinary Germans?

2. How were the Nazis able to turn the German language to their ideological purposes?

Lecture Thirteen—Transcript
Nazism

In our previous lecture, we examined the darkening storm clouds over Europe, over much of the world, over the course of the troubled decade of the 1930s. In today's lecture, we'll examine one very prominent feature of that trajectory: The rise of the disturbing movement of Nazism in Germany.

In this lecture, we'll be examining the origins, the ideological beliefs, and rise to power of the Nazi movement in Germany. As we'll see, many of the origins for this phenomena lay even further back than the 1930s, troubled as they were: The legacy of the First World War.

We will discuss, in particular, the Nazi worldview, and its promises for a fundamental reordering of German society along racial lines, after coming to power in 1933, their fusing of terror with modernizing programs for superhighways, super weapons, and super men, in the promise of a German utopia.

We turn, first of all, to the question of the origins of Nazism. One particular point that we want to underline is just how much these origins owed to the effects of that first great war, World War I. Time and again, we see that the features of the Nazi movement, and its ideology, tie back to roots in the First World War. The impact of that war on culture, politics, and society, truly lay the groundwork for the emergence of the Nazi movement in Germany, and crucially informed its ideology.

Some historians have traced back the energies, the mobilization of the masses that the Nazis sought, to those days at the start of the First World War, or the so-called "August madness," in which, in a moment of ecstasy which was supposed to overcome the earlier divisions in society, Germans had allegedly felt lifted up into a sense of national unity and national purpose. The analyst, whom we have discussed in earlier lectures, of the dynamics of crowds, and of masses, Elias Canetti, had already written in his book, *Crowds of Power*, that in some sense, the national Socialist movement, began, not nearly in 1919 with the formal founding of the party that became the Nazi Party, but began, in fact, in those August days of 1914. He argued that Hitler and the Nazis, ever after, would seek to reclaim or re-create by artifice, that emotion that Germans had supposedly felt in 1914.

It was following upon such a sense of national mobilization that defeat had hit Germany particularly hard in 1918. Many ordinary Germans were left embittered, unable to accept the fact of failure, and historians of Germany are emphasizing ever more strongly today that it was not the harshness of the postwar settlement that was crucial in setting Germany upon its troubled path in the years after 1918, but rather the fundamental inability of ordinary Germans to accept defeat. This had crucial consequences. Faith in the democratic Weimar Republic, as it was called, after the town of Weimar in which the constitution of this new democracy was written, was crucially undermined by those things that it was associated with in the minds of Germans. It was associated with German defeat, what Germans denounced as the Versailles Treaty, universally condemned in German society, and a legacy of economic hardship, carrying over from the dislocations of the First World War.

In spite of a period of stability from 1924 to 1929, German democracy still remained fragile. German Nationalists had an explanation for what they saw as the humiliation of their nation. They propagated what came to be called the "stab-in-the-back legend," which claimed that in fact German armies had not been defeated on the battlefield, but that Germany's war effort had been betrayed by forces on the homefront. In a sort of scapegoating of minorities in German society, it was claimed that German democrats, German Socialists, and in particular, a religious minority, German Jews were responsible.

In the postwar turmoil of Germany, a small new party, calling itself the German Workers' Party, its acronym was the DAP, was established in turmoil-filled Munich in the south, in January of 1919, by Nationalists who had earlier been active in the German war effort and had earlier been active in the Fatherland Party, established to bolster German morale, in the last stages of the First World War. This small group was just one among hundreds of such radical, small groups in German society. However, it was destined for a different fate than those of the small parties that tended to fade with time. In part, this was due to chance.

In September of 1919, one meeting of this German Workers' Party was visited by a then-unknown soldier by the name of Adolf Hitler. The German army, as part of its intelligence-gathering operations, had charged him to collect information on such small political gatherings. He soon became a member, I'm pretty sure, even though the observers were not supposed to do this, and soon had a meteoric rise within the party. By 1921, he was the party's chairman. At his urging, the party renamed itself, taking on the name National Socialist German Workers' Party. It was known by its full acronym, NSDAP, or for short, as the Nazi Party.

That very name was significant. The words "national" and "German" tended to appeal to Nationalist conservatives, while the words "socialist" and "worker" tended to appeal to those on the left side of the spectrum. With this very name announced, it was a crucial attribute of this young radical movement, the attempt to reach out to a broad constituency in German society, promising something for everyone. Hitler was in process of remaking this party in his own image.

The very figure of Hitler would be crucial in this context. Hitler presented himself, and was presented through the propaganda of the young Nazi party as the "unknown soldier," who had emerged from the trenches of the Great War, transformed by that experience, carrying a message of renewed greatness to a humiliated nation.

The obscure man, Hitler, presented himself as the embodiment of all those millions of unknown trench soldiers, who had experienced the fighting on the Western front. Hitler's own conception of his role changed over time. He had at first seen himself as, he put it, a "drummer," summoning a new political coalition, a group of forces opposed with democracy in Germany, to do away with the democratic experiment.

Over time, however, he would come to see himself not simply as a summoner of energies, but as the prime leader himself. Due to his skills in oratory, as well as that organization, and the hard work of propaganda, Hitler himself became ever more crucial to the fortunes of the Nazi movement. Indeed, very often among ordinary Germans, as the Nazi movement gained prominence, it was often called the "Hitler movement." Hitler's followers began to call him by a very messianic title, the *Führer*, the "leader," a man of destiny.

In urban legend, Hitler's oratorical skills were ascribed to his experiences in the First World War. Supposedly having been gassed in the trenches of that conflict, it had done something to his vocal cords, had changed the nature of his voice, had given it a hypnotic quality.

Well, this was urban legend, speculation, the sort of supernatural myth that would surround the figure of Hitler in the expectations vested in him. What was indisputable and true was the Hitler clearly knew his audience. He was able to speak to their deepest fears and desires. He himself explained that he saw himself as channeling his audience's innermost feelings and convictions. He was careful to take the pulse of the crowd, and tell that crowd what it wanted to hear. This was the reality of his oratorical skills.

Another crucial element in the Nazis' rise to power was also calculated use of terror. In particular, Nazi storm troopers, called the SA, were the enforcers of this terror on the streets of German towns and cities.

Nazi organization and ritual within the party was permeated with the influences of that great experience of the First World War. This was most clearly the case when we examine the storm troopers, the *Sturmabteilung*, or SA, as it was called.

They were organized in 1921 as the political arm of the party. They saw themselves as political soldiers. Essentially, however, they were thugs, dressed in brown-shirted uniforms. They drew their inspiration from Mussolini's Italian Fascist black-shirt movement, and indeed it was clear that they imitated this effective model. It was joked that the time that indeed Hitler had sought black shirts for his storm troopers, but that the stores had been out of them at that time. There had been a sale on brown shirts, hence the uniforms.

It was joked at the time that in one characteristic of the party after another, in its ritual and symbols, one could see very clearly the tremendous debt that Hitler, as a would-be dictator, owed to Mussolini and his Italian Fascists, from the Roman salute to the imitation of the shirts for the thuggish storm troopers. It was joked that Hitler could visit Italy in the future, and would then have to hail his earlier patron, or the man he'd modeled himself on, Mussolini, with the words "Hail Emperor," or "Hail to the Emperor." The joked then continued that Mussolini is would have to answer, "Hail Imitator," or "Hail, you Imitator," of Mussolini's own tactics.

The storm troopers of the SA grew out of a wider, thuggish milieu in the troubled German society. More than a million men had belonged to the paramilitary organizations of the Freikorps that had arisen in defeated Germany in 1919 to 1920, and many such men were sluiced into the storm troopers ranks.

The storm troopers leadership prided itself on a gangster style, on their toughness, indeed, on their brutal violence. A man who excelled at this, of course, a former *freikorps* captain, Ernst Röhm, was the leader of the SA. He now pursued what he thought was a clear and determined plan for power. It was to be an imitation of Mussolini's own tactics that had been successful in Italy. He aimed to imitate Mussolini's March on Rome, in an incident that has come to be called by the faintly ridiculous name of the Beer Hall *putsch*.

Imitating Mussolini's determined march on Rome, Hitler aimed to start a march on Berlin, on November 8, 1923. This was something out of a comic opera. The storm troopers didn't even make it out of downtown Munich in their march on Berlin, as the police fired on them, and the marchers scattered. This revolt ended in failure, but what followed was key in the rise of Hitler. At the treason trial, Hitler, in part due to sympathetic judges, exploited this opportunity to win a media victory, turning the tables on the German democracy that was putting him on trial. His name now gained national resonance, and was crucial in relaunching the party in 1925, when he was released from his ludicrously short term in prison.

We now turn to examine the Nazi ideology that the Nazis championed. At its ideological core were the ideas of racism and anti-Semitism. Hitler had a brutal social Darwinist worldview that looked out on the world and saw a reality of constant struggle, and in fact, constant racial war, pitting peoples against peoples, races against races, as a constant struggle for survival. It was a struggle in part for *Lebensraum*, or "living space," in which a people could expand and grow.

Thus, the applications for the Nazis were obvious. One needed to consciously seek racial strategies, to embrace natural conflict that they understood as the key to history, in order to win triumph for the German people. The Nazis posited the existence of a superior race, which they aimed to recreate. This was the superior "Aryan" race. The Aryans, of which the Germans are supposed to be the finest surviving exemplars, though by no means pure themselves, were supposedly, in the stereotypes of the Nazis, champion: Blonde, tall, honest, good, and embodying all that was creative and healthy. Of necessity, they were juxtaposed with the demonic stereotype of the exact opposite. Those were the Jews, depicted by the Nazis as parasites, incapable of creating culture on their own, eternally contaminating influences upon other peoples, and by definition the eternal enemies of all that the Aryan race, for the Nazis, stood for.

The Germans were supposedly the purest remnants of the original Aryans, and would now have to be re-created. The Nazis promised the creation, within Germany, of a true racial unity. The charged term that they used for this idea was the *Volksgemeinschaft*, the "people's community." This was to be a racial utopia of rough egalitarianism among those who belonged to this racial unity. This racial utopia would be achieved by the purification and consolidation of the German people within, the elimination of the Jewish minority, and then aggressive expansion abroad.

Other elements of the Nazi ideology included opposition. Opposition to democracy, which was considered weak and individualistic; opposition to Marxism, though the Nazis claimed to represent a truer German socialism not based on materialism; opposition to pacifism, to individualism, which was considered self-serving; opposition to capitalism; opposition to what was called the "soulless rationality," and against the intellectual life.

Influenced by the model of mobilization of the masses that occurred in World War I, the Nazis valued a strong state, which stood above individuals, military mobilization, and war, which they considered the guarantee of the health of the nation. How was it that the Nazis championing this extreme ideology could come to power? In part, it was due to the hard work of organization, as they sought to come to power, using democracy to destroy democracy.

While in prison until 1925, Hitler had dictated a manifesto, which he called *Mein Kampf*. This might be translated as "*My Struggle*," "*My Battle*," or "*My War*." In it, in this otherwise unreadable book, full of bad prose and ludicrous ideas, Hitler did announce, in a prophetic way, his route to power. This was summed up as, the "legal route to power." Using the ballot box to come to power legally, and then to destroy German democracy, to enter Parliament and destroy it.

Hitler outlined his plans to create a mass party, and in the original sections of this book, he discussed remarkably innovative ideas on the use of manipulative propaganda to win the confidence of the masses.

The Nazis, motivated by their fanatical hatred of the system, outdid other parties in organization and intensive activity. In some cases, they borrowed models from their ideological enemies, the Communists, as when they set up a nationwide party network imitation of the Communist Party cells permeating other countries.

However, the Nazis were first disappointed by the results of their attempts to propagandize and mobilize Germany. They only gained less than three percent of the vote in 1928 parliamentary elections. The true opportunity would come with crisis, the crisis of the Great Depression.

From 1929 on, the Great Depression, destroying developed industrial economies and hitting the United States and Germany especially hard, sped the Nazis' way to power in Germany.

Weimar democracy, as historians have pointed out, was already often in a bad way, perhaps even moribund, before the Nazis came to power in 1933. From 1930 on, Parliament was hard put to pass effective legislation.

In the 1930 election, the Nazis scored a breakthrough success, becoming the second-largest party, a true mass movement within German society. In the July 1932 elections, they built on this success, becoming the largest party in Germany. That dream of Hitler, of the legal route to power, seemed almost within their grasp.

We want to briefly outline some of the remarkably innovative means of Nazis propaganda. Above all, these included mass meetings. These meets were supposed to be a vivid symbol of the gathering together of Germans into the people's community, or the *Volksgemeinschaft*. They generated an image of excitement and of dynamism for the Nazi party.

In 1932, the Nazis organized up to 3000 meetings every day nationwide, in the large German cities as well as small towns and villages. The Nazis used modern technology, including airplanes, to orchestrate their campaigns. They were also aided by another feature of the Nazi party's self-image, and that was the image of the youthfulness of this movement.

The youthfulness of Nazi party members and activists was another crucial element in selling the Nazi movement to Germans at large. The average age of a new member of the Nazi party in the course of the 1920s was 29 years. Compared to the relatively older demographic of established German parties, this was striking for its youthfulness. Again and again, the Nazis emphasized one symbol of their movement: Coordinated marching of masses, of true believers, of storm troopers, that were intended to have an exhilarating effect. The Nazi movement anthem stressed that the storm troopers were on the march; Germany was on the march towards a Nazi future.

The Nazis were also aided in their rise to power through the remarkable polarization of German politics. Within German politics, the Marxist parties of the left, the Social Democrats, and the German Communist Party, who might otherwise have cooperated to stop to rise of Nazism were, in fact, bitter rivals. The Comintern, the Communist international organization, following Stalin's orders, had directed the German Communist Party to denounce the Social Democrats as nothing better than "Social Fascists." They argued that in the coming struggle, German Communists were confident of being able to pick up the pieces after the collapse of German democracy, after the collapse of the Nazi movement, and after the collapse of the social democratic rivals.

The Communist slogan, which as we now know was self-deluding, was "After Hitler—Us." The Communists hoped to come to power. Thus, opportunity was lost to forestall the Nazis' rise to prominence.

By contrast, in this remarkably fragmented, polarized German political scene, the Nazis presented themselves in a remarkably self-serving way as the only party the reached out to the broad masses of German society, the only party that was a natural alternative to Communism now that democracy had failed.

Curiously, indeed, while these parties were ideologically at loggerheads, a strange, reciprocal, antagonistic relationship emerged between the Nazis and the Communists in this crisis. They both hoped to benefit from the collapse of German democracy, and they both, in practice, cooperated to make the German parliament impossible.

Moreover, the Nazis were very proud of opportunities to win followers from the Communists, feeling that this was a true symbol of their promise to own the future by winning over such former true believers.

The Nazis would now come to power. Ironically, in spite of Hitler's ambitions to come to power through the ballot box, the Nazis, in fact, entered government in January of 1933 through backroom intrigues, not through a clear-cut election victory.

In the November 1932 elections, the Nazis were stunned and horrified to see their percentage of the vote dip, suggesting at long last that their growing support had peaked, and now was on the decline. Nonetheless, on January 30, 1933, Hitler became Chancellor in coalition and in cooperation with conservative Nationalists who had placed him in power, but who planned to manipulate him. He would end by manipulating them.

The Nazi worldview was now in power, and the Nazis would seek to Nazify German society through their policy called *Gleichschaltung*. Once in power, Hitler outflanked his conservative Nationalist allies by securing control of the police forces. Then, after the mysterious Reichstag fire on February 27, the so-called "enabling act" of March 23, 1933, sometimes called the "suicide note of the German Parliament", gave Hitler legal control of authority in Germany. This impression of legality would be important in the Nazi's' consolidation of power.

In the following six months, the Nazis pursued their policy of *Gleichschaltung*, which might be translated as "coordination" or "consolidation" of control, to Nazify Germany. They purged the civil service, outlawed other political parties, shut down labor unions, and relentlessly terrorized political opponents.

At the same time, they promised the *Volksgemeinschaft*, the "people's community", was supposedly coming into being. This was to be a community of solidarity, in which it was said "the common good would come before the individual good," an appealing slogan to many Germans. The Nazis' striving for total power was presented as a transcendence of earlier divisions. In the August 1934 plebiscite, not an election, but a poll, as it were, the German people, 85 percent of the voters approved the Nazi regime. It was not a free election, but nonetheless it was a measure of how the Nazis felt about the legitimacy given to their regime.

At the same time, the Nazis made open use of terror to quell resistance or challenges. In 1934, the SA, the storm troopers, now consisted of four million men, a formidable force. The established concentration camps openly throughout Germany, not hidden. They announced that the camps' purpose was supposedly the "reeducation," or the "protective custody" of those who had opposed the Nazi regime. A "model camp" was established in March of 1933 in Dachau, outside of Munich, which was later imitated widely throughout Germany, a model of terror.

In spite of their brutality, these concentration camps were not as yet places of mass murder, as the death camps of World War II would be, but they certainly prefigured them in their coordinated, calculated use of violence.

As this was going on, the Nazis announced that they were building the German future, rebuilding the country with vast public works projects, including the *autobahn* superhighway that one can still see in Germany today. The German people were promised that the *Volkswagen*, which one can also still see today, the "people's car," would allow the German people to enjoy a level of prosperity and equality of life that they had not known before. At the same time, however, rearmament began.

In 1936, in imitation of Stalin's industrialization drives, the so-called Four-Year Plan was announced, to ready Germany for prosperity and greatness on the international scene.

By 1939, the Nazi machine was boasting of full employment in Germany. For ordinary Germans, this certainly made the Nazi regime popular. Society was on its way to being Nazified. Nazi propaganda urged an idealized utopia of a united folk, working and acting together. The images that celebrated this were the common images of shared meals of communal stew, which is not very appetizing, perhaps, today, the so-called *eintopf*, or winter relief campaigns, in which charity was organized by the state.

To shape popular opinion, in March of 1933, the Ministry of Popular Enlightenment and Propaganda is established, led by Josef Goebbels. He was a Rhinelander, one of the few highly educated members of the Nazi elite, and a propaganda mastermind. His talents were exemplified by his earlier listing off of "Ten Commandments for

National Socialists," transmuting the religious impulse into political religion.

Moreover, the regime subsidized a particular piece of physical equipment, which was supposed to spread its message far and wide. This was the production of millions of so-called *volkssender*, or "people's radios," that were now proliferated throughout Germany in order to spread the message of the regime. At this point, Germany had the highest rate of radio ownership in the world. In this modern measure of a society's advancement, 70 percent of households in Germany had access to these radios. For those who did not, thousands of loudspeaker pillars, as they were called, were set up in public places throughout Germany, so that the booming voice of Hitler, the Führer, could be heard throughout the nation.

Goebbels announced that the radio would mediate to the masses, in this age of the masses. He announced that the Nazi revolution would not have been possible without the radio, and he aimed to use it for propaganda.

The regime also intervened energetically in the family. Women's chief role was now to be breeders of new soldiers, just as in the Soviet Union. Metals were awarded to women who were producing large numbers of children. They were hailed for their contribution to the national cause.

Special attention was also given to young people. They participated in the ritual burning of books, to show the downgrading of traditional education. This was now replaced with the induction of boys into the Hitler Youth for military training, and girls into the League of German Maidens, to take them out of the family, and instead, conduct the them into a Nazified society.

Finally, there was the Nazis' perverse triumph in Nazifying the German language itself. A German Jewish philologist, a student of language by the name of Victor Klemperer who survived the Nazi regime, has been famed in our present day for his diaries, which recorded his experiences. He also made a fascinating study of the Nazi perversion of the German language, which felt that this was one of their keys to power. He had the evidence of this ready to hand. He had been horrified to discover himself, an opponent of the Nazi regime, sometimes falling into their rhetorical phrases.

He observed with horror that the Nazis had turned terms that had earlier been negative, like "fanaticism," into the very highest praise of all. The Nazis also set about a program of racial persecution, to bring about their racial utopia. In their future, they promised racial solidarity, which was defined not simply by being German, but also by being against others, those who were labeled "outsiders." These included German Jews, gypsies, Slavs, homosexuals, and other minorities. The Nazi state would attack these groups with growing radicalism, and the man who steered these policies, Adolf Hitler, is the man we'll discuss in our next lecture.

Lecture Fourteen
Hitler

Scope:

This lecture illuminates the man behind the Nazi movement, indispensable to both its success and its growing radicalism, Adolf Hitler. His beginnings were obscure and unpromising, yet his mastery of techniques of political manipulation would make him *Führer*, "leader," of the German people. This lecture profiles the man and his distinctive characteristics as a dictator and considers the keys to his effectiveness, in particular his capability for boundlessly cynical propaganda. His long-range ideological goals were revealed in his foreign policy revolution, upsetting the postwar international order and the launching of programs for the racial persecution of the Jews.

Outline

I. The man.

    A. Youth.

        1. Hitler was born in 1889 to a middle class family in Braunau am Inn in Austria.

        2. His youth was unremarkable and directionless; he dropped out of high school to go to Vienna in 1907 to become an artist.

        3. After rejection by the Academy of Fine Arts, Hitler slipped into a Viennese netherworld of poverty. He claimed that this "down and out" period was decisive in his development.

        4. He soaked up the radical influences aswirl in the imperial capital: the populist anti-Semitism of Mayor Karl Lüger, racialism, the extreme Nationalism of the Pan-Germans, and the heroic artistic stances of Richard Wagner's operas.

        5. In spite of his personal failure, the arts and architecture would remain important to him.

    B. Hitler in the First World War.

        1. The coming of the war fired Hitler's imagination and finally gave him a sense of purpose and belonging. He was caught up in the August Madness in Munich and was captured on film.

2. Shortly after he evaded military service in Austria, Hitler volunteered for a German regiment. He served on the western front and earned a rare Iron Cross First Class.

3. While recovering at a hospital from being gassed, Hitler learned that Germany had sued for peace. He was devastated and underwent a breakdown, in the course of which he became convinced that he had a political mission to save Germany.

C. Launching a political career.

1. Remaining in the army even after the armistice, Hitler was sent to observe radical parties in Munich.

2. On visiting the German Workers' Party (DAP) in September 1919, he made a speech and was enrolled as a member.

3. By 1921, he had risen to the chairmanship of the party. Members called him the Führer.

4. Hitler renamed the party the National Socialist German Workers' Party (NSDAP), seeking to appeal across the political spectrum.

5. After the failed Beer Hall *putsch* of 1923, Hitler's "legal route to power" used Weimar democracy to destroy parliamentary government. Growing mass support and intrigue brought Hitler to the chancellorship in January 1933.

D. Psychological background.

1. Psychohistorians have sought to analyze Hitler's childhood or upbringing to account for his later role.

2. However, authoritarian childrearing common to the era or disappointed career goals alone obviously cannot explain Hitler.

II. The dictator.

A. Method to the madness.

1. Hitler's work methods were unsystematic and his delegation of authority, chaotic. His personal habits were eccentric, and he kept unusual hours.

2. Historians have referred to his duplication of authority as "bureaucratic Darwinism" and argue over whether this was a deliberate tactic or unconscious.
3. The outcome of his style of authority was a dynamic that favored radical solutions. Nazi followers spoke of "working towards the Führer."
4. Hitler's unsystematic approach has led some historians to suggest that he was a "weak dictator." In fact, in matters of ideological importance to him, Hitler always intervened effectively.

B. The cult of the Führer.
1. A carefully cultivated myth of Hitler as the infallible Führer of the Third Reich was deliberately constructed by Josef Goebbels.
2. It took on religious overtones, as did other imagery of the Third Reich.
3. This charismatic element included an erotic charge for some followers; to preserve this, Hitler's mistress, Eva Braun, was kept out of sight.
4. Letters from enthusiastic followers testified to the effective cult of the leader.
5. Remarkably, the leader cult also insulated Hitler himself from criticism, which was deflected onto the party and state, until nearly the end of his rule.

III. The keys to his effectiveness.
A. Underestimation.
1. Throughout his rise to power and once installed as dictator, Hitler repeatedly benefited from being underestimated and misunderstood.
2. Even movies, such as Charlie Chaplin's *The Great Dictator*, popularized a comic image at odds with his true menace.
3. In what Hitler considered the most perilous period of his plans, the consolidation of this rule and rearmament, he repeated claims that he desired nothing more than peace.

B. Ruthlessness.
1. Hitler also showed the readiness to use ruthless violence to achieve his ends, beyond bloodthirsty rhetoric.

2. This was made especially clear early on, on June 30, 1934, when scores of his own SA storm trooper leaders and other targets were murdered by the SS in the Night of the Long Knives (Stalin expressed his admiration).
3. In secret deliberations, such as those recorded in the 1937 Hossbach memorandum, Hitler charted an aggressive foreign policy of rearmament and future conquest.

C. SS as security.
1. After the 1934 purge, Heinrich Himmler's SS commenced a dramatic institutional growth, taking on ever larger responsibilities, becoming a pillar of the Nazi regime and a state within the state.
2. The SS carved out a special role in executing the racial initiatives of the Third Reich.

IV. The diplomatic revolution.
A. The foreign policy vision.
1. Hitler envisioned a new order in Europe and the world, with Germany holding a dominant position.
2. Following the ideas of geopolitics, Hitler believed in the paramount need for increased *Lebensraum*, or "living space," for the reconstituted German master race.
3. In this future order, small nations were to be eliminated, creating consolidated great power blocs.

B. Hitler's demands for revision of the Versailles Treaty were enthusiastically seconded by ordinary Germans, though his aggressive long-range plans were not yet revealed.

C. The Axis.
1. Mussolini coined this term in 1936 to describe the solidarity of Germany and Italy in a new era of changed alignments. Nazi Germany later signed the Pact of Steel with Italy in 1939.
2. In 1936, Hitler signed the anti-Comintern Pact with Japan, directed against Communism.

D. Appeasement.
1. Misunderstanding Hitler and determined to avoid a repetition of the world war, the Western democracies sought to meet Nazi Germany's demands.

2. Hitler systematically broke the Versailles Treaty's strictures and effected a diplomatic revolution: leaving the League of Nations, rearming Germany, moving troops into the Rhineland, and annexing Austria.

3. When Hitler prepared to move against Czechoslovakia over the Sudetenland border region, Britain and France gave in to Hitler's demand for the area at the September 29, 1938, Munich Conference. In March 1939, he nonetheless occupied the rest of the country.

4. Appeasement had failed in both political and moral terms.

V. Anti-Semitic programs.

   A. The longer European history of anti-Semitism.

      1. Centuries of religious anti-Semitism, discriminating against or abusing minority Jewish populations in Europe, were the background to the growth of a new variety of virulent hatred.

      2. Often called *radical racial anti-Semitism* or *biological anti-Semitism*, this Social Darwinist and racist ideology called not for conversion, but separation and elimination. The libelous "Protocols of the Elders of Zion," an 1890s forgery of the Russian Tsarist secret police, claimed a world conspiracy.

      3. The supposedly scientific nature of this new anti-Semitism and its promises of social integration caused it be labeled "Socialism for idiots."

   B. Nazi hatred in action.

      1. Historians debate how the Nazi regime reached the destination of genocide. Was the road to Auschwitz direct and premeditated from the first, or was it a twisted path?

      2. In this debate, *intentionalists* argue that the Nazis pursued a blueprint for genocide from the outset. *Functionalists* contend that the Nazi regime grew more radical in its policies over time.

      3. At first, the Nazis sought to encourage emigration of German Jews through intimidation and violence.

      4. The 1935 Nuremberg Laws took away the citizenship and rights of Jews and isolated them socially.

5. In the *Kristallnacht* of November 9, 1938, Jewish homes, synagogues, and businesses were attacked and Jews were arrested.

6. With the coming of World War II, forced emigration would be replaced with murderous policies.

Essential Reading:

Brigitte Hamann, *Hitler's Vienna: A Dictator's Apprenticeship.*

Ian Kershaw, *Hitler.*

Supplementary Reading:

Ian Kershaw, *The "Hitler Myth": Image and Reality in the Third Reich.*

Questions to Consider:

1. What aspects of Hitler's background and youth might be useful to the cult of the leader, and which ones might need to be hidden?

2. How did the cult of the Führer compare to the cult of Mussolini as the Duce? What similarities and contrasts are notable?

Lecture Fourteen—Transcript
Hitler

In our previous lecture, we considered the rise of the Nazi movement in Germany, and its coming to power. In this lecture, we'd like to concentrate on the man behind the Nazi movement, who was key to its success and to its growing radicalism, Adolf Hitler.

He came from beginnings that were obscure and unpromising, but would rise to become leader of the German people, the Führer. This lecture profiles the man, the dictator, his distinctive characteristics as a political leader, and then considers the keys to his effectiveness. His long-range ideological goals were revealed in aggressive foreign policy, the launching of murderous programs, and ultimately, World War II.

We considered, first of all, Hitler's youth. He was born, not in Germany, but in the Austrian Empire, in 1889, to a middle class family in Braunau am Inn. His father was a customs inspector, a bureaucrat of the empire. Hitler's youth was unremarkable, and directionless. He was considered a slacker, a dreamer, who dropped out of high school to go off to the big city, to Vienna, in 1907, to become an artist, to seek fame.

However, he was rejected by the Academy of Fine Arts, which considered him a capable enough draftsman, but lacking that spark of artistic genius. After this disappointment, Hitler slipped into a sort of netherworld of poverty, in the Viennese capital.

We're accustomed to thinking of Vienna as a beautiful world capital of art and cultivation. That it is, but it also had its ugly side at the start of the 20th century. Hitler claimed that this down-and-out period in the underworld of Vienna was decisive in his development, because he soaked up those many radical influences that were aswirl in the imperial capital: The anti-Semitism of the popular mayor, Karl Lüger, the racialist ideas that circulated on the fringes of its society, the extreme nationalism of the Pan-German movement in the empire, which denounced the non-German nationalities ruled over by the Habsburgs, and the heroic artistic stances and mythological scenarios of Richard Wagner's operas. Later in life, Hitler would observe that no one could understand his political career without first understanding Wagner.

Hitler subsisted in the flophouses, men's hostels, and rescue missions of Vienna in poor circumstances. He was also fascinated by the scenes that unfolded in the streets of Vienna, people for whom he had no political sympathy, but whose talent for the organization of the masses he admired. He was fascinated by the Socialist Mayday parades. He saw how, for hours on end, the long rows of workers would march by in their celebrations, seeming to him to be, as he put it, "a dragon," nearly a superhuman organism, and this would prefigure his attempts to mobilize the German masses on his own.

In spite of his personal failure at attempting to become a great artist in Vienna, the arts and architecture would remain important to him forever after, but he would seek to place his mark upon the world in politics.

The coming of the First World War was decisive for Hitler. It fired his imagination, and gave him a sense of mission that he had not had before. The declaration of war, he later observed, gave him a sense of purpose and belonging. We've described in our earlier lectures so-called August Madness of 1914, when crowds had celebrated the onslaught of war at last. Hitler was caught up in those crowds during the August Madness in Munich.

Indeed, he was captured in a photograph of those days. A photographer who had heard that Hitler had been among the crowds celebrating the news of the war in Munich went back years afterward, and looked through each of the faces in the crowd that he had photographed that day, with a magnifying glass. Indeed, as we can observe in photographs today, Hitler's ecstatic, cheering, shining face was to be found among those crowds.

The analyst of crowd behavior, Elias Canetti, whom we've mentioned a few times in our lectures, claimed that this was Hitler's decisive experience, forming him in his later career. This fostered a sense of belonging to a larger group, and a sense of having a place, something that Hitler would try to re-create for himself, as well as the German people, in the future.

Shortly after having evaded military service in Austria, because Hitler objected to the multinational nature of the Austrian army, he volunteered for a German regiment. He served on the Western front in the trenches, and was distinguished with a rare award of an Iron Cross First Class. Despite having a military career that was distinguished in certain ways, Hitler didn't rise through the ranks. In indeed, he was considered even by fellow soldiers to be a little bit odd. Something was slightly off about this character. In part, it was his propensity to lecture other soldiers about the greatness of Germany's national cause, the slightly too gung-ho attitude that he evidenced in the trenches.

Hitler was sent to a hospital after being caught in a gas attack in the trenches on the Western front. It was there that he would learn that Germany had begged for peace from the Allies. This news struck him like a thunderbolt. He was devastated, and underwent a psychological breakdown. In the course of the breakdown, as he later claimed in *Mein Kampf*, he had had a vision. This vision convinced him that he had a political mission to save Germany, and to restore it to its greatness. He would announce that this was the launching of his political career.

At loose ends when peace had come about in 1918, Hitler remained in the army, that place where he had found a sense of belonging, even after the Armistice. He was hired by the army to observe radical parties in Munich. In the process of visiting one such party, the German Workers' Party, in September of 1919, he had been spontaneously moved to make a speech, and was enrolled as a member, one of about 50 in number at that time. In order to make the numbers seem larger, however, they added several hundred to their party books, identifying themselves as party members, to give the impression of being a mass movement.

By 1921, Hitler had risen dramatically within the movement to become chairman of the party. Members were now calling him the Führer, or the " leader," in the nearly religious devotion, a sense of the infallibility, supposedly, of this leader, hovered around the figure of Hitler.

Hitler renamed the party the National Socialist German Workers Party, or "Nazi" for short, seeking to appeal across the political spectrum. After the failed Beer Hall *putsch* of 1923, Hitler's "legal route to power" used Weimar democracy and the ballot box to destroy parliamentary government. Growing mass support and intrigue brought Hitler to the chancellorship of Germany in January of 1933.

Historians have tried to puzzle out what tantalizing clues we have about Hitler's psychological background and his early youth as well. Such historians are sometimes called by the unfortunate label of "Psycho historians," as they aim to understand psychological background.

Such "psycho historians" have sought to analyze Hitler's childhood, or his upbringing and education, to account for his later political career. However, many of these attempts, tantalizing and intriguing as they can be, are often, in fact, not quite satisfactory, because placing all of our explanatory weight upon the authoritarian childhood, or the child rearing that Hitler was subject to, and indeed was common to many in that era, doesn't begin to explain why this man was launched upon a career of political evil, while so many others went on to seemingly normal adulthood. Even the disappointed career goals obviously alone cannot explain Hitler. Rather, we see questions of choice as well. There was the choice to pursue political radicalism, and the choice to pursue the route to dictatorship.

We turn, now, to an examination of Hitler as dictator. We want to point out that there was a method to the madness in Hitler's approach to dictatorship. Hitler's work methods were, even to some of his own followers, maddeningly unsystematic and chaotic. His way of delegating authority often seemed to lack reason or rationale. He would often charge different followers with the same task, duplicating authority. His personal habits were eccentric. He would keep unusual hours. He loved to watch movies late at night. This is perhaps a recurring feature of dictators. He also would not keep regular office hours.

In particular, historians have referred to Hitler's tactic of duplicating authority, giving the same task different followers, and letting them contend to see who could best fulfill that task as "bureaucratic Darwinism." I think that's a very apt name. The notion that the better of the two, the more forceful, the more radical, the more determined, would win out, was something that Hitler was putting into practice. Historians have argued over whether this was a deliberate tactic, or perhaps unconscious. I feel that much speaks for it having been deliberate and a characteristic mode of operation for Hitler.

The outcome of his style of authority was, in fact, a radicalizing dynamic. It was a way of operating, a way of setting about dealing with political challenges that favored radical solutions, because as followers contended to please the Führer, the most radical one could, in many cases, be sure of the Führer's approbation. The Nazi followers, indeed, would sometimes speak of "working towards the Führer." The term is significant. By anticipating his radical beliefs and anticipating his preference for a radical solution, Hitler's followers, coupled with his often chaotic, unsystematic approach to delegating authority has led some historians to suggest that he was a "weak dictator."

In fact, however, in matters of ideological importance to Hitler, he always intervened effectively. He could see himself as delegating authority, or not dealing with matters that were of less ideological importance to him. In cases that were of such importance to him, such as racial policy, however, he was sure to be the determining voice.

Hitler's dictatorship was also marked by the effectiveness, the aura that was given by the cult of personality, the cult of Hitler as Führer. This was not accidental. This was a carefully cultivated myth of Hitler as the infallible leader of the Third Reich. At first, this cult had grown up around Hitler, perhaps out of the spontaneous devotion of his followers, in the early days of the party. Over time, however, it was later deliberately constructed by Josef Goebbels, the propaganda minister of the Third Reich.

These two men worked in tandem to produce perverse masterpieces of propaganda. The cultive Hitler as a Führer, delighted Goebbels, and believed it as well, in a paradox. What office sees this phenomenon of ministers of propaganda coming to believe their own propaganda, over time. That probably makes them more effective in their presentation of propaganda messages.

Over time, this propaganda also took on quite explicitly religious overtones, as did other imagery of the Third Reich. Hitler was hailed as the "messiah," the "savior" of Germany, using, or hijacking, earlier religious imagery.

The charismatic element that hovered around Hitler and his carefully choreographed and stage-managed appearances could often include an erotic charge for some followers, who would be able to project upon this figure of desire. To preserve this erotic charge, Hitler's mistress, Eva Braun, was kept out of sight. He was presented as an austere, chaste representative of the leadership living for the German people, in a mission that transcended such ordinary human concerns.

In a bizarre phenomenon, letters flowed into the chancellery from enthusiastic followers, addressed to Hitler. Some of these were embarrassing letters that testified to dreams, in some cases even erotic fantasies about the Führer, and they all testified to the remarkably spontaneous effective cult of the leader in Germany.

There was another remarkable phenomenon that was tied into this cultivation of a cult of personality. That was the way in which Hitler himself was often isolated or insulated from criticism of the regime's shortcomings. Often, the party, the state, even some of Hitler's most senior followers would be blamed by public opinion for this or that shortcoming of the regime, while Hitler himself was considered to be "out of the loop," concerned with the "big picture," and not to blame for the day-to-day dissatisfactions of Nazi Germany. A recurrent phrase was, "If only Hitler knew." Hitler was remarkably exempted from blame for the failings of the regime, until nearly the end of his rule, in the Third Reich.

What were the keys to Hitler's effectiveness, in his rise to power, and in his rule over Nazi Germany? There were several. One that we need to keep in mind, first of all, was that he had a persistent pattern of being underestimated.

Throughout his rise to power, and even once installed as dictator, Hitler, both at home and abroad, repeatedly benefited from being misunderstood and underestimated. This took place in the international arena as well. Even movies, like Charlie Chaplin's fantastic lampoon of Hitler and Mussolini, *The Great Dictator*, popularized the comic image, at odds with Hitler's true menace. Some historians have pointed out that this was, perhaps, a message that came at the wrong time. This was precisely when Hitler needed to be stopped, energetically. A picture of a buffoon who was ineffective was being propagated in this otherwise comic classic.

In what Hitler considered to be the most perilous, dangerous, risky period for his plans, which was the consolidation of his rule and rearmament in Germany, in the first years after 1933, he repeatedly claimed that he, as a former soldier, desired nothing more than peace. He hid his true, aggressive, foreign policy goals for the future.

Another key Hitler's effectiveness was a remarkable ruthlessness. Hitler showed a readiness to use ruthless violence to achieve his ends, beyond the bloodthirsty rhetoric so common in his speeches. Early on, this was made especially clear when he massacred some of his own loyal followers, when they seemed to be interfering with his plans.

This was made clear on June 30, 1934, in the so-called "Blood Purge." Scores of Hitler's own the SS in what came to be called the Night of the Long Knives murdered SA storm trooper leaders and other targets. Hitler feared that these earlier "bully boys," the brown shirts, had done their task, had accomplished their political role of helping him come to power, and now could only be an element for disorder and chaos, a liability for the regime. Thus, he had them executed.

In a remarkable tribute, Josef Stalin of the Soviet Union, upon hearing news of the "Night of the Long Knives," expressed his admiration for Hitler's character and strength.

In Hitler's secret deliberations with his generals and diplomats, such as those recorded in the secret Hossbach Memorandum of 1937, Hitler, while he talked peace in public, was already charting an aggressive foreign policy of rearmament and future conquest.

Another key in Hitler's success was being able to rely on security forces of remarkable capacity for terror, in particular, the SS. After the purge of the SA in 1934, the SS, Hitler's own protective *Schutzstaffel*, or bodyguard, led by Heinrich Himmler, commenced a dramatic institutional growth. It took on ever-larger responsibilities, growing from a small force of bodyguards into a huge empire within an empire, a pillar of the Nazi regime.

Heinrich Himmler was in many ways a wan and remarkably pale, unremarkable individual. He was a former failed chicken farmer. He was not a man who seemed remarkable in anyway, but he did have a genius for bureaucratic empire building. Under his leadership, the SS, as a Nazi elite, would carve out for itself a special role in executing the racial initiatives of the Third Reich.

A final point that was a key to Hitler's effectiveness was not only the use of terror, but also drawing on terror in combination with a remarkable conviction and popularity on the part of the German population at large.

One needs to keep in mind that the population was not merely terrorized into obedience, but rather, in many cases, it enthusiastically integrated itself into the Nazi vision of society. In the many organizations that the Nazis used to Nazify German society, ordinary Germans found a place.

A joke from the period testified to what many ordinary Germans understood as the all-pervasive nature of the Nazification of Germany. In this joke, a little girl in Nazi Germany said that her entire family was very actively involved in the movement: Father was in the storm troopers, her older brother was in the SS, for smaller brother was in the Hitler Youth, her mother was in the Nazi women's organization, and she was in the girls' organization, the League of the German Maidens. As the joke continued, the little girl was asked, "How does your family find time to actually get together as a family?" The little girl answered, "That's no problem. We meet at party rallies every year in Nuremberg."

This joke was significant not only for revealing the Nazification of German society. It was also significant in that the Nazis themselves might not have objected to this joke. They might have felt that it was a tribute to the thoroughness of their accomplishment in Nazifying German society. Thus, Hitler was able to draw not only upon terror, but also upon remarkable popular enthusiasm, especially for his diplomatic revolution.

The Hitler's foreign policy vision was now one that he tried to put into effect. He envisioned, in private, a new order in Europe and in the world, with Germany holding a dominant position. In public, however, he spoke of merely restoring German repute and German standing in the world.

Following the ideas of geopolitics that had been articulated in previous decades, Hitler believed that the paramount need for Germany, then, was increased living space, or *Lebensraum*, for his reconstituted German master race. In the future order, small nations were to be eliminated. Their day was over. Instead, great consolidated power blocks of superpowers would rule the world. This was Hitler's long-range aim. He now set about it with an innocuous self-image of a man who was asking, he claimed, reasonably enough, for revision of the Versailles Treaty. Hitler's demands for the revision of the Versailles Treaty, from the end of the First World War, were, in fact, enthusiastically seconded by ordinary Germans, though his aggressive long-range plans were not yet revealed, and probably would not have been as popular.

Hitler could also count on allies, that is to say, the so-called "Axis." His earlier model, later associate, and later, junior associate, Benito Mussolini in Italy, coined the term "axis" in 1936 to describe the new friendship, the new solidarity of Nazi Germany and Fascist Italy in a new era of changed alignments. The Nazi Germany would later sign the Pact of Steel with Italy, in 1939. One sees these rhetorical flourishes in international politics.

In 1936, then, Hitler also signed the anti-Comintern Pact with Japan, directed against international Communism. Hitler could also benefit from the stance of the Western democracies, which was a stance of appeasement.

Misunderstanding Hitler and his true intentions, and, understandably enough, determined to avoid a repetition of the horrors and suffering of the World War, the Western democracies sought to meet Nazi Germany's demands insofar as they could be met. Hitler, however, exploited this willingness for compromise by systematically breaking the Versailles Treaty and effecting a diplomatic revolution.

He took Germany out of the League of Nations, in which so many hopes for peace had been vested, rearmed Germany, in violation of the Versailles Treaty, moved troops into the Rhineland, and annexed Austria, proclaiming that he was bringing it back into the German Reich.

When Hitler was prepared to move against Czechoslovakia, over the Sudetenland border region, where German minorities were exploited as an issue to provoke a conflict, the Munich Conference took place, September 29, 1938. This was where Britain and France gave into Hitler's demand for the area without a fight.

Hitler had gotten what he wanted, without violence. In March of 1939, however, he occupied the rest of Czechoslovakia, making a mockery of the hopes for peace.

Appeasement by the Western democracies had been a failure, both in political as well as moral terms. The Western allies had sold out the sole functioning democracy in Eastern Europe, Czechoslovakia, and they had not managed to take a stand against Hitler, when such a stance might truly have brought significant results.

Hitler would now also pursue another priority, anti-Semitic programs. These anti-Semitic programs were not merely a new feature on the political landscape of Germany, or indeed, of Europe. They drew upon a longer European history of anti-Semitism in Western civilization.

Centuries of religious anti-Semitism, Christians discriminating against or abusing the minority Jewish populations in Europe, were the background and the context to the growth of a new variety of a virulent, radical hatred. This new variety, which built upon, but also differed significantly from earlier, religious anti-Semitism, was often called *radical, racial, anti-Semitism*, or *biological anti-Semitism*.

This ideology, which was racist and social Darwinist, not religious, didn't call for conversion, as had once been the case, but rather, it called for the separation or elimination of the Jewish minority.

The libelous, forged, so-called "Protocols of the Elders of Zion," which was a clumsy forgery from the 1890s of the Russian Tsarist secret police, claimed that the Jews were organizing a world conspiracy. In act of psychological projection, anti-Semites would use such fabricated forgeries as an excuse for mounting an international campaign against what they claimed was an international Jewish threat.

The supposedly scientific nature of this new racial, or biological, anti-Semitism, and its far-reaching promises of social integration and social good, if only this one direct could be eliminated, caused it to be labeled by its critics as "Socialism for Idiots." The notion was that socialism promised social cohesion and unity, while anti-Semites were promising a radical utopia of hatred against the Jews, which they promised, if put into action, could yield goods for society. The Nazis, however, would set about using the tools of the state to put their hatred into action.

Historians continue to debate today, about precisely how the Nazi regime reached the destination of genocide: By what route? This question has sometimes been formulated thusly: Was the road to Auschwitz, to the death camps of eastern Europe, directed, premeditated, and planned out in advance from the first, or was the road to Auschwitz, as other historians have argued, a twisted path? Was it a road toward destruction that might have taken other turns, one that was not foreordained of necessity?

In this debate, there are two schools: The intentionalists, and the functionalists. The intentionalists, as they're called, have argued that the Nazis pursued, indeed, a blueprint for genocide from the outset, that this was implicit from the very earliest articulation of Nazi ideology, and that Hitler pursued the realization of this genocidal agenda with a clear, step-by-step plan.

Other historians who oppose aspects of this argument are known as functionalists. They're sometimes also called structuralists. They contend that the Nazi regime's functioning, or its structure, in fact, did much to set it upon its murderous route. They argue that the functioning of the Nazi regime grew more radical in its policies over time, and that the growing radicalism of these policies eventually led to the realization of a genocidal program.

Many historians today have recognized that this debate, in fact, perhaps poses false alternatives in too stark, too schematic a form. Many historians today, who study these historical events call themselves "moderate functionalists," and try to, as it were, find a middle ground between the positions. The argue that, from the first, the intention was a radical treatment of this group defined as the enemy of the Nazis, but that on the other hand, certainly, those policies could grow ever more radical over time.

We can see, indeed, an escalation of Nazi policies against those whom they termed their racial enemies. At first, the Nazis sought to remove the Jewish population from Germany, by encouraging emigration. This was not done by means that were legal, but rather through intimidation, and violence. In 1935, these policies were ratcheted up further, in the infamous "Nuremberg Laws," which took away the citizenship, and human rights of German Jews, and increasingly isolated them socially. The Nazis were adept at prying apart earlier social solidarities and in dividing up society.

Many ordinary Germans, now barred from interaction with those who had earlier been their German neighbors, might more easily assimilate the demonized stereotypes of the Jews in German society, propagated by the Nazis.

The next step was a massive act of violence, the so-called *Kristallnacht* of November 9, 1938. In German towns and cities, Jewish homes, synagogues, and businesses were attacked. Jews were arrested and brutalized. The Nazis, now, had stepped towards state policies of massive violence against this targeted minority.

There was yet another escalation to come, however. With the coming of World War II, the Nazis would have cover, as well as rhetorical arguments, for a further escalation of their policies. Forced emigration would now be replaced with a murderous program of what the Nazis, with their perverse skill euphemism and perversion of the German language, would call the "Final Solution" to their racial utopia, which we'll be examining in our following lectures.

Lecture Fifteen
World War II

Scope:

The Second World War was unleashed by Hitler in 1939 with some help from his newfound friend, the Soviet Union's Stalin. Recently ideological mortal enemies, these former foes aimed to usher in a new international order by swearing friendship in the Nazi-Soviet Pact. Affinities between their regimes were remarked on at the time by contemporary observers and are discussed here. The war saw more violence directed at unarmed people: the Nazi terror bombings of civilian centers and killing squads sent into Poland, Soviet executions of Polish officers at Katyn, and mass deportations from newly seized countries. In 1941, Hitler turned on his former ally Stalin and launched an invasion of the Soviet Union as a racial war. On all sides, this "perfected" total war took massive civilian casualties, especially in war from the air, culminating in the opening of the atomic age with the bombing of Hiroshima and Nagasaki.

Outline

I. The road to war.

    A. World War II was Hitler's war. Although historians debate the First World War's causes, the Second World War's origins are far clearer.

    B. Gathering forces.

        1. Fascism and Nazism saw war not as a necessary evil, but as a positive thing.

        2. As Mussolini drew closer to Hitler (earlier his disciple), he adopted anti-Semitic racism from 1938. Contorted racialist justifications were found for alliance with Japan.

    C. Enabling invasion.

        1. Convinced of Western democracies' weakness, Hitler resolved to attack Poland, disregarding British security guarantees.

        2. To avoid two-front war, Hitler sought cooperation with Stalin.

3. The start of World War II thus was a common project of the two dictators. Both believed it would usher in a new epoch, reordering Europe and hurrying democracy's abolition.

II. The Nazi-Soviet Pact.

   A. The Treaty.

      1. News of the Nazi-Soviet Pact by Joachim von Ribbentropp and Vyacheslav Molotov on August 23, 1939, came as a shock around the world.

      2. Given that the regimes were sworn ideological enemies, this pact seemed impossible.

      3. Propaganda machines of both states turned on a dime, reversing denunciations, to herald new friendship.

      4. Formally called a nonaggression treaty, it had secret protocols dividing Eastern Europe into spheres of influence.

      5. Western Poland and Lithuania were the Nazi share, while Latvia, Estonia, Finland, and eastern Poland were allocated to Stalin. Later, the Nazis exchanged Lithuania for more Polish territory.

   B. Consequences.

      1. Hitler was now freed to attack Poland. World War II was enabled by cooperation between the dictators.

      2. The Soviets provided shipments of raw materials and supplies to Germany.

      3. An era of population movement began, with ethnic Germans transported from the Baltic states to be used as settlers in conquered Poland.

   C. Why would Stalin do this?

      1. Stalin's decision is obscure but would be entirely unfathomable without considering his ideological mindset.

      2. Convinced that Nazism represented capitalism's last, most brutal phase, Stalin sought to redirect Hitler westward against the capitalist powers.

      3. In the meantime, Stalin sought more time to prepare for war and to mend damage done by his purges.

4. In the coming world struggle that would wear down all the capitalist powers fighting in the West, much like World War I, Stalin hoped to pick up the pieces.

III. Totalitarian affinities.

    A. The term: definitions and origins.

        1. *Totalitarianism* denotes regimes unlike earlier tyrannies, aiming at total control of populations through both terror and ideological belief, demanding not merely passive assent but active participation and mandatory enthusiasm.

        2. In 1923, a journalist critical of the Fascists applied the label to them, and Mussolini took it up, accepting it.

    B. Hannah Arendt.

        1. In 1951, Hannah Arendt (1906–1975) published *The Origins of Totalitarianism*, on the development of modern dictatorial systems, such as Nazi Germany and the Soviet Union.

        2. Arendt drew on personal observations as a German-Jewish refugee from Nazi Germany, settling in the United States.

        3. Arendt remains controversial. As a student in philosophy in Germany, she had an affair with Martin Heidegger, who supported Nazism. Her 1963 *Eichmann in Jerusalem* was criticized for its concept of the "banality of evil" and other assertions.

    C. The essence of totalitarianism.

        1. Others before Arendt noted similarities between ideologically opposed regimes, suggesting that "extremes meet."

        2. Arendt, however, systematically traced the model's origins as an extension of imperialism after the breakdown of 19th-century liberalism.

        3. Similarities across regimes included: the cult of the leader, dynamic claims of ideological infallibility, use of violence to fulfill those claims, concentration camps as microcosms of totalitarian aims, hierarchies of believers and elites, secret police, atomized masses, and similar monumental art and propaganda.

4. A final, essential feature was constant motion, pursuing universal, global aims.

D. Continuing debate.

1. After the 1960s, the concept was criticized as a Cold War rhetorical tool, inaccurate in describing everyday life under dictatorships.

2. From the 1990s, however, Eastern Europeans enthusiastically endorsed and revived this description of regimes they had endured.

IV. The war.

A. *Blitzkrieg.*

1. *Blitzkrieg* ("lightning war") was a strategy to overcome the immobility of World War I.

2. Instead, tanks and planes acting in unison would decisively annihilate the enemy.

3. Quick victory would allow the enemy's territory and population to be exploited for the next war.

4. The *Blitzkrieg* idea was also a symptom of Hitler's mistrust of ordinary Germans, avoiding total mobilization.

B. Destroying Poland.

1. The attack on Poland commenced on September 1, 1939. Britain and France declared war on September 3, and World War II began.

2. In spite of heroic resistance, Poland was quickly overrun. Airplanes bombed Polish cities, underlining the radical nature of this war.

3. Special SS *Einsatzgruppen* were sent in to "decapitate" Polish society by murdering intellectuals, political leaders, and clergy.

C. Stalin's share and "cleaning" in the Soviet sphere of influence.

1. Stalin moved to take his share and to impose his order.

2. On September 17, the Soviet army moved in to claim eastern Poland.

3. Stalin had thousands of Polish officers shot and buried in mass graves in Katyn (a crime denied until 1990).

4. After forcing the Baltic states (Lithuania, Latvia, and Estonia) to accept bases in 1939, Stalin annexed them as Soviet republics in August 1940.

5. Stalin began mass deportations of Baltic civilians in June 1941, aiming to remake the territories.

6. When the Soviet Union invaded Finland in the Winter War of 1939–1940, the army's dismal performance revealed the cost of Stalin's purges.

D. Assault on the West.

1. In 1940, Hitler attacked in the West, overrunning Denmark and Norway, then defeating France by June (in six weeks). Hitler celebrated the overturning of World War I.

2. Though Britain remained undefeated, Hitler turned to his next goal, conquest of living space in Eastern Europe. He attacked his Soviet ally.

V. Hitler's attack on the Soviet ally.

A. Barbarossa.

1. Operation Barbarossa began June 22, 1941. With three and a half million men, this was the largest invasion in history.

2. In spite of repeated warnings, Stalin did not believe the attack was coming. Ideological assumptions blinded him.

B. A radical form of war.

1. Hitler declared this a new kind of war, freed of civilized constraints: a war of ideologies and racial enemies.

2. This was underlined in the *Kommissar* Order of June 6, 1941, instructing soldiers to kill Soviet political officers, orders later extended to Jews in the occupied territories.

3. Soviet prisoners of war were captured in enormous numbers, put in camps, and allowed to die of hunger and neglect, considered to be Slavic subhumans. By the end of 1941, two million Soviet prisoners of war had died.

VI. Total war intensified.

A. The nature of improved total war.

1. World War II saw intensification of trends already evident in World War I, especially in mobilization and targeting of civilians.
2. Nazis used slave labor, which became crucial to their war economy.
3. In occupied territories, especially in Eastern Europe, the Nazis killed civilians in reprisal for partisan activity.
4. Bombing of civilian centers became common, beginning with Nazi attacks on Warsaw in Poland, Rotterdam in the Netherlands, and Coventry in Great Britain.
5. Air war came to Germany, where bombing killed between 350,000 to 650,000 civilians. In a raid on Dresden near the war's end, around 80,000 were killed.
6. Japan's surprise air attack on Pearl Harbor on December 7, 1941, brought America into the war.
7. In August 1945, the United States dropped atomic bombs on the Japanese cities of Hiroshima and Nagasaki, killing an estimated total of 110,000.

B. The Nazi regime, embracing total war, made deliberate murder of civilians a special aim and project.

Essential Reading:

Hannah Arendt, *The Origins of Totalitarianism*.

John Keegan, *The Second World War*.

Supplementary Reading:

Abbott Gleason, *Totalitarianism: The Inner History of the Cold War*.

Questions to Consider:

1. How did the Nazi and Soviet regimes explain their friendship to their respective populations?
2. Without ideological blinders, how might a Russian leader more pragmatic than Stalin have acted in this era?

Lecture Fifteen—Transcript
World War II

In our previous lectures, we've discussed Hitler and the Nazi party. In this lecture, we turn to a discussion of Hitler's war, World War II. The Second World War was unleashed by Hitler in 1939, with some help from an unlikely, newfound friend, the Soviet Union's dictator, Josef Stalin. Until recently, they had been ideological mortal enemies. These two dictators, aimed, by swearing a pact, the Nazi-Soviet Pact, to bring about fundamental change in the world. Contemporaries had already remarked on some similarities, some intriguing resemblances between their regimes. We'll be discussing them today.

The Second World War would see more violence directed at unarmed people. It would be an intensification of the patterns of total war that target evident to a degree in the First World War. On all sides, this perfected model of total war would take civilian casualties on a massive scale, especially in the terrifying war from the air, which at the end of the Second World War would usher in the atomic age.

We need first to consider the road to war. World War II was very clearly Hitler's war. Historians have now been debating for nearly a century the reasons for the causes of the First World War, but they debate far less the origins of the Second World War. Those origins have to do with Hitler's will, Hitler's desire for a great conflict, and what he hoped to gain from it.

Forces had already been gathering for war in Hitler's attainment of an ally in Fascist Italy, and later in his approach towards Japan. Both Fascism and Nazism were distinctive as ideologies in the sense that they saw war not merely as a necessary evil, but looked upon it as a positive thing. Peace was the exception, as they saw it, in human affairs. War was the natural state. For this reason, they would collaborate in the approaching conflict.

As Benito Mussolini, who had been an earlier model to Hitler, and was now increasingly his junior associate, drew nearer to his earlier disciple, he began to imitate certain features of the Nazi regime. From 1938, anti-Semitic racist policies were adopted, and thus, it was hoped, to give some racial coherence to the alliance between Italy and Germany.

It was more difficult to explain why Japan should be an ally. The Nazis, after all, in their racist ideology, saw Asians as being inferior to the European races, and thus, some contorted racial justifications were found for alliance with Japan by claiming that they were, in a sense, the Aryans of the Asian part of the world, and thus, worthy allies.

At the same time, Hitler and his associates viewed the Western democracies as weak, and was convinced that, in all likelihood, further aggression, further invasion, following that of Czechoslovakia, would not be met with decisive resistance either. Convinced of the Western democracies' weaknesses, Hitler resolved to attack Poland, disregarding the security guarantees that had been given by Britain.

There was one other fear, however, that Hitler needed to deal with. That was the anxiety about the position the Soviet Union would take in such a conflict. Hitler aimed to avoid a two-front war, the perennial nightmare of German politicians and diplomats, by a diplomatic revolution. He sought the cooperation of Stalin.

This was an unlikely alliance, to put it mildly, because the Communists and Nazis had been ideological mortal enemies. By the start of World War II, it would thus be a common project of the two dictators, who cooperated in facilitating its outbreak. Both of these dictators vested utopian hopes in this war, moreover. They believed that the conflict would usher in a new epoch, reordering Europe, maybe even the world, and hurrying the abolition, the demise of their common enemy, democracy.

Thus, we need to consider a truly remarkable document, the Nazi-Soviet Pact. When news of the Nazi-Soviet Pact, Pact of Non-Aggression, as it was formally known, signed on August 23, 1939, became known, it sent shock waves around the world. It had been signed by the German foreign minister, Joachim von Ribbentrop, and the Soviet foreign minister, Vyacheslav Molotov, but it still seemed hard to believe. These regimes, after all, were sworn ideological enemies. They had vowed to fight for their respective extinctions. This very pact, now announced as an accomplished fact, seemed impossible. Nonetheless, the propaganda machines of both states, of Nazi Germany and the Soviet Union, literally turned on a dime, reversing their earlier denunciations of their respective mortal ideological enemies. Now, instead, they heralded a new friendship, facing off against the moribund democracies of the West.

This news came as a dreadful shock to true believers in either regime. In Nazi Germany, a joke circulated during the time that underlined the improbable nature of this new treaty of friendship. The joke said that after the treaty had been signed, Hitler had sent a special gift to Stalin as a seal of friendship. That special gift had been a copy of Hitler's *Mein Kampf*, in which he had laid out his plans for destroying Communism, with certain sections personally erased by the Führer himself. What this underlined, in joke form, was the very improbability, the implausibility of what had just taken place. We need to explore this phenomenon a little further, to understand its deeper significance.

Formerly, the Nazi-Soviet Pact, as it was popularly called, was a non-aggression treaty, pledging not to go to war against one another. It had secret paragraphs, however, secret protocols, which divided up Eastern Europe, independent countries not belonging to either side, into respective spheres of influence. These two cannibals, in other words, Hitler and Stalin, were engaged in the exercise of carving up Eastern Europe among themselves. Western Poland and Lithuania, independent countries, were given to the Nazis, while Latvia, Estonia, Finland, and eastern Poland were allocated to Stalin. Later, the Nazis exchanged Lithuania for more Polish territory. The cannibals were capable of polite negotiation over the fate of others.

The consequences of this improbable treaty were significant. Hitler was now truly freed up to launch his attack on Poland. World War II, which broke out as a consequence, was enabled in this sense by cooperation between the two dictators. The Soviets continued to cooperate in this friendship by providing promised shipments of raw materials and supplies to Germany, as a pledge of cooperation. Another consequence was that, in earnest now, an era of massive, modern population movements began.

Population movements, the shifting of peoples from one region to another, existed earlier in human history. The historical accounts are full of the notion of peoples being removed from their original homelands. This was truly a traumatic experience, when it happened in such ancient times. It had been a practice of the Ottoman Empire, for instance, to use this for political purposes, to shift populations around from areas where it was felt they couldn't be trusted. It was this tradition that was ultimately radicalized in the Armenian massacres of the First World War, that we've discussed in an earlier lecture.

Now, however, the principal of political population movements became an organizing idea of the modern age, on a scale that had not been seen before. As a first step, ethnic Germans were transported from the Baltic states, which were now taken over increasingly by the Soviet Union, and settled as colonists in conquered Poland, established in farms and houses, whose Polish inhabitants had been expelled only days or hours previously. This ushered in a new age of despotic movement of populations.

We need to pause for a moment, however, to dig more deeply into the mystery of this tale of two dictators. Why would Stalin do this? Why would a man whose paranoia, whose distrust was legendary, who distrusted his own followers, and probably all of mankind, choose this one man, Adolf Hitler, as a man in whom to repose his confidence?

This is a mystery that likely will never entirely be satisfactorily solved. Stalin's decision to trust Hitler remains obscure in the absence of Stalin's own personal testimony. However, we can at least begin to understand this mystery by considering Stalin's ideological mindset. Without it, we'll simply be at a loss entirely. The ideas in his mind, his expectations, his sense of what the future held in store, are in part the key to this mystery.

The Stalin's Marxist ideology suggested to him that the Nazis were not so much a rival ideological modern movement of the sort that he spearheaded in the Soviet Union. Rather, they were the last gasp of capitalism. Nazism was capitalism at its most naked, undisguised, brutal self. It was the last episode of a world historical stage, not a modern contender for ideological supremacy. Thus, Stalin felt that playing for time would be crucial, and would allow history to work its way out towards the inevitable triumph of the Communist ideology.

For Stalin, then, it might have made sense to seek to placate or appease Hitler, insofar as that was possible, in dividing up Poland and the rest of Eastern Europe, as a way of then redirecting Hitler's energies and ambitions westward, away from the Soviet Union, away from Stalin's own regime, and against the other capitalist powers, to let capitalist forces battle it out among themselves in a battle royale. In the meantime, Stalin seems to have expected that he would've gained time, time to prepare, if necessary, for a future war, and incidentally, to mend the damage that he had done by his own self-inflicted purges that had done so much to cripple the functioning of the regime.

Thus, in his expectations, we might surmise, in the coming world struggle, in some sense a replay of World War I, the capitalist powers fighting in the West would be worn down, would exhaust one another in a battle of attrition, and Stalin, then, might ultimately hope to pick up the pieces of this world historical climax, ushering in a final triumph.

If Stalin and his followers had paused to really carefully read Hitler's *Mein Kampf*, they might have had a more sober understanding of precisely where the ambitions of their Nazi ally lay in the long-term, and they would have been less optimistic about the chances for avoiding this conflict.

It was precisely this moment, this bombshell of the news of the Nazi-Soviet Pact, that seemed to bring into focus for many contemporaries, at least briefly, some resemblances, some common ground, some occasions when the Communist and Nazi regimes could make common cause revealing what some contemporaries felt to be affinities between these regimes. These were regimes that were sometimes summed up in one word, in spite of their ideological conflicts, as totalitarian regimes. I want to examine the definition of this form of rule and its origins.

The term *totalitarianism* is used to denote regimes that were unlike the earlier tyrannies or despotisms of the pre-modern age. In fact, these were supposed to be a new form of tyranny. They didn't just aim at acquiescence, not simply at repressing populations and fighting off their resistance, but at something more: Aiming at total control of populations through both terror and ideological belief and enthusiasm, demanding not just passive assent, but active participation and mandatory enthusiasm on the part of subject populations. These were total regimes, wanting total control of their populations, heart and soul.

The origins of the term are fascinating. In 1923, an Italian journalist who was critical of Mussolini's Fascists had used the word "totalitarian" in his criticism of the Fascists, saying that they wanted it all. Their ambitions were total; hence they were totalitarian. When Mussolini heard this term of criticism, he and the Fascists rather liked it and accepted it as a self-definition.

A philosopher, I think one of the truly important political philosophers of the 20th century, Hannah Arendt, who was a witness to this period of turmoil in human history, used the concept of totalitarianism as part of an extensive study of the dynamics of such politics in the modern age.

In 1951, at the dawn of the Cold War that we'll be discussing in a later lecture, Hannah Arendt published a large work called *The Origins of Totalitarianism*, which compared and contrasted the development of modern dictatorial systems, Nazi Germany and the Soviet Union, to try to tease out this new form of rule, this, as Arendt felt, very modern form of rule.

Hannah Arendt, in her theoretical treatment of totalitarianism, didn't rely only on ideas and theoretical models. She also drew on personal observations. She herself was a German Jewish refugee from Nazi Germany, who later settled in the United States and taught at the University of Chicago. Hannah Arendt remains a significant but controversial figure. As a student of philosophy in Germany, she had had an affair with one of her professors, Martin Heidegger, a philosopher who supported Nazism. This was a mystery of her personal life.

Her later book, published in 1963, *Eichmann in Jerusalem*, was both widely read and widely criticized for its concept of the banality of evil and other assertions about how the Nazi regime had operated, how the victims of this regime had responded. She had claimed, in her concept of the "banality of evil," that the perpetrators of the violence of the Nazi regime, in many cases, were bureaucrats whose capacity for simply doing their job, even in genocide, revealed something disturbing about modern bureaucracies as such. She remains controversial.

Let's examine, now, the essence of Hannah Arendt's concept of totalitarianism. Arendt was not the first thinker to note similarities between ideologically opposed regimes, even mortal enemies.

Indeed, other contemporaries had suggested that "extremes meet," that there were factors in common between Fascists, Communists, and the Nazis, in how they practiced the politics of violence.

Arendt, however, went beyond just this anecdotal observation. She, instead, systematically traced the model's origins. She saw totalitarianism as a new form of rule they grew out of the breakdown of 19th-century classical liberalism, the breakdown of the nation-state, with its concept of equal citizens protected by the law. This breakdown had further been evidenced in the concept of imperialism, and its rule over subject populations who were not accorded rights and privileges, as at least had been the case in theory, in the liberal nation-state.

The totalitarianism, in Hannah Arendt's model was thus, in a sense, imperialism coming back to Europe. Modes of rule and terror that had earlier been practiced out in the periphery were now reimported into modern societies as a form of rule that was emphatically opposed to democracy and liberalism.

Hannah Arendt cataloged, in a structural analysis, the similarities that could be observed between regimes like Stalin's Soviet Union and Hitler's Nazi Germany. Just to mention a few, those similarities included the cult of the leader, dynamic claims of ideological infallibility on the part of the leader and the government, the use of violence to fulfill those claims or to make good on those prophecies, concentration camps as microcosms or laboratories of the most total achievement of the most radical aims of totalitarian regimes, and hierarchies of true believers and elites, who could cynically manipulate the masses of believers.

Institutions of enormous significance in such regimes, like the secret police, the enforcers, and then the raw material of these regimes, atomized masses of people, no longer bound together in other social identities, but rather, isolated individuals, facing the government alone, and organized by the regime into mass organizations. It was almost superfluous to note here that there were uncanny similarities in the monumental art and in the propaganda of the regimes Hannah Arendt described.

As a final, and essential feature of these totalitarian regimes, Hannah Arendt observed, "They shared in common the need for constant motion." Hannah Arendt observed that when these regimes lost the impetus of forward movement, they threatened to topple over. For that reason, these regimes tended to grow more radical over time. They pursued evermore ambitious, universal, global, utopian aims. The need to move toward that future would give them dynamism and force.

Debate on the concept of totalitarianism raged after Hannah Arendt had articulated her theory. In the 1960s and afterward, the concept was criticized very heavily. Some argued that, in the context of the Cold War, the assertion that Communism and Nazism had similarities was merely a Cold War rhetorical tool. They further pointed out that, in many ways, it could be inaccurate in describing everyday life under dictatorships where total control had, in fact, not been achieved by the governments, but where pockets of resistance could remain.

In fact, this was perhaps somewhat unfair to Hannah Arendt, whose theory had not claimed that totalitarian regimes had achieved total control of their subject populations. Rather, she had emphasized that while that total control might elude them, what was crucial was the aim, the ambition, the harboring of the notion that total control should, and could, be realized. Some political science studies, in fact, following up on some of Hannah Arendt's insights, were, in fact, perhaps too schematic, too rigid, and didn't take into account the pockets of resistance that might still exist in totalitarian societies.

However, then something remarkable happened the 1990s, closer to our own times. After the revolutions in Eastern Europe, many Eastern Europeans who read Hannah Arendt's book enthusiastically endorsed her theoretical notion, and revived this description of totalitarian regimes as they felt was the accurate depiction of the sort of life they had endured. We've seen, thus, a fascinating renaissance of the term, and of Hannah Arendt's thought. It's my conviction personally, that Hannah Arendt's book, *The Origins of Totalitarianism*, is likely to be read hundreds of years from now, for an understanding of the violent trajectory of the 20th century.

Hitler, now, had been enabled, through this cooperation of unlikely ideological opponents, to fight his war. This war was to be a "lightning war," *Blitzkrieg*, a strategy that the Germans had developed to overcome the immobility and stasis of the trench warfare of World War I. Instead, in this "lightning war," tanks and planes, acting in unison, would decisively annihilate the enemy.

Quick victory would allow the enemy's territory and population to be occupied, and then exploited, to pay for the next war. *Blitzkrieg*, thus, was supposed to be a self-perpetuating war machine.

However, the *Blitzkrieg* idea, historians have pointed out, was also, in some other paradoxical ways, a symptom of Hitler's mistrust of ordinary Germans. To fight quick wars that could pay for themselves was supposed to allow Germany to avoid total mobilization. Thinking back to the First World War, Hitler was afraid of what might happen if the morale of the homefront buckled. He believed in the "stab-in-the-back legend," and thus, he aimed to spare Germany mobilization.

Poland was soon destroyed. An attack on Poland had commenced on September 1, 1939. Britain and France then declared war, and World War II had begun. In spite of truly heroic resistance, Poland was quickly overrun. German airplanes bombed Polish cities and civilian centers, underlining the radical nature of this war. Special SS death squads called *Einsatzgruppen*, or "special forces units," were sent in to "decapitate," as the term went, Polish society, by murdering those who were understood to be natural leaders: The intellectuals, political leaders, and clergy.

For his part, now, Stalin moved to "clean" and claim his share of the Soviet sphere of influence. Stalin moved into his territories to impose his Communist order. On September 17, while the Nazis were with quelling their portion of Poland, the Soviet army moved in to claim Eastern Poland. Those Polish officers who had retreated eastward, in a fighting retreat, were now captured by Stalin. Thousands of them were shot and buried in mass graves in Katyn. This was a crime that the Soviet Union denied until 1990, at almost the very end, until finally admitting Stalin's role.

Stalin soon forced the Baltic states, the previously independent republics of Lithuania, Latvia, and Estonia, to except Red Army bases in 1939, and then annexed them as Soviet republics, which supposedly had asked for voluntary admission into the Soviet Union, in 1940.

He soon began mass deportations of Baltic civilians in June of 1941. Scarcely a family was not affected by these deportations. Overnight, civilians suspected of potential political disloyalty were rounded up, put in to train cars, or cattle cars, and sent on the long road to Siberian exile, and the death that awaited many of them there.

When the Soviet Union invaded Finland in the Winter War of 1939 to 1940, Fins reacted with a ferocious resistance and guerrilla warfare. The Red Army's dismal performance against Finnish irregulars revealed the cost that Stalin's purges had taken on the Red Army. Hitler, now, was free to turn towards the West.

In 1940, Hitler attacked in the West, overrunning Denmark and Norway, and then defeating France in the course of six weeks by June. Hitler celebrated what he saw as the overturning of the verdict of World War I. What the German armies hadn't achieved in four years of protracted trench warfare, that he himself had participated in, the German armies had achieved now, in the course of several weeks.

Though Britain remained undefeated, Hitler now turned to his next goal: The conquest of living space for his master race in Eastern Europe. He now turned on his Soviet ally.

Hitler's attack on the Soviet ally began with the so-called Operation Barbarossa, launched on June 22, 1941. With 3.5 million men, this was the largest invasion mounted in history until that time. In spite of repeated warnings, Stalin had refused to believe that the attack was coming. His ideological assumptions had blinded him to the treacherous nature of his own ally.

Stalin reeled before the impact of this treachery, which essentially anyone but he could certainly have anticipated. Some historians suggest that he might have suffered a nervous breakdown in those first days of the attack by his former ally. However, when he emerged afterwards and spoke to the Soviet population, he appealed to them to fight in a war against the foreign invader. He appealed, in particular, to Russian nationalism. This was a remarkable reversal. He announced a great patriotic war, to expel the German enemy, not a great Communist war, not a great Bolshevik war, but instead, a holy war for holy Mother Russia, to expel the foreign invader.

Many ordinary Russians took this to be an implicit promise that if only they mobilized for the sake of Russia, then, after the war, after its successful end, liberalization would follow. Indeed, mobilization was impressive.

Part and parcel, Stalin's new tactic, was an increased rapprochement with the Orthodox Church, which now was instructed to "preach the message" of a nationalist uprising against the German invader, now enjoying better relations with the Soviet government that for decades previous had persecuted the Church.

Hitler, for his part, declared that the war in the East would be a new kind of war, freed of the constraints of civilized warfare. This was to be a war of ideologies, racial enemies, a war to the death. This fact was underlined, in fact, in orders that Hitler handed down to the German armies, such as the *Kommissar* Order of June 6, 1941. It instructed German soldiers to kill Soviet political officers, upon capturing them. These were the propaganda chiefs who were appointed to the units of the Red Army. These orders were later extended to another group the Nazis would target, the Jews in the occupied territories, because they were considered racial enemies.

The Soviet prisoners of war, many of whom didn't feel any particular compunction to die for Stalin, were captured in enormous numbers, in the first battles of the invasion of the Soviet Union. They were put in camps, and the Nazis allowed them to die of hunger and neglect, considering them to be Slavic sub-humans. When incidences of cannibalism broke out in these camps, the Nazis chiefs considered that funny.

By the end of 1941, two million Soviet prisoners of war had died as a result of their mistreatment in the Nazi camps. Total war was now intensified. World War II would see an intensification of those trends that were already evident in World War I, especially in the mobilization and targeting of civilians. The Nazis used slave labor, which became a crucial component of their war economy. In the occupied territories, especially in the harsh treatment of the Eastern European territories, the Nazis killed civilians in reprisal for partisan or guerrilla activity. Bombing of civilian centers became common, beginning with Nazi attacks on Warsaw in Poland, Rotterdam in the Netherlands, and Coventry in Great Britain, but then air war came back to Germany. Allied bombing there killed between 350,000 and 650,000 civilians in a raid on Dresden, near the war's end. Up to 80,000, many of them refugees, were killed in this intensification of total war.

Half a world away, the Japanese, in their surprise attack on Pearl Harbor in December of 1941, brought America into the war, making it even more total. In August of 1945, the United States dropped fearsome new weapons, atomic bombs, on the Japanese cities of Hiroshima and Nagasaki, killing an estimated total of 110,000.

The Nazi regime, however, enthusiastically embraced total war, and made the deliberate murder of civilians a special aim and project of its conduct of the war, making it a cornerstone of its legacy, that we'll discuss in our following lecture on the Final Solution.

Lecture Sixteen
Nazi Genocide and Master Plans

Scope:

This lecture considers the Nazis' program of mass murder against the Jews and Hitler's future plans for construction of a racial utopia. The Nazis set off on the road to mass murder with escalating persecutions, euthanasia programs of medicalized killing, and execution squads sent into occupied countries. Their program culminated in the factories of death—extermination camps, such as Auschwitz, where killing was mass-produced on an industrial scale. For the future, the General Plan for the East foresaw German settlement of Eastern Europe. Nazi architecture and monuments hinted at the vast scale of Hitler's ambitions for world domination, reflected also in his views of the United States. Only the end of the war in 1945 foreclosed these megalomaniac plans.

Outline

I. The road to murder.

   A. Eugenics.

      1. Eugenic thinking, widespread worldwide during the first half of the century, urged planning of a superior population through encouraging "good births" and discouraging reproduction of those judged unfit.

      2. German eugenics was not limited to Nazi medical experts but was a strong tradition long before 1933.

      3. American eugenic measures provided inspiration to German eugenicists.

      4. Soon after coming to office, the Nazis passed a July 1933 law authorizing sterilization of those with hereditary diseases (including mental illness, epilepsy, blindness, and alcoholism). Hundreds of thousands of Germans were sterilized.

      5. Nazi schools propagated eugenic thinking with readings and math problems about the social costs of "useless eaters" and "life unworthy of living."

   B. Euthanasia.

      1. In 1939, a program of "mercy killing" was instituted, using the war as cover to justify these measures.

2. Departments in hospitals collected information on children, then adults with handicaps and mental illness, referring them to SS experts. An estimated 100,000 people were killed.
3. The program was halted in August 1941 for reasons that are still debated.

C. The SS.
1. The SS was a key institution in the Third Reich's racial policies.
2. SS medical personnel were involved in euthanasia, gaining experience in scientific, medicalized mass murder.
3. The Reichsführer SS, Heinrich Himmler, sought a new racial elite, devoted to breeding of a master race. In 1939, he became Commissar for Strengthening of Germandom.
4. Under Himmler's deputy, Reinhard Heydrich, the SS pressed forward with a policy of *Entjudung*, "removal of Jews" from Germany. By 1939, more than a fourth of all German Jews emigrated.

D. Master executioners: the *Einsatzgruppen*.
1. SS *Einsatzgruppen* were sent into Poland to eliminate intellectuals and leaders.
2. Tens of thousands of Polish Jews were also deported to occupied Poland, which the regime planned to use as a dumping ground or reservation for Jews from the rest of their sphere of influence, which was to become "cleansed of Jews."
3. With the attack on the Soviet Union, *Einsatzgruppen* followed the armies and committed mass murder of the Jewish communities behind the lines, killing one million Jews by the end of 1941.
4. However, Nazi leaders judged this mode of killing too open and inefficient and, thus, laid new plans.

E. The final solution.
1. The Wannsee Conference took place January 20, 1942, in a villa outside Berlin. There, the operations already underway were systematized into a comprehensive "final solution."

2. When the meeting protocol, couched in bureaucratic euphemism, was discovered after the war, it was called one of the most shameful documents in world history.
3. Europe's Jews were to be shipped to the East and exterminated there.
4. The introduction of an obligatory yellow star for Jews in Germany in 1941 marked them and singled them out for this fate.

F. Hitler's role.
1. Historians debate Hitler's precise actions in launching the Nazi genocide.
2. Hitler's aversion to written orders and caution about leaving paper trails make tracing the documentary evidence complicated.
3. Clearly, Hitler's role was pivotal, because he established the goals of the regime and endorsed programs of growing radicalism.

G. The circle of complicity.
1. It is crucial to note that a program of this scope and magnitude involved more than a small circle of planners. In fact, enormous numbers of officials, at the highest and lowest levels of the state and party, from generals to station masters, were implicated and were needed to make the final solution happen.
2. Collaborators who helped the Nazis in their programs turned up in every country.

II. The factories of death.
A. The institutions.
1. By early 1942, death camps were operating under SS control in the occupied eastern territories, at Auschwitz, Belzec, Treblinka, Chelmno, Majdanek, Sobibor.
2. Jews concentrated in ghettoes were shipped to the camps by train.
3. Gas chambers disguised as showers were used to kill millions, a machinery of death.
4. Unlike in earlier concentration camps, here, secrecy was emphasized, to avoid news affecting world opinion or the German homefront or provoking more desperate resistance among intended victims.

5. Yet millions of Germans and others were involved, directly or indirectly, and had some measure of knowledge about the program's details.

6. Ironically, when news of the death camps did leak out to the West, it was often initially not believed, because of skepticism engendered by World War I propaganda.

B. The toll.

1. The Nazis killed an estimated six million Jews in camps and elsewhere during the Holocaust and were responsible for the deaths of millions of others as a result of abuse, slave labor, and executions.

2. Primo Levi (1919–1987) gave a searing account of his experiences in *Survival in Auschwitz*, showing how the camp universe was designed to destroy human identity itself, demonstrating that there were no limits and fulfilling ideological prophecies.

III. Future plans.

A. The Nazi vision of the future.

1. Hitler foresaw a Europe dominated and "organized" by Germans, spreading into living spaces of the East as colonial overlords.

2. The German people were to grow from 80 million to 250 million in one century and would be racially reengineered.

3. The Third Reich was to last a thousand years and dominate world politics.

B. GPO: the general plan for the East.

1. An actual blueprint of Nazi plans was the *Generalplan Ost* produced in the SS planning office and reviewed by Himmler in June 1942.

2. It projected what Eastern Europe would look like 25 years after the war and coolly calculated removal and decimation of 31 million non-Germans, along with the use of slave labor and planned colonization.

3. These projects were already underway with movement of ethnic Germans from Eastern European countries.

C. Nazi architecture.

1. Nazi architecture matched the regime's ambitions and was declared to be ideology in stone.

2. Hitler compulsively planned the rebuilding of Berlin on a grand scale as a new capital, with vast parade grounds and assembly halls.

3. These buildings were to be cultic centers replacing traditional religion, which was expected to wither away.

4. The grandiosity of Nazi architectural plans has suggested to some historians larger aims, including world domination.

IV. World domination.

    A. Superpower visions.

        1. Hitler envisioned a postwar order of large blocs of superpowers contending for supremacy.

        2. There is evidence of global goals in planning for an invasion of India, plans for superbattleships and superbombers capable of reaching America.

    B. Hitler's view of the United States.

        1. Hitler's views of Americans had been ambivalent, and he seemed to expect a showdown, perhaps in another generation.

        2. On December 11, 1941, Hitler declared war on the United States after Japan's attack on Pearl Harbor.

V. The war ends.

    A. The battle over Stalingrad in late 1942 and 1943 was an emblematic struggle between the dictators. German surrender there in January 1943 marked a turning point of the war.

    B. Mussolini was deposed and arrested in July 1943, ending his domination of Italy. After the Nazis rescued him, he was set up in a puppet state, the Republic of Salo.

    C. The war turned against Germany.

        1. In spite of total mobilization of the economy, the Soviet army advanced relentlessly on Germany and was joined by American and British forces in the West in 1944.

        2. Goebbels manipulated the Stalingrad defeat to motivate Germans through fear.

    D. The bunker.

1. Hitler retreated to a bunker in Berlin, losing touch with reality.
2. Goebbels sought to choreograph the fall of Berlin as a film, the final act of the "Twilight of the Gods" as the last element of the myth of the Führer.
3. With the so-called Nero Order of March 1945, Hitler ordered the "scorched earth" destruction of Germany.
4. After leaving a hate-filled final testament, Hitler committed suicide on April 30, 1945, in the bunker.

E. In Asia, Japan was defeated with the dropping of atomic bombs, opening the atomic age.

Essential Reading:

Michael Marrus, *The Holocaust in History*.

Supplementary Reading:

Primo Levi, *Survival in Auschwitz*.

Questions to Consider:

1. What were the crucial milestones on the Nazis' road to genocide?
2. Was world domination a logically implicit aim in Nazi ideology, or were more limited goals likelier?

Lecture Sixteen—Transcript
Nazi Genocide and Master Plans

In our previous lecture, we had discussed World War II, the war unleashed by Hitler, as a way station onto the realization of his ultimate goals. In this lecture, we'll examine in detail Nazi genocide and future master plans. We'll consider the Nazis' program of mass murder against the Jews, and Hitler's future plans for the construction of a racial utopia.

The Nazis set off on the road to mass murder with escalating persecutions, with medical killing, and execution squads, sent into occupied countries. These programs would lead to the construction of those institutions, the "factories of death," the extermination camps of Eastern Europe, during World War II.

For the future, Hitler and the Nazis looked forward to a colonial utopia in the East. Nazi architecture and monuments would suggest the vast scale of Hitler's ambitions, and only the end of the Second World War in 1945 and the defeat of Germany, would bring these plans, and their megalomania, to an end.

The Nazis had been quite explicit about their goals of achieving a racial utopia. Now, within German society in this period, a joke circulated, which cast doubt on the validity of this racial aim. The joke went as follows: "What should an ideal German look like?"— representative of Hitler's planned German race. The joke said, with conscious irony and paradox, that the ideal German should be as blond as Hitler, who, in fact, had dark hair, as slim as Goering, the notoriously fat fighter ace and Nazi leader, as tall as Goebbels, who was, in fact, diminutive, and as chaste as Rohm, the storm trooper who had decidedly not been so.

In fact, this joke, while it certainly stripped away the veneer of ideological hypocrisy in these leaders, who were presenting themselves as model Germans in terms of their own racial criteria, the Nazis would have responded by arguing that they were in the process of reshaping the raw material of the German people, unsatisfactory as it might be at present by their standards. They were on the road to creating, or breeding, the master race of the future. This program, this impetus, this dreadful dynamism, would lead to murder as a tool in the realization of these utopian nightmares.

The road to murder led, first of all, through eugenics. Eugenic thinking, was, in fact, not a German monopoly. We've discussed it in an earlier lecture. It had been a remarkably widespread mode of thinking worldwide during the first half of the century. This mode of thoughts, often associated with social Darwinism, had urged social policies that would plan a superior population for the nation, through the encouragement of "good births," as they were called, and discouraging, as a flip side, the reproduction of those who were judged unfit. German eugenics was not initiated only by Nazi medical experts, but in fact, had a strong tradition in Germany long before 1933.

It's also a dreadful commentary that American eugenics measures, in particular the forced sterilization laws that were common to many American states in the 1930s, were often held up by German eugenicists as a model, an inspiration for their own movement. The existence of such laws, I think, has been largely suppressed from the collective memory in United States, but it deserves to be recalled.

The Nazis would make eugenic policy one of their keynotes. Soon after coming to office, the Nazis passed a law in July of 1933, which authorized the forced, involuntary sterilization of those with hereditary diseases. Those could include mental illness, epilepsy, blindness, or alcoholism, which was judged to have a genetic basis. Hundreds of thousands of Germans were sterilized involuntarily.

The Nazi education, preparing the way for even more radical policies in the future, sought energetically to propagate eugenic thinking in the younger generation, with readings, or math word problems, about the social costs of what were considered those who were unfit.

In the Nazi genius for perverting the German language for their ideological aims, new phrases, terms, and names were crafted to label those who were considered unfit. These were chilling terms. They included the term *nutzlose Fresser*, or "useless eaters," or *Lebensunwertes Leben*, or "life unworthy of living." Nazi doctors would decide who was worthy of living and who was not.

The policy that came into being next was the euthanasia policy. In 1939, a program of euthanasia, or so-called "mercy killing," was instituted in Germany secretly, using the Second World War as a cover to justify these measures. We need to look back for a moment to the phenomenon of the First World War, and some of its devaluation of human life, to see that there were, in fact, earlier precedents for such a policy.

It is now emerging, in current research that is being done on German asylums and hospitals during the period of the First World War, that what amounted to a policy of euthanasia was perhaps—the historical record is now in the process of being researched more carefully—but perhaps there were policies that amounted to passive euthanasia, as those who were considered mentally ill or physically unfit were considered less deserving of limited food and other resources, in the time of total war. The research is still ongoing, but some historians are arguing that this experience of the First World War in some sense informed, and prepared the way, for active euthanasia in the Nazi regime during World War II.

The Nazis now set about establishing an active program to kill those whom they considered to be a drag on the national unity and resources. Departments and hospitals were ordered to collect information on children, and then on adults, who had handicaps or mental illness. Those who were so referred were passed into the hands of SS experts who would, in essence, condemn them to death. An estimated 100,000 people were killed in the course of this euthanasia program.

Then, the program was halted precipitously in August of 1941, for reasons that are still being debated by historians. Some argue that the very beginnings of growing resistance and unease on the part of some in German society who objected to euthanasia, were instrumental in bringing the program to a halt. Other historians have argued that, in fact, a simpler bureaucratic feature was at work. The euthanasia program had killed as many people as they had planned it to kill initially, and thus, was halted for the time being.

An institution that would play a very important role, and was now stepping into the forefront, executing the racial plans of the Nazi regime was the SS, under Heinrich Himmler. It was to be a key institution in the Third Reich's racial policies. SS medical personnel had been involved in the euthanasia program, where many of them had gained experience in the business of scientific, medicalized mass murder. The Reich's Führer SS Heinrich Himmler now sought to craft within the SS a new racial elite devoted to the breeding of the master race.

In 1939, Himmler became the Commissar for the Strengthening of Germandom, a title which, in essence, gave him enormous powers in the occupied Eastern territories, to seek to realize the racial utopia. Under Hitler's deputy, Reinhard Heydrich, the SS pressed forward with a policy of, and this was a consciously ugly word in German society, *Entjudung*, the "removal of the Jews" from Germany.

By 1939, more than a fourth of all German Jews had emigrated. Those who were left were those who could often not find refuge elsewhere in the world, the most vulnerable in society, who awaited their fate.

The SS also provided master, experienced executioners, the *Einsatzgruppen*. They were the special forces task groups, or strike groups of the SS. They were first sent into Poland, in 1939, to eliminate intellectuals and leaders, and to quell potential resistance. They and other Nazi officials then set about also deporting tens of thousands of Polish Jews from those areas in Western Poland that were to be annexed to the greater German Reich. Those tens of thousands of Polish Jews were now essentially expelled into the remaining areas of occupied Poland, which the regime planned to use as a so-called "dumping ground," or reservation for Jews and others who were considered racially undesirable. The areas otherwise in Nazi influence were to be "cleansed of Jews."

With the attack on the Soviet Union, the *Einsatzgruppen* followed right behind the German armies as the front moved forward. Behind the lines, they committed mass murder of the Jewish communities in Eastern Europe. They killed an estimated one million Jews by the end of 1941.

However, Nazi leaders judged that this mode of killing, the open executions, the shooting into pits full of men, women, and children of Eastern Europe by the *Einsatzgruppen* was too open and too inefficient, in essence. Anxieties were voiced about what effect face-to-face killing would have even on ideologically motivated killers like the *Einsatzgruppen*. Heinrich Himmler, who witnessed an execution, apparently fainted upon viewing its barbarity face-to-face, rather than from behind a desk. The thus, new plans were laid for a more efficient, regularized, bureaucratic plan. This was known as the "Final Solution," using the Nazis' perverse talent for bureaucratic euphemism.

The Final Solution was to eliminate the Jews. The Wannsee Conference, as it was called, took place on January 20, 1942, in an opulent villa outside of Berlin. There's a remarkable museum there today. It's a place around which an aura of evil hovers, in our historical memory. In this villa, even as operations were already underway, and the "final solution" was being put into effect, discussions took place on how to systematize the comprehensive Final Solution.

Contrary to popular memory that circulates out there, the Final Solution was not planned at the Wannsee villa. Rather, the discussion wasn't about whether the program should take place, but merely about how to fine-tune it. When the meeting protocol, the minutes of the meeting, couched in bureaucratic euphemism, in an attempt to cloud or veil, as much as was possible, the reality of what was being discussed, mass murder, were discovered after the war, with justice, they were called some of the most shameful documents in world history. What had been agreed?

Europe's Jews, not just in Germany or in Poland, but from all of Europe, already occupied or yet to be occupied, were to be, euphemistically "shipped to the East." There, they would be worked to death or exterminated outright. Within Germany itself, the obligatory yellow star was introduced for German Jews in 1941, and had already taken place in other occupied territories in Eastern Europe. Thus, this community was now singled out, set apart for this fate.

Hitler's role in the launching of the Nazi genocide is still being debated, as historians trace his precise actions in the available documentation. Hitler's aversion, both to regular, bureaucratic functioning, as well as putting orders down on paper, written orders, were due to his caution about leaving a paper trail that could be traced back to him. This makes tracing the documentary evidence complicated. Clearly, however, Hitler's role was pivotal, as he established the long-term goals of the regime and endorsed programs of growing radicalism in the racial sphere. One needs to keep in mind, nonetheless, the larger circle of complicity around Hitler as well.

It's crucial to note that a program of this scope and this magnitude, involving the planned murder of millions, involved more than just

Hitler himself, more than a small circle of planners, such as a Wannsee. In fact, enormous numbers of officials at both the highest and lowest levels of the state and the party, from generals, to mayors of towns, to station masters, to ordinary guards, were implicated and were needed to make the Final Solution happen. Indeed, wherever the Nazis gained power in the occupied countries of Europe, they found collaborators who turned up in every country to help them in this program.

The program culminated in the erection of what were essentially "factories of death," institutions, the death camps, that produced not goods, not materials, but death itself. By early 1942, death camps were operating under SS control in the occupied Eastern territories, with names that still ring with horror for us today, names like Auschwitz, Belzec, Treblinka, Chelmno, Majdanek, and Sobibor.

These were, as distinct from the earlier concentration camps, devoted to the extermination of those who were sent there. Europe's Jews were concentrated in ghettos in Poland and elsewhere and then were shipped to the camps by train. Gas chambers were disguised as showers, and were used to kill millions in all rationalized machinery of death. Unlike in earlier concentration camps set up in the first years of the Nazi regime, where their existence was relatively open, here, secrecy was emphasized, to avoid having news spread that might affect neutral world opinion, or to avoid having news spread to the German homefront, which then would be confronted with the immediate reality of what was being done in Germany's name. They were also kept secret to avoid provoking more desperate resistance among intended victims.

Yet, one thing is clear. In spite of the secrecy that was ordered, such a program could not be kept entirely secret. Millions of Germans and others were involved, directly or indirectly, and thus had some measure of knowledge about the program's details.

There was a further irony. When news of death camps did leak out of Germany and the occupied territories to the West, those rumors were often initially not believed. This was another legacy of the First World War. Propaganda in the First World War had announced news of atrocities, some without basis, some with. After the First World War, a great skepticism had grown up about such stories. It was precisely this skepticism which, in this case, led to such true rumors, such first portents, of the atrocities being committed by the Nazis in their full scale, to be dismissed, at first.

The toll of such policies was dreadful. The Nazis killed an estimated six million Jews in the camps and elsewhere during the Holocaust. They were further responsible for the deaths of millions of others, due to abuse, slave labor, and executions. One Italian Jewish survivor of Auschwitz, Primo Levi, gave a searing account of his experiences in what amounts to a classic of this barbarous era, his book, *Survival in Auschwitz*.

It showed in detail, from his own experiences, how the camp universe, the parallel universe set up by the Nazis, was designed specifically for the aim of destroying human identity itself, demonstrating to the prisoners that there were no limits in how they might be treated, and to fulfill the ideological prophecies of the Nazis, who had announced that the world was broken down on racial lines, and that some races would be slated for extinction, while others dominated. The camps were where those prophecies were to be brought to pass, as Primo Levi suggested.

Primo Levi's *Survival in Auschwitz* also had one haunting image. He recounted an experience he had of a meeting with an educated German, a doctor by the name of Pannwitz, who was looking for educated prisoners who knew something about chemistry, in order to use their knowledge at least for awhile, to use them economically. Pannwitz interviewed Primo Levi. Levi explained that if he were able, as a survivor of the camp, to communicate to people who had not known that reality how that German doctor had looked at him, that look, that gaze, he could communicate the entire barbarity of Nazi Germany.

He explained that that look was not the sort of look that would pass between two human beings. There was no flicker of fellow feeling, no recognition of common shared humanity on the part of that German doctor as he looked at the prisoner in front of him. Levi explained that instead, that it was the sort of look that one might see at a zoo, between a creature of one race and another who was there to be exploited, used, and cast aside, not a fellow human being. Levi understood that his very humanity was under assault.

The Nazis had further future plans beyond even their barbaric perfection of the Final Solution. We need to discuss, in brief, some of the Nazi visions for the future, in essence, the science fiction of the Nazi utopia, which they projected for the future.

Hitler foresaw a Europe, which would be dominated and "organized" by the Germans as a master race, spreading into the living spaces of Eastern Europe as colonial overlords. The German people were to grow from 80 million, at that time, to 250 million in one century. They were to be racially reengineered, purified, the dross melted away, stripped away, and instead, leaving the racially pure. The Third Reich was to last 1000 years and to dominate world politics.

In some sense, we don't need merely to look at Nazi propaganda to understand their plans for the future. We can actually view another document, which gives us a glimpse of what they wanted their future to be like.

This is the GPO, as its known in its bureaucratic acronym, the general plan for the East, the *Generalplan Ost*. This was an actual blueprint of Nazi plans, produced in the SS planning office for the future of Eastern Europe. It was reviewed by Heinrich Himmler in June of 1942, and was sent back to the planning office by Himmler with the comment that it was still too gentle, still too mild, and that they should continue to work on it. What this document say, in that form?

It projected what Eastern Europe would like 25 years after the war had been successfully fought by the Nazis. It was, in essence, work of science fiction. It coolly calculated the removal and annihilation of some 31 million non-Germans from Eastern Europe, the Slavic and other non-German pupils living there at that time. Those who would be allowed to remain would not be free. Rather, they would provide slave labor for awhile, and their areas would be colonized by the German master race.

These projects were already, in part, under way, with the movement of ethnic Germans from Eastern European countries to the new colonial empire. Nazi architecture also gives us a vivid visual way of understanding some of the vastness of the regime's ambitions. The Nazis declared that their architecture was "ideology in stone." It was bombastic, it was neoclassical, and expressed some of the compulsions of the Nazis for monumentality and the dwarfing of the individual.

Hitler, himself a frustrated architect, compulsively planned and re-planned the rebuilding of Berlin as a new German capital, to be renamed "Germania," on a grand scale, with vast party buildings, vast parade grounds, assembly halls, and marching fields where a million Germans could gather to parade in the marching that was so important to Nazi imagery.

These buildings were to be cultic centers, replacing traditional religion, which was expected to wither away. Hitler was especially pleased with the work of his personal architect, Albert Speer, was charged with the mission of realizing some of Hitler's fantasies, who would achieve the so-called "Cathedral of Light," a massive projection of pillars of light in the Nuremberg party rallies, to imitate a traditional cathedral.

The grandiosity of Nazi architectural plans has suggested to some historians larger aims, including world domination Nazi architecture was preplanned to leave tremendous dramatic ruins for the future, thousands of years hence. Some historians have argued that it's also a blueprint for world plans.

Hitler clearly had superpower visions. He envisioned a post-war order of large blocs of superpowers contending for supremacy, certainly Germany, maybe Great Britain, maybe the United States, maybe others. There is evidence that there were global goals in Nazi planning for such seemingly improbable things like an invasion of India, in order to strike at the British Empire through Afghanistan and plans for super battleships and super bombers that would be capable of ranges to reach America in a coming war.

Hitler's view of the United States was a very interesting feature in his thinking about the future. His views of Americans had always been very ambivalent. At certain times, they were largely negative. At certain times, though, Hitler had thought that the preponderance of German ancestry among many Americans might represent a racial core that meant that America might still be revived. At other times, he and the Nazis were scathing, considering America, as they put it, a "mongrel nation" of racial mixing, which doomed it, in racial terms, in coming confrontations.

Hitler seemed to expect a showdown between the German superpower and the United States, perhaps in another generation, after his time. When it came to war, however, between Japan, his ally, and the United States, Hitler declared war on the U.S., on December 11, 1941, after Japan's attack on Pearl Harbor and cast the die in this gamble.

The Second World War would also be brought to an end, which would spell the conclusion to these bombastic plans. The battle over Stalingrad in the Soviet Union, in late 1942 and 1943, had grown into an emblematic struggle between the dictators. It had enormous symbolic significance. In this sense, it bore some similarities to that great industrial battle of Verdun that we've discussed, in the First World War, both in mistakes as well as in the ferocity of the fighting.

Hitler had announced how important it was to take this city, Stalingrad, which literally means "Stalinville," to show that Stalin's own city, Stalin's own place of honor, was not immune from German victories. When the Red Army surrounded the German army there, however, Hitler refused to countenance the idea of a retreat. When the German army surrendered there finally, in January of 1943, against Hitler's orders, this marked a symbolic turning point of the war. The veneer that had surrounded the supposedly inevitable victory in the field was now lost. The fortunes, the tides of war, had begun to turn.

This was clear in Fascist Italy as well, which had increasingly come under the orbit of the Nazis. Benito Mussolini was deposed by some of his own Fascist allies and was arrested in July of 1943, ending his domination of Italy. This fact in and of itself is significant. One can't imagine Hitler being deposed by some of his closest followers in this same way. Clearly, Benito Mussolini, though he was proud of being, supposedly, the archetypal totalitarian dictator, in fact, had not achieved that measure of total control.

Hitler, who felt that he would ever after owe Mussolini a debt of gratitude for showing the way in his political career, sent special forces to rescue him from his captivity. Mussolini was then finally set up rule over a rump little puppet state in northern Italy, the Republic of Salo, where, towards the end of his career, he came full circle almost, some have suggested, pursuing more socialist policies, coming back to some of the affinities of his youth. Eventually, however, as Italy itself was lost to the Germans, as the allies fought their way up the Peninsula, Mussolini himself would be hunted down by partisans, killed, and ignominiously hung upside down, a bitter end for man who had wrought such destruction in Italy.

The war had turned against Germany in spite of the belated total mobilization of the economy, which Hitler had deferred out of fear for how the German homefront might react. The Soviet army now advanced relentlessly on Germany, and was joined the West by American and British forces in 1944 as the noose tightened on Hitler's Third Reich.

Goebbels, meanwhile, pulled off some remarkable propaganda stunts, even as defeat grew near. Goebbels argued that Stalingrad's defeat should not be hidden from the German people, but should, in fact, be played up. Germans could be motivated to fight, not through confidence in victory, he said, but even more effectively through fear. He would now play masterfully upon the anxieties and the consciences of those who felt what retribution might be in store after the Nazis' reign of terror.

Hitler now retreated to the bunker in Berlin, awaiting the end. In the bunker, underneath the center of Berlin, he began to lose touch with reality. In the strange last days of Nazi Germany, Goebbels sought to produce a final triumph of propaganda. This already suggested his own loss of reality, the way in which this propaganda chief had come to believe his own propaganda, about the inevitable victory, or the glory of the Third Reich.

Goebbels sought to choreograph the fall of Berlin itself, as a film that wasn't on film, but rather, would be enacted with real actors, real fighters, and real leaders going down in defeat. This was to be the final act in a Wagnerian opera made real, the "Twilight of the Gods," as the final crowning element of the myth of the Führer that he had crafted. Goebbels, after killing his children and his wife, would follow his Führer into death.

With the so-called Nero Order of 1945, Hitler, without a trace of remorse, ordered the destruction of Germany itself, to be sure that the Allies would gain nothing after he was defeated. After leaving a hate-filled final testament, in which Hitler announced, with no trace of remorse, that his hatred would arise again, he committed suicide, on April 30, 1945, in the bunker.

In Asia, Japan was defeated with the dropping of atomic bombs, opening the atomic age. What would follow upon the horrors of the Second World War, however, contemporaries would be horrified to discover, was not the hoped-for peace, but rather, a new standoff, the ideological conflict of the Cold War, to be discussed in our next lecture.

Lecture Seventeen
The Cold War

Scope:

No sooner had World War II ended than a new ideological confrontation emerged. This lecture considers the Cold War and how ideological blocs of countries faced off against one another. It discusses Stalin's renewed consolidation of control in the Soviet Union, as liberated Soviet prisoners of war were sent to the Gulag camps and societies were remade by force, with the mass deportations of Baltic peoples, Tatars, and Chechens. Before his death in 1953, Stalin seemed to be preparing a new round of persecutions, now targeting the Soviet Union's Jews. In the decades that followed, a new worldwide fear became almost ordinary: the nuclear balance of terror, with "mutually assured destruction" precariously maintained by the Cold War opponents.

Outline

I. Aftermath of World War II.

   A. The costs.

      1. The war, involving more than 40 nations, left over 50 million dead.

      2. Roughly half were civilians (versus an estimated 10 percent in World War I).

   B. The atomic age.

      1. Invention of atomic weapons opened a new age of potential destruction.

      2. By 1949, the Soviet Union also produced a nuclear weapon (aided by espionage).

   C. Onset of the Cold War.

      1. The uneasy alliance of the United States and Britain with Stalin was already strained, but hopes remained that international cooperation could continue, despite stark ideological differences.

      2. These differences, however, soon led to *Cold War*, armed ideological confrontation lasting nearly half a century.

II. International efforts and human rights.

   A. The United Nations.

      1. The United Nations Organization was founded at the San Francisco Conference (April–June 1945).

      2. The Charter defined aims: peace through collective security, self-determination, international cooperation and progress, and respect for human rights.

      3. Above the General Assembly, the Security Council wields power. Its five permanent members are victors of World War II (the United States, the Soviet Union, Britain, China, and France).

      4. Cold War tensions impeded its functioning. The Soviets demanded and received extra seats.

      5. Vetoes in the Security Council immobilized the body.

      6. The Universal Declaration of Human Rights, approved December 10, 1948, in Paris, remained a nonbinding expression of ideals, which many member states violated and continue to violate.

   B. Nuremberg war crime trials.

      1. From 1945 to 1947, Nazi leaders were tried in Nuremberg by Allied judges for crimes against humanity, placing a new emphasis on human rights.

      2. Critics pointed out the irony of Soviet judges passing verdicts while Soviet crimes, such as the events at Katyn, were not considered. Nonetheless, the sentences were richly deserved.

   C. Genocide Convention.

      1. In 1948, the United Nations General Assembly passed the Genocide Convention, making genocide (a term invented by crusading jurist Raphael Lemkin) an international crime.

      2. The term was defined in special ways that are still controversial today.

      3. The convention's effect has been slow to be felt.

III. George Orwell's vision of 1984.

   A. British journalist George Orwell wrote his dystopian novel *1984* in 1948, drawing on contemporary trends and his reading of Zamyatin's *We*.

B. Protagonist Winston Smith lives in a society dominated by the omnipresent, mysterious Big Brother. Inner resistance dooms Smith and his love for a young woman.

    1. He works in the Ministry of Truth, revising historical records and purging the past.

    2. A political language, Newspeak, eliminated "thoughtcrime."

    3. Smith resists the system but is tracked down and broken, betraying his love for Julia and his own humanity.

C. Orwell's vision is dark and pessimistic.

    1. The future is presented as "a boot stamping on a human face—forever."

    2. Details of his story matched many of the features of contemporary regimes.

    3. Yet the message was a wider one, on the human susceptibility to tyranny.

IV. Forced population movement and ethnic cleansing in Europe.

A. The war left 11 million refugees, bureaucratically labeled "displaced persons."

B. Expulsion of ethnic Germans.

    1. Some 15 million ethnic Germans fled or were expelled, especially from Poland and Czechoslovakia.

    2. At the Potsdam Conference (July–August 1945), the United States, Britain, and the Soviet Union approved their "humane and orderly transfer," referring to the 1923 Lausanne Treaty as precedent.

    3. The process was, in fact, violent, with an estimated three million dead.

C. Over two million refugees from Eastern Europe were forcibly deported, returned to Stalin's control, killed, or jailed.

V. The Cold War and Stalin.

A. Outer empire and inner empire.

    1. Claiming security needs, Stalin established an "outer empire" of Eastern European People's Republics, ruled by Communists after a period of coalition governments.

2. In the "inner empire" of the Soviet Union itself, Stalin clamped down again, betraying implicit wartime promises of liberalization.

B. Soviet prisoners of war.
1. Stalin considered captured soldiers to be traitors.
2. Instead of being returned home, they were shipped by cattle car to labor camps.
3. Solzhenitsyn's *One Day in the Life of Ivan Denisovich* portrayed his own experiences in the Gulag of this period.

C. Punished peoples.
1. Entire nations suspected of disloyalty were deported and decimated.
2. Before the war's end, in 1944, Chechens, Ingush, and Crimean Tartars were all deported from the Caucasus and Crimea to Central Asia.
3. Half a million Chechens and Ingush were deported, and 189,000 Tartars, with great losses.
4. Conflict in Chechnya today cannot be understood without this background.
5. Mass deportations resumed in the Baltics (following on deportations of 1941). Several hundred thousand people were deported to Siberia. Scarcely any families were left untouched, and 15 percent of the Baltic populations were gone by 1950.
6. World War II continued in Eastern Europe even after 1945. The Baltic Forest War saw guerrillas fighting Soviet forces into the 1950s.

D. Growth of the Cold War.
1. Stalin stated that a territory's occupier determines its social system and worked with allies in Eastern European countries to consolidate Communist rule.
2. In 1947, non-Communist parties were dropped from government in Hungary, Romania, and Poland. In 1948, a Communist coup in Czechoslovakia created sole rule.
3. In October 1947, the Comintern, shut down when Stalin had looked for support in the West against Hitler, was revived under the name of *Cominform*.

4. Communist parties in Italy and France enjoyed considerable popularity and prestige because of their anti-Nazi resistance.

E. Stalin's death.
1. Stalin died in March 1953, perhaps on the eve of another wave of purges.
2. In January 1953, Soviet authorities announced discovery of an alleged "doctor's plot." Government doctors, mostly Jewish, were accused of a wide conspiracy to poison Soviet leaders.
3. Stalin's regime seemed to be taking a radical anti-Semitic turn before his death.

F. De-Stalinization and changes.
1. In 1956, Nikita Khrushchev's speech at the 20th congress of the Communist Party denounced Stalin's crimes, especially those against the party.
2. Khrushchev announced a new policy of coexistence and competition, promising to bury the West technologically.
3. Soviet forces suppressed uprisings in East Germany (1953), Poland (1956), Hungary (1956), and Czechoslovakia (1968).
4. Sputnik (1957) and nuclear weapons gave the Soviet Union an image of progress, belied by failures of development, such as Lysenkoism's crackpot agricultural theories.

G. Dividing lines.
1. Aleksandr Solzhenitsyn compared ideological conflicts of the Cold War to a line running through individuals.
2. The blocs of East and West were not monolithic. Individual sympathies and allegiances varied greatly.
3. Although the Cold War did not erupt into a full-scale clash, it did cause "proxy wars," such as America's Vietnam War and the Soviet invasion of Afghanistan.
4. Alliances on both sides contradicted ideological consistency.

VI. The Berlin Wall.
A. Division of the Germanies.

1. On occupying eastern Germany, Soviet forces engaged in abuse of civilians and mass rape, in a cycle of revenge for Nazi atrocities. This experience undercut support for German Communists.
2. In the eastern Soviet zone, the German Democratic Republic was declared in October 1949.

B. After massive population flight, the Berlin Wall was built on August 13, 1961.
1. Called an "anti-Fascist protection wall," extending through the border between the Germanies, the wall became a symbol of division.
2. Some 900 people died trying to escape westward.

VII. M.A.D.: mutually assured destruction.

A. Cuban missile crisis.
1. The 1962 Cuban missile crisis over the stationing of Soviet missiles in Cuba (where Fidel Castro had taken power in 1959) seemed to bring the world to the brink of nuclear war.
2. It was followed by attempts at détente, relaxing tensions.

B. Balance of terror.
1. A key concept of deterrence, *assured destruction*, sought to prevent nuclear aggression by the implicit threat of a second nuclear strike that would obliterate the attacker and render victory meaningless.
2. Globally, this balance of terror kept an uneasy peace.

Essential Reading:

Brian Moynihan, *The Russian Century*, pp. 183–222.

George Orwell, *1984*.

Supplementary Reading:

Samantha Power, *"A Problem From Hell": America and the Age of Genocide*, pp. 17–85.

Norman M. Naimark, *Fires of Hatred*, pp.85–138.

Aleksandr Solzhenitsyn, *One Day in the Life of Ivan Denisovich*.

Questions to Consider:

1. Was the Cold War a period of stability or instability in international politics? Why?
2. Could the Cold War have been avoided? How?

Lecture Seventeen—Transcript
The Cold War

In our previous lectures, we had been discussing the ordeal of the Second World War, and we had further discussed the plans for the future that the Nazis had hatched, which were forestalled by their defeat in that conflict.

When World War II had ended, however, it didn't bring with it the peace that so many people longed for, but rather a new ideological confrontation, the *Cold War*, which we'll be discussing today.

A point that we've underlined before in the context of our discussion of the First World War, and of other conflicts, is that even when they're brought to a formal, or juridical end, they still continue in aftershocks. In some sense, the Cold War would represent an aftershock, a settling of accounts that had built up during the Second World War, as a new ideological confrontation loomed.

As people took stock of the world in the aftermath of war, the costs were borne in upon them. The war, which had involved more than 40 nations, making it truly a global conflict, had left, by a conservative estimate, over 50 million dead. Some estimates range far higher.

Historians estimate that roughly half of those who were victims of the war were civilians. This represented an intensification of that feature of total war that we'd already remarked on in our discussion of the First World War. In the First World War, it's estimated that some ten percent of the victims of that conflict were civilians. Now that number, that proportion, had jumped to 50 percent. This represented a terrible intensification. Moreover, as a signal emblem of that intensification, the end of World War II had also ushered in a new age of weapons that had even more formidable destructive power: The atomic age.

A new age of potential destruction had been opened up, heretofore unknown to man, and these weapons would proliferate. While the United States had been first to use atomic weapons against Japan, by 1949, the Soviet Union had also produced a nuclear weapon, in part aided by espionage against its former allies. The Cold War now set in.

According to many historians, the Cold War had already, in essence, started to play itself out in the Second World War, especially in its closing stages. World War II had seen an uneasy alliance of the United States and Britain, Western democracies on the one hand, with Stalin and his Soviet Union on the other side. This uneasy alliance had already been strained during the war, but as the war ended, hopes, reasonably enough, were still present that international cooperation might be continued past the conflict despite the stark, some argued, irreconcilable ideological differences between the former allies.

These differences, however, soon led to what came to recall a "cold war," not a "hot war" of active armed conflict, but rather, a tense standoff that threatened, at any moment, to turn into an all-out armed confrontation, an ideological standoff that lasted nearly half a century, and did much to shape our world in the present day.

With the end of the Second World War, and its closing stages, people, quite understandably, were gathering their thoughts on the sort of international efforts that might pool the resources of an international community, that might assure human rights, that might seem to ground hopes in peace. The United Nations, in particular, was held up as one such international institution, that as a successor to the League of Nations project, might finally vindicate those hopes.

The United Nations organization was founded at the San Francisco Conference, from April to June of 1945. The United Nations' charter defined its aims. These were the noble aims of peace through collective security, the promise of self-determination, the notion of international cooperation and shared progress, and respect for human rights.

The structure of the United Nations was one that was intended as a compromise between these ideals and the demands of political realism and diplomacy. There is a General Assembly, in which nations would participate, at least in theory, as equals, while above the general assembly a so-called Security Council wields real power. Its five permanent members are the victors of World War II: The United States, the Soviet Union, Great Britain, China, and France.

To the dismay of those who invested such hopes in the United Nations, however, the recognition soon dawned that Cold War tensions impeded its functioning along the lines that they had imagined. To give but one example, the Soviets demanded and got extra seats in the General Assembly for constituent republics of the

Soviet Union, Ukraine and Byelorussia. Within the Security Council, vetoes by the Soviet Union, or by its opponents in the Cold War, tended all too often to immobilize that body, and prevented its effective functioning.

Nevertheless, further hopes were vested in an articulation of what were taken to be shared, common principals. One very important example of just such a public articulation of shared ideals, at least shared in theory, was the Universal Declaration of Human Rights. This was approved on December 10, 1948, in Paris. It remained, moreover, a non-binding expression of the ideals of aspiring for the respect of human rights, which unfortunately, all too many member states of the United Nations violated, and still continue to violate, to this very day.

There were also other accounts that needed to be settled in the aftermath of the Second World War. One outstanding issue was: What should be done with the defeated Nazi Germany? The regime that its authors had expected would last 1000 years, Hitler's Third Reich, had collapsed. What was now to be done to reckon up the crimes of that regime?

Contemporary observers, including Hannah Arendt, noted that when one traveled in postwar Germany, one could note a bizarre phenomenon. It seemed as if all the Nazis had disappeared. People now presented themselves as either having been active resistors or passive inward objectors to the Nazi regime, and Hannah Arendt and others observed that it was very difficult to find publicly professed Nazis in the aftermath of this war. It seemed that the collapse of the regime had been total, and the regime's ideology had been discredited. Now, however, the question still presented itself: How should its crimes be dealt with?

This was, in part, answered at the Nuremberg War Crimes Trials. In the city of Nuremberg, in southern Germany, from 1945 to 1947, prominent Nazi leaders were tried by Allied judges for crimes against humanity. The very term was significant, because it emphasized that new stress on human rights, which was so hopefully current in the immediate postwar period.

Some critics of these war crimes trials pointed out the irony of Soviet judges passing verdicts against their ideological allies from before, now defeated ideological former allies, while Soviet crimes like

Katyn were, in fact, not even considered. One thing was clear, however. The sentences that were finally leveled against these Nazi leaders were richly deserved.

The war crimes trials also accomplished something far larger than holding individuals accountable. They were also important in setting down the historical facts of the regime and its crimes. It laid down a historical record, which would be of enormous significance in spreading common knowledge of these events. We had discussed in an earlier lecture how, in the aftermath of the First World War, in Germany, there had arisen a "stab-in-the-back legend" that argued that, in fact, Germany had never really been defeated, but that inner enemies were to blame. The finality of Germany's defeat in the Second World War, and the Nuremberg War Crimes Trials, with their registering of a public record, made it clear that no such legend or paranoid myth was tenable in the postwar period.

The process of an entire society, of German society coming to terms with and acknowledging the crimes that had been committed in its name was not simply one limited to the immediate postwar period, but indeed, was a longer process, only really gaining steam in the '70s and '80s; indeed, it's still ongoing, a wrenching confrontation with a burden of the past.

Another legacy of the immediate postwar period and the emphasis on human rights, was the Genocide Convention. In 1948, the United Nations General Assembly passed the Genocide Convention, which made genocide an international crime. The term "genocide" was a new one; the phenomenon, obviously, was one that had a much longer history. In part, its popularization of this term was due to one man, a crusading jurist by the name of Rafael Lemkin.

Rafael Lemkin was a Polish Jewish refugee who had come to the United States. He represented a lonely, prophetic voice in arguing that people who committed what before then had been crime without a name, needed internationally to be held to account.

In fact, he had already been thinking in these terms before the Nazi genocide. In the course of the 1920s, he had been shocked and dismayed to hear of the Armenian genocide of the First World War, and had struggled with the implications, both legal and moral, of the existence of such crimes. He crusaded, ultimately successfully, for the prescription of this crime of genocide, a word that he had invented by combining the Greek word for "tribe" or "an ethnic group", *genos*, with the Latin word for "murder", *cide*.

The term was defined in ways that were controversial then, and are still controversial today. The convention defined the crime of genocide as, "The intent to destroy, in whole or in part, national, ethnic, racial or religious groups."

Some critics argued that this particular definition might set the bar too high; certain crimes might be downplayed, as it were, because they didn't meet all of the definition's requirements. Others argued that the bar might be set too low, pointing out that the question of determining intent was a notoriously difficult one, and people are still wrestling with the question of which particular atrocities qualify for the full term of "genocide," and which fall short of it. Thus, the question remains controversial today. The Convention's effect has also been slow to be felt, as we'll see in our following lectures, when we examine particular cases of international inaction in the face of what clearly meets these criteria of genocide.

At the same time as laws and conventions were seeking to draw some conclusions from the experience of the previous decade, in the terms of literature, another lesson was drawn. That was to be seen in George Orwell's great novel of dystopia, *1984*.

The British journalist George Orwell wrote his dystopian novel, *1984*, in the year 1948. He simply reversed the years of his writing to indicate a coming future, not all too distant. He depicted a society of totalitarian rule, drawing on contemporary trends, particular modes of government, and modes of politics that he observed in his own world around him. In addition, and this is significant, he drew on his own reading of Zamyatin's classic dystopian novel of the Soviet Union, written in 1920, *We*.

In *1984*, perhaps the most famous of the dystopian novels of the 20th century, his protagonist, by the name of Winston Smith, lives in a society totally dominated by the omnipresent, mysterious "Big Brother," and a dominant party. In terms of the novel's plot line, outer repression, as well as inner resistance within Winston himself, dooms him, and his love for a young woman.

Winston Smith works in the Ministry of Truth, which is devoted entirely to the task of revising historical records, to bring them into line with the shifting version of the truth of the Party. It is engaged in the constant purging of the past, throwing out data, now untrue historical records, into what Orwell very notably called "the memory hole," a sort of incinerator.

A political language was developed by Big Brother's regime, entitled New Speak. It was aimed at the task of eliminating thought crime, eliminating the very possibility of thinking thoughts that were not approbated by the regime. We consider the resemblance that this sort of linguistic control of a society depicted in Orwell's novel; we think of Victor Klemperer, that analyst of Nazi perversion of the German language, and see some remarkable parallels.

In the novel, Winston Smith resists the system, but ultimately, he's tracked down and broken. He betrays his love for Julia and his own humanity.

In this novel, Orwell's vision is dark and pessimistic. The future is presented in the words of one of the interrogators of Winston Smith as he's being broken, as "a dark one, full of hatred forever." This interrogator tells his victim, "If you want a picture of the future, imagine this: A boot stamping on a human face—forever." The interrogator promised that what would follow upon the triumph of the regime, upon suppressing the last resistance, would be a world of terror, not a utopia of love or peace, but a world of terror based on hatred and domination, which were equally parts of human nature.

It's remarkable to observe that in this story, in which George Orwell emphasized the conviction that totalitarian regimes had of the malleability of human nature and their ability to manipulate, that one could actually see many of the features of contemporary regimes, or in some cases, even anticipations of later authoritarian practice in the world at large.

George Orwell's novel was not simply about the regimes that he observed in the present day, however. His pessimistic message was a wider one. It had to do with the human susceptibility, as he saw it, to the lure of tyranny, the promise of order and stability, even at the price of the extinguishing of human nature.

Indeed, even in these hopeful times of the first years of the postwar period, observers who looked around could certainly see portents that were far more troubling than the high hopes of this postwar period. These included massive forced population movements and ethnic cleansing in Europe itself.

World War II had left 11 million refugees on the European continent, and many more millions in other parts of the world. These were now, as it were, a new kind of person: Stateless, unmoored, homeless. Bureaucratically, they were labeled "displaced persons." In Hannah Arendt's reflections on the 20th century, she argued that the 20th century might have to be considered the century of the displaced person or of the refugee.

Among those who were displaced or were actively expelled were ethnic Germans in Eastern Europe. Some 15 million ethnic Germans fled or were expelled from Eastern European countries, where they had lived as minorities, in some cases for centuries previous, especially from Poland and Czechoslovakia. They were expelled, in part, as part of a cycle of revenge against Nazi crimes committed against Eastern European peoples. To note that this human tragedy in no way minimizes the guilt of the Nazis, in no way exculpates their crimes, but rather underlines the vicious nature of cycles of revenge and violence in modern history.

At the Potsdam Conference, where Great Britain, the United States, and the Soviet Union gathered from July to August of 1945, the Allies approved what they called the "humane and orderly transfer" of such people. They referred, in particular, to a precedent that we've already discussed in earlier lecture, the precedent of the 1923 Lausanne Treaty, which had established were supposed to be, at least in theory, humane population transfers between Greece and Turkey in the aftermath of the First World War. That process had been violent. This new, underwritten process of population transfer after World War II was also enormously violent, with an estimated three million dead. The rhetoric of humanity and concern for humanitarian issues covered up a brutal reality.

Beyond this, over two million refugees from Eastern Europe were also forcibly deported or returned to Eastern Europe and to Stalin's control, where they were killed or jailed. A terrible fate had awaited them.

Within the areas of his control, Josef Stalin now clamped down in recognition of the growing tensions of the Cold War. One needs to distinguish between Stalin's policies in an outer empire, of the areas dominated by the conquering Red Army, and his policies of reconsolidating his control in an inner empire, the Soviet Union itself. Let's consider first the outer empire of Eastern Europe.

Claiming security needs and omitting to mention that the Nazis had been an invasion of his own allies, Stalin demanded an "outer empire" of Eastern European so-called People's Republics, ruled by Communists after a period of shared government in coalition. Within the "inner empire" of the Soviet Union itself, Stalin now clamped down again. You'll recall that at the start of the battle between the Nazis and the Soviets, Stalin had implicitly seemed to offer the promise of liberalization, if only ordinary Soviet citizens would rally to the cause of defending the motherland. These promises were now betrayed. Stalin returned to his rhetoric of addressing the peoples of the Soviet Union no longer as "fellow Russians" or "fellow members of the homeland" but rather, as "comrades." A very vivid example of this was the fate of Soviet prisoners of war.

You'll recall that those Soviet prisoners of war who had fallen into Nazi hands were often allowed to die of neglect, in the millions. Stalin now meted a cruel fate out to those who survived. Ipso facto, Stalin considered soldiers who had allowed themselves to be taken prisoner traitors. As they were loaded onto trains, and brought back home, to Moscow and other Russian cities, their trains didn't stop to unload them there. Instead, these trains with prisoners of war, now "liberated," sped on through to Siberia. They were shipped there by cattle car to labor camps, to pay for the crime of having been captured.

Alexandr Solzhenitsyn's novel, entitled *One Day in the Life of Ivan Denisovich*, portrayed this man's own experiences in the Gulag of this period. He had been an artillery officer in the Red Army, had been a committed fighter in the Russian cause, but he'd been arrested in 1945 for making critical remarks about Stalin, and was subjected to eight years in prison. He depicted, in this novel, the brutal realities of the Gulag camp, and later would be awarded the Nobel Prize, in 1970, for this depiction. This account of the brutal existence of ordinary prisoners, *One Day in the Life*, bore a punchline that was ironic. That punchline was, essentially, that this, on balance, had been a good day for a prisoner, since he had survived.

Other peoples were to be punished wholesale for their real or suspected disloyalty. They were deported or decimated. Before the war's end in 1944, Chechens, English, and Crimean Tartars, non-Russian peoples living in the Soviet Union, were all deported from the Caucuses in the Crimea to central Asia, because of Stalin's suspicions. Half a million Chechens and English were deported, and 189,000 Tartars, with great losses to their populations. The conflict that still rages in Chechnya, in the Russian Federation today, cannot be understood without this long-term background.

Mass deportations also resumed in the Baltics, following on earlier deportations of 1941. Hundreds of thousands were deported to Siberia. Scarcely any families were left untouched. It's estimated that 15 percent of the Baltic populations were gone by 1950. In a sense, World War II also continued in Eastern Europe, even after 1945. The so-called "Baltic Forest War" also saw guerrillas fighting Soviet forces well into the 1950s.

The Cold War would also grow in intensity in the following years. Stalin stated that a territory's occupier determined, and had a right to determine, its social system. He worked with Communist allies in Eastern European countries to consolidate their rule. In 1947, non-Communist parties were dropped from government in Eastern European countries, one after the other: Hungary, Romania, Poland. In 1948, a Communist coup in Czechoslovakia also created sole rule on the part of the Communists. In October of 1947, the Comintern, which had been shut down to continue good relations with the Western democracies, was now revived under the new name of the *Cominform*.

Communist parties in Italy and France also enjoyed considerable popularity and prestige, due to anti-Nazi resistance, and it seemed to many hopeful internationalists that Communism was progressing on all fronts. However, Stalin then died, in 1953. It's been suggested that he was, perhaps, on the eve of another wave of purges. Authorities had announced in months previous the discovery of an alleged "doctor's plot." Government doctors, mostly Jewish in origin, were accused of preparing a wide conspiracy to poison Soviet leaders. Stalin's regime seemed to be taking a radical anti-Semitic turn before his death. It's suggested that the Jews of the Soviet Union might have been the next target of his paranoia.

What followed in the Soviet Union was a process of de-Stalinization. In 1956, Nikita Khrushchev, the following leader, gave a speech at the congress of the Communist Party, in which he denounced Stalin's crimes, especially those against the Communist Party. Khrushchev now announced a new policy of coexistence in competition with the West, promising that the West would be buried technologically. Nonetheless, Soviet control in Eastern Europe often needed to be secured through violence. Soviet forces suppressed uprisings in East Germany and Poland, in Hungary, and then in Czechoslovakia.

At the same time, Soviets hoped to forge ahead with new science and technology that would put them in the forefront of development. The launch of the Sputnik satellite in 1957, and the prestige of nuclear weapons, gave the Soviet Union an image of progress. Below the surface, however, there were significant failures of development, some of which can be summed up in one example, that of the crackpot agricultural theories of Trofin Lysenko. Lysenko believed that genetic theories were invalid, a bourgeois invention, and that in fact, characteristics that had been taught to plants could be passed on through the generations. He urged a socialist Communist model of agriculture. Plants could cooperate to grow better, he argued. Thus, he urged that grain and other crops be planted very close together. The predictable thing happened. All of these plants died, starved of the opportunity to grow individually.

Further, he hatched a plan called the Great Stalin Plan for the Transformation of Nature. It, he urged the warming of Siberia's climate by planting trees, and urged the transformation of the physical environment of the Soviet Union itself. Such theories would be disastrous in practice, and they clue us into an abiding paradox. Regimes of the nature of the Soviet Union claim to be scientific, but they would often fall prey to such pseudoscientific disastrous theories.

The Cold War involved choices and dividing lines. They didn't run neatly in a geographical sense between one Eastern and one Western world. In fact, Aleksandr Solzhenitsyn had compared the ideological conflicts of the Cold War to a line running through individuals themselves, who needed to determine where their sympathies lay. The blocs of East and West, in spite of our talking that way, were, in fact, not monolithic. Individual sympathies and allegiances could vary greatly.

While the Cold War did not erupt, thankfully, into a full-scale clash, it did cause "proxy wars," substitute wars, such as America's involvement in the Vietnam War, or the Soviet invasion of Afghanistan. Indeed, as has been pointed out, alliances on both sides could often conflict ideological consistency, and lead them into relations with unsavory regimes.

There was one symbol, above all, of the Cold War that deserves mention. That was the wall that divided the Germanys, with Eastern Germany under Communist control and a Western Germany under the sponsorship of the Western Allies.

Upon occupying Eastern Germany, Soviet forces had engaged in abuse of civilians and mass rapes, in a cycle of revenge for Nazi atrocities. It's been argued that this experience would fatally undercut support for the German Communists, that might otherwise have arisen. In the Eastern Soviet zone, a German Democratic Republic was declared in October of 1949, in reaction to the setting up of a Western German republic, under Western sponsorship, earlier in that year.

This was a regime that experienced massive population flight, a "brain drain," especially, of the best and brightest, who flocked, instead, to the West. In order to deal with this hemorrhaging of the population, the East German authorities, with the sanction of the Soviet Union, built the Berlin Wall, on August 13, 1961.

This wall, which at first ran through the divided capital of the Germanies' Berlin, soon extended across the breadth of Germany itself, from north to South, dividing Eastern Germany from the West. In significant ideological terms, it was called an "anti-Fascist protection wall." In fact, however, this symbol of division was meant to keep people in. In the course of the following decades, some 900 people died trying to escape westward.

A further phenomenon, which was indicative of the tense standoff of the Cold War was the phenomenon of what was called, in a suitable acronym, M.A.D., or mutually assured destruction. It became especially clear in the Cuban missile crisis of 1962, over the stationing of Soviet missiles in Cuba, where Fidel Castro had taken power in 1959, and had come under the orbit of the Soviet Union, which seemed to bring the world to the brink of nuclear war. This frightened both opponents, and was followed by attempts at détente, to relaxing tensions.

Nonetheless, what followed in the subsequent decades was a balance of terror. A key concept of deterrence *assured destruction*, argued that nuclear aggression could be prevented by the implicit threat of a second nuclear strike, which would meet any first attack, obliterating the attacker, and rendering victory and defeat meaningless to both sides. Clearly, this was a balance of terror that globally kept the world in an uneasy peace, but threatened at any time to tip over into Armageddon and apocalypse.

In our next lecture, we'll be considering another player emerging in the Cold War, the great China of Chairman Mao.

Lecture Eighteen
Mao

Scope:

After decades of civil war and struggle over the future of China, Chinese Communists came to power in 1949. The "People's Republic" was declared under the leadership of Mao Zedong. This lecture examines the society formed by the ideology of "Mao thought," as it revised and adapted Marxist ideas. We examine the *Little Red Book*, the uniform dress of "Mao suits," and the cultural break with a rich past forced through by the regime. Mao commanded massive campaigns with the goal of developing the country. The failed *Great Leap Forward* in the 1950s led to massive violence against civilians and a famine. Renewed inner turmoil came with the *Cultural Revolution*, as young Red Guards terrorized and "reeducated" millions, ending only with Mao's death.

Outline

I. The Communists come to power.

  A. Preludes.

  1. After the collapse of the Manchu dynasty, China became a republic in 1911. When the country dissolved into warlord rule, Sun Yat-Sen founded the Guomindang (GMD) Nationalist Revolutionary Party to promote national independence, progress, and science.

  2. The GMD was at first supported by the Chinese Communist Party (founded in 1921).

  3. By 1927, the earlier allies came into conflict. General Chiang Kai-shek attacked Communists, destroying them in Shanghai and in urban areas. Communists needed to pull back to peasant areas.

  B. Mao Zedong.

  1. Mao (1893–1976), called the "Great Helmsman," was born in 1893 in Hunan province, son of a peasant landlord. In his youth, he admired Napoleon.

  2. He became a revolutionary activist from 1911, active in both the Nationalist movement protesting the Paris Peace Conference and the Communist Party, and serving as chairman of the Chinese Soviet Republic established in Jiangxi in 1931.

©2003 The Teaching Company Limited Partnership

3. When the GMD encircled their Communist enemies in 1934, 100,000 Communists were forced to undertake the *Long March* to Yanan in 1934–1935.
4. Some 60,000 died on the march, which was turned into a foundational myth of Communist propaganda, underlining the notion that determination could overcome material obstacles.
5. With this march, Mao became principal leader.
6. In particular, Mao understood how to use peasant unrest to mobilize for revolt. To set peasants against one another, he called for a short reign of terror in the countryside.
7. Mao stated that "political power grows out of the barrel of a gun."
8. Unlike such men as Zhou En-Lai, who became a Communist in France in 1921, or Deng Xiaoping, who studied in the Soviet Union, Mao's experience was limited to China.
9. From 1935, Mao clearly headed the leadership of the party.

C. Communist victory.
1. Communists took over northern areas during Japanese occupation and enacted land reforms.
2. Once World War II ended, civil war intensified between the GMD and Communists.
3. After their defeat, the GMD withdrew to the island of Taiwan in 1949.
4. On October 1, 1949, Mao declared the People's Republic of China in Beijing's Tiananmen Square.

II. Red dawn in China.

A. The founding.
1. Mao later admitted that 800,000 people were "liquidated" in the first five years of the People's Republic.
2. After an initial "New Democracy" policy (modeled on Lenin's NEP), Mao commanded collectivization, following (and perhaps seeking to surpass) Stalin's campaigns against the *kulaks*.

3. Farmers were reorganized into communes in the countryside, though small private plots were allowed, as in the Soviet Union.
4. Activists agitated for radical social change, working to eliminate illiteracy, footbinding, and traditional medicine and to replace these with a modern social organization.
5. They also launched attacks on the past and traditional life, banning songs and opera, destroying temples, and plowing over ancestral graves.

B. Industrialization
1. The first Five-Year Plan was launched in 1953.
2. The Soviet Union was the model for development. A common slogan of the 1950s was: "The Soviet Union's today is our tomorrow."
3. At the same time, Mao was determined to outdo the Soviets.

C. Communist fraternity breaks down.
1. Relations worsened with the Soviet Union.
2. Stalin pressured Mao to help North Korea. Mao came to resent being treated as a junior partner.
3. After Stalin's death and de-Stalinization, Mao despised the Soviet Union and declared that torch passed to China.
4. By 1958, the Chinese-Soviet split was increasingly clear, and border clashes took place between their armies in the late 1960s.
5. In 1964, China exploded a nuclear bomb, underlining its independence.

D. Purges.
1. In 1956–1957, in the *Hundred Flowers Campaign*, Mao encouraged the blossoming of a "hundred flowers and a hundred schools of thought."
2. This seeming liberalization lured forth dissidents, whom Mao then attacked. An estimated half million were killed in the purges that followed.

III. The Great Leap Forward, 1959–1961.

A. The Great Leap Forward was announced in 1958 as a revolutionizing of the country.

1. Mao wanted to "strike while the iron is hot" and press forward through will.
2. Official slogans promised "hard work for a few years, then a thousand years of happiness."

B. Measures.
1. Collectives were consolidated into larger "people's communes."
2. The fraudulent agricultural ideas of Lysenko were copied.
3. Harvests failed.

C. The great famine.
1. By 1960, famine was raging, and cases of cannibalism were recorded.
2. The famine left up to 40 million dead.
3. By 1960, the project was abandoned, but the commune structure remained in place.

IV. The Great Proletarian Cultural Revolution.

A. Cultural Revolution, 1966–1976.
1. Fearing a slowing of revolutionary fervor, Mao sought to regain the initiative by encouraging youths to move against established party officials, teachers, and elders.
2. "Enemies of the people" were accused of trying to move China over to a "capitalist road."
3. A smaller group of party leaders, including Mao's wife, Jiang Qing, supported this campaign.

B. Red Guards.
1. Young people were organized into Red Guard units, several million strong, organized on military lines.
2. They were charged with the duty of purging the party and society.
3. Accused of revisionism or capitalist betrayal, millions were killed or sent to *laogai* camps for "reeducation."

4. Ordinary people were forced to participate in rituals of self-criticism to show the proper revolutionary consciousness. Party General Secretary Deng Xiaoping and other rivals of Mao were purged.

5. Campaigns also focused on traces of the past, Western influences, education and teachers, books, and old art.

6. The *Four Olds* (old thought, old culture, old customs, old habits) were to be obliterated.

C. Mao Zedong's thought.

1. A collection of Mao's sayings, gathered in the *Little Red Book*, was hailed as a replacement for education.

2. Standardized "Mao suits" became approved garb.

D. Mao later used the army to suppress the Red Guard movement when he feared it was going too far. Mao's death brought an end to the Cultural Revolution.

E. Mao's personality.

1. Mao's overriding conviction of the power of will was not orthodox Marxism.

2. Mao praised ordinary people as a beautiful blank page on which new characters could be written.

3. Chairman Mao was puritanical in his views but indulgent toward himself.

V. Aftermath.

A. Mao died on September 9, 1976.

B. After his death, following a leadership struggle, Deng Xiaoping and his allies emerged victorious and put Mao's wife and her associates, the *Gang of Four*, on trial.

C. Results.

1. Even after a turn toward more pragmatic policies, the Communist government still hailed "Mao Zedong thought" and claimed that his contributions outweighed any mistakes.

2. An honest reckoning with this period has been slow to emerge in China. One bizarre result is that advertisements intended to appeal to nostalgia use propaganda styles of the Cultural Revolution.

Essential Reading:

Jonathan Spence, *Mao Zedong*.

Supplementary Reading:

Jasper Becker, *Hungry Ghosts: Mao's Secret Famine*.

Questions to Consider:

1. In what specific ways did Mao aim to surpass the Soviet Union?
2. What were the keys to Mao's success in coming to power and keeping power?

Lecture Eighteen—Transcript
Mao

In our previous lecture, we discussed the growing ideological conflict of the Cold War. We now turn to examine one of the players in the Cold War itself, the rising of Communist China.

One of the essential points that we've tried to underline again and again in these lectures is that the sort of ideological regimes we've described and have been discussing needn't, and mustn't be viewed in isolation. Rather, in many cases, they have, been in relation to one another, sought to outdo each other, or been in conflict with each other. When we discuss the case of Communist China, we'll see how a Western ideology, Marxist ideology, was adopted to Chinese culture, and changed in the process.

The Chinese Communists would come to power in 1949, and would form a society informed by the ideology of Mao thought, which adapted Marxist ideas. We'll examine the forms of this society, its emphasis on a radical break with a rich past. We'll see how Chairman Mao commanded massive campaigns, using human beings as material, with the goal of developing the country, most notoriously in the failed Great Leap Forward, in the 1950s, and the inner turmoil of the Great Cultural Revolution that followed.

We first begin by an examination of the Communists' long march to power. In the course of the early 20th century, China had been in turmoil. With the collapse of the Manchu Dynasty, China had become a republic in 1911. However, the country dissolved into warlord rule, threatening to split apart into what amounted to independent regions. To deal with this situation, Sun Yat-sen founded a nationalist party known as the Guomindang, or GMD. As a revolutionary party, it sought to promote the goals of national independence, unity, progress, and science.

In an alliance founded on certain shared ideas, this nationalist party, the Kuomintang, was at first supported by the Chinese Communist Party, founded in 1921. In classical Marxist thought, it was thought necessary for a country to move through the stages of revolutionary development, including a stage of bourgeois dominance, before moving to full-fledged revolution; thus, this cooperation was seen as ideologically sensible. By 1927, however, these earlier allies had come into to conflict.

The successor to Sun Yat-Sen, General Chiang Kai-shek, attacked the Communists, seeing them as a threat to his dominance. He destroyed them in Shanghai and other urban areas, where they had their bases. The Communists now had to pull back to peasant areas, where they sought to build a new base of support.

What was crucial in this context was an emerging leader in the young Communist movement in China, Mao Tse-tung. He would come to be called the "great helmsman" of China. Who was this man who would steer his nation?

He was born in 1893 in Hunan Province, son of a peasant landlord. In his youth, he admired Napoleon. He especially admired Chinese emperors, and steeped himself in reading and history. Nonetheless, in spite of this fervent desire for education, he remained an outsider for much of his formative years, because of his rural origins. He was never quite able to measure up to the educated elites he aspired to be.

His independent reading, done in time spent between schools, filled him with admiration for the concept of a new culture, a modern, transformative culture that was shaping the world, and, as he saw it, expressing itself in one particular country at the time, the Soviet Union, the building of a new experiment that he would like to participate in.

Mao became a revolutionary activist early on, already beginning in 1911. He was active in both the nationalist movement, which protested the Paris Peace Conference ending the First World War, for what were seen as unjust impositions upon China, and he joined the Communist Party. He became the Chairman of the Chinese Soviet Republic, established in Jiangxi in 1931, and began to move up through the ranks.

When the Kuomintang launched their offensive against their earlier allies, but now Communist enemies, in 1934, they had encircled 100,000 Communists. These Communists were now forced to undertake a breakout attempt, and to move to a new base of support. This was the, later legendary, "Long March" of the Communist Party. This took place in 1934 and 1935, and sent them on a long trek towards the Yunnan, where they would re-establish their control.

This march, constantly harried and harassed by nationalist forces or locals, led to massive losses. It's estimated that some 60,000 or more may have died on this march. This march, this elemental movement of the Communists, was later turned into a foundational myth of propaganda. It underlined an essential, cornerstone notion that determination, fanaticism, and will could overcome even the most incredible material or military obstacles. This Long March also had another significance. In its course, Mao became principal leader of the party.

Only 8000 of those who had started this trek survived and made it to Yunnan. Mao would soon represent the leadership of this hardened corps of believers. Mao soon was the object of legend, and of a charismatic myth of the leader. In Yannan, Mao lived in a cave in a hillside, in a spartan, simple way of life, focused on the political goals of his movement. He would become a legend for his austerity and commitment.

In particular, Mao had one insight, which I think had a lot to do with his own personal background, and it would shape some distinctive features of Chinese Communism. In particular, Mao understood and emphasized the potential of using peasant unrest, mobilizing the elemental powers and desires of the peasantry, which was inchoate and inarticulate itself, to mobilize them and to send them off in the direction of revolution, revolt, and transformation. Mao's own peasant upbringing, and his roots in the countryside, certainly had much do with this insight.

Mao felt that in order to unleash this enormous revolutionary potential that was present there in the peasantry, it would be necessary first to set the peasants against one another, in order to eliminate those elements of the peasantry he felt stood in the way of the truly revolutionary potential that was implicit in their masses. In particular, they needed to be directed against slightly richer peasants, those who were denounced as the exploitative landlords.

Mao called for a short reign of terror in the countryside that would set the peasant masses aflame and unleash their potential for his political purposes. In one of his much-quoted phrases, Mao insisted that revolution was not a dinner party, not embroidery, but an uprising. It would involve violence, upheaval, and this was seen as necessary. We think back to that phrase from the French Revolution, of it being necessary to break eggs in order to make an omelet. Here, one hears the echoes of that earlier revolutionary slogan.

It has been suggested by some historians that Mao might have had even earlier models in mind when he spoke of the revolutionary potential of the peasantry that were not orthodox Marxist. In fact, in the course of the 19th century in China, which had been utopian and revolutionary in its scale, a movement called the Taiping Rebellion arose. The Taiping rebels had promised a heavenly kingdom on Earth for Chinese peasants, and also promised the redistribution of land, shared property, and equality. For a long period, it certainly had enormous appeal in parts of the Chinese countryside.

Such older historical models, it's been argued, were important in adapting the message of Marxism to China's realities. In conclusion, Mao stated that "political power grows out of the barrel of a gun," and that one had to not merely wait for revolutionary transformations, but to unleash them if necessary through violence.

Mao's peasant identity, and his identification with the peasant masses and the revolutionary potential he saw in their nature, set him apart from other men who were playing a very important role in the Communist Party at the time. Unlike men such as Zhou En-Lai, who became a Communist in France, where he been studying in 1921, or men like Deng Xiaoping, who would become Communist as a result of study in France, again, or in the Soviet Union, Mao's experience was limited to China.

In many cases, one can trace a certain tension throughout his political career between identifying himself with his Chinese rural roots and those with foreign education and experience in the ranks of the Chinese Communists, as well as the advisors of the Comintern, the Communist International, who'd been sent to China. Mao felt that it was necessary to draw on his experience in order to move China in a revolutionary direction.

From 1935 on, Mao clearly headed the leadership of the party. A cult of Mao, and what was called "Mao thought," based upon his ideas about the peasantry and their revolutionary potential, grew up, especially from 1943 on. As was mentioned, Mao was hailed as the "Great Helmsman," steering China. It was said that Mao was the man who managed to unite Marxist-Leninist theory with Chinese revolutionary practice. The Communists now moved towards victory.

In the course of the Japanese occupation, and then of World War II, the Communists gained control over northern areas and gained the support of many peasants there by enacting land reforms immediately. Once World War II ended, a civil war continued in China between the Kuomintang and the Communists. After their defeat, due largely to their own incompetence, the Kuomintang withdrew to the island of Taiwan, in 1949. The Communists now reigned on the mainland. On October 1, 1949, Mao declared the existence of the People's Republic of China, from an important symbolic spot, Beijing's Central Tiananmen Square. Now, one saw a Red dawn in China, the founding of a new state.

The founding of this new state, however, would be marked by enormous violence. Mao is later said to have admitted that somewhere on the order of 800,000 people were "liquidated" in the first five years of consolidating control.

After an initial "New Democracy" policy of stabilization, which was modeled largely on Lenin's New Economic Policy that we've discussed in an earlier lecture, Mao announced that the time had arrived for full steam ahead towards Communism.

He commanded collectivization of agriculture, following, and perhaps seeking to surpass Stalin's campaigns against the kulaks in the Soviet Union. Farmers were reorganized into so-called communes in the countryside, though they were still often allowed small private plots in which they could farm for themselves, as was the case in the Soviet Union. It was, at least, an intermediate compromise.

Activists within the Communist Party, however, were not satisfied and continued to agitate for even more radical social change. They affected remarkable transformations within China. They worked to eliminate the endemic illiteracy in the countryside, to eliminate vestiges of traditions like the foot-binding of women, which were already in decline, to eliminate traditional medicine, which they saw as superstitious, and illegitimate, and to replace these features of traditional society with modern social organizations.

In the process, such activists also launched attacks on the Chinese past and on traditional life, banning popular songs or opera, and replacing them with approved, politicized forms of song and theater, destroying temples, and plowing over ancestral graves. These policies would later be at intensified in the Cultural Revolution.

One aim of the regime was to move forward with great force towards industrialization. In this, they imitated the Soviet Union, the model to follow in forging ahead to becoming a socialist society.

The first Five-Year Plan was launched in 1953, and the Soviet Union was always held up as the model for development. Even films of the Soviet Union were shown to peasants and ordinary Chinese, to show them what to aspire to. A common slogan in the 1950s summed it up: "The Soviet Union's today is our tomorrow."

At same time, however, one can detect within Mao's policies and statements the growing determination not merely to follow the Soviet Union, but in fact, to outdo it, by leaping ahead of it. One could see, in spite of all the pledges of Communist fraternity that unity was beginning to break down in these great Communist powers. The Soviet Union was the largest Communist state in a geographical extent. China, however, was the most populous.

Stalin viewed Mao as a junior partner. He pressured Mao to help North Korea in the Korean War. Mao, understandably, soon came to resent being treated as a junior partner. After Stalin's death and after de-Stalinization, Mao grew to despise the Soviet Union, feeling that it had deviated from the true path towards Communism, and now declared that the torch had been passed to China, which had a revolutionary calling.

By 1958, the Chinese-Soviet split was increasingly clear, and border clashes took place between their armies in the late 1960s. In 1964, China exploded a nuclear bomb, underlining its independence in military terms as well. Mao would move towards an imitation of other patterns of Stalin's rule in the Soviet Union, with purges.

In 1956 and 1957, in what came to be called the *Hundred Flowers Campaign*, Mao first encouraged the blossoming of a hundred flowers and a hundred schools of thought." This was an invitation to independent-minded thinkers and those who showed initiative in society, to criticize and to present new ideas. This seeming liberalization lured dissidents forth, who now felt they could speak up. Then, Mao attacked. An estimated 500,000 people were killed in the purges against such deviationists that followed. Some historians argue that in fact Mao himself had not expected the extent of criticism, or, as he saw it, deviation that followed, and he panicked. In other words, this is still a period of some controversy.

This opened the way towards an even greater determination through will to forge ahead towards the future, in what was called the Great Leap Forward, from 1959 to 1961. The Great Leap Forward had already been announced in 1958, as a revolutionizing of the entire country. Mao argued that it was necessary for China to "strike while the iron was hot," and press forward through will, willpower and dedication. He praised the Chinese as an especially disciplined people, who would do as their government demanded. Official slogans promised something in return. One sonorous slogan of this time said, "Hard work for a few years was then to be followed by a thousand years of happiness." What was involved in this policy?

Mao explained that if one followed industrialization and the agricultural reforms that he had in mind, China would become a utopia, a paradise on Earth. He explained that new ideas about deep plowing in agriculture would produce food so bountiful that China would no longer even have any food problems, but in fact would export food. Food would be distributed for free. Hard work would make people healthy, and doctors would soon be unemployed. Education and production would somehow be fused into one and work together in a synergy. Clothes would be free in this abundant state. All would be equal; all would enjoy the benefits of this new quality of life.

Others further built on his promises and expanded on them, arguing that ordinary Chinese peasants would soon be living in skyscrapers. Ordinary Chinese people would have airplanes as their mode of transportation. What was needed, however, they underlined, was hard work and fanatical self-sacrifice.

Workers were to sleep at their machines, to fulfill their quotas, and to make this plan a reality. Peasants could be expected to sleep in the fields, to be able to leap into work from the earliest morning hours.

The measures involved, the consolidation of collectives into huge, gigantic, "people's communes," which aimed to achieve economies of scale. In these people's communes, it was expected that the peasants and the workers would practice what was called, theoretically, "mixed and intensified production." Backyard furnaces, on a primitive enough scale, were supposed to produce steel, even if this meant melting down ordinary household items to produce what was essentially worthless scrap metal.

The problems of agricultural food being eaten by birds of the fields, sparrows, were to be eliminated by a campaign against birds, against sparrows, in order to wipe them out. This turned into an ecological disaster, because as these predators of insects were eliminated, the insects proliferated at a horrific rate.

Common dining halls were to replace individual households. The fraudulent agricultural ideas of Trofin Lysenko, from the Soviet Union, which we've mentioned in an earlier lecture, were copied, and indeed, intensified. Deep plowing, which had been hailed as the revolutionary transformation of agriculture, now saw plowing not just a foot into the soil, but 10 feet into the soil. Predictably enough, the result was agricultural disaster. However, propaganda would announce successes. It was announced that pumpkins of a vast new size were being grown, weighing 132 pounds, and that pigs had been crossbred with cows, in order to yield a new, dynamic breed. This was the propaganda, but the reality was that harvests failed. The Great Famine followed.

This has been called the greatest, largest famine in human history. In some sense, it was perfectly predictable, because it matched the pattern of events unfolding in the "terror famine" of Ukraine, in 1932 and 1933, in the Soviet Union.

By 1960, famine was raging in the provinces, and cases of cannibalism were recorded. Dining halls in the communes broke out into food riots. The famine left up to 40 million people dead as a result. The event was denied by the Chinese government, but those who had a chance to travel through the provinces had one particular haunting impression: The silence in the Chinese countryside, with people and animals all gone.

By 1960, the project of the Great Leap Forward was abandoned, but the communes structure would remain in place.

The next wave of revolutionary transformation, as it were, to redeem these failures, was called the Great Proletarian Cultural Revolution, from 1966 to 1976. Mao, who was already growing old, feared that the revolutionary fervor and determination of China was fading and slowing. Thus, he sought to regain the initiative by encouraging a young generation, those who had been born after the revolution, to move against those he saw as established authorities. These included party officials, teachers, and elders. In fact, these were some of his own allies from the route to power.

These people were now announced to be "enemies of the people." In many ways, this is reminiscent of the cases we've seen in this course of dictators moving against their own former allies. They were now suspected of betraying China's revolution, of trying to move the country over to a "capitalist road" and away from that close future of Communism. A smaller group of revolutionary elites around Mao, including his wife, Jiang Qing, supported this campaign, as Mao pledged that it was necessary to set China on fire once again.

The young people who were vested with this task were known as the Red Guards. They were organized into Red Guard units, several of which were millions strong. They were actually several million strong in extent, organized on military lines. These Red Guards were charged with the duty of purging the party, and society. Those who were accused of "revisionism" or "capitalist betrayal," as it was called, were killed in the millions, or sent to *laogai* camps for "reeducation," to redeem their potential.

Ordinary people were forced to participate in public rituals of self-criticism, to show the proper revolutionary consciousness, and that they were not deviating. These were often called "struggle sessions." Party General Secretary Deng Xiaoping and other rivals of Mao were purged. Campaigns associated with this Great Proletarian Cultural Revolution also aimed to eliminate corrupt traces of the past, such as Western influences, especially in education, and in the teaching staff, in books, and in old art.

Propaganda denounced the *Four Olds*: Old thought, old culture, old customs, and old habits. These were to be obliterated.

Mao Tse-tung's thought was now made obligatory, and was emphasized in even more frenetic propaganda, that had already been the case before. A collection of Mao's sayings, *The Little Red Book*, first published in 1964, was now hailed as a replacement for traditional, laborious education. Everything one needed to know about the keys to the future was there in the book of Mao sayings.

Standardized "Mao suits," drab uniforms of plain tailoring, became approved, and indeed, necessary garb. These uniforms were to show the equality, the sameness of society. It was, indeed, dangerous to wear anything else, because it would show that one was perhaps a bourgeois individualist. Wearing jeans was prescribed, and the Mao suits would now be worn by a quarter of humanity.

Over time, Mao grew worried that this force he'd unleashed, the Red Guards, was starting to go too far. Indeed, certain Red Guard units essentially devolved into street gangs and could fight one another. Mao now fell back on using the army to suppress the Red Guard movement. Mao's own death finally brought an end to the Cultural Revolution in 1976.

Mao's personality had done much to shape the regime. At its core had been his overriding conviction of the power of will. This clearly was not orthodox Marxism. Marx had stressed material forces, but Mao had felt that it was necessary to adapt this ideology. At one point, in a chilling quote, Mao appraised ordinary people, the Chinese masses, as a "beautiful, blank page upon which new characters could be written." A new humanity could be formed.

Chairman Mao was puritanical in his views in public, but became notoriously indulgent towards himself, especially later in life. In his own train, he would entertain scores of mistresses and live the good life. In a kind of grimly joking way, he would be called "the Red Emperor," by some Chinese, because he mimicked, in his luxury and self-indulgence, the emperors of the Manchu period.

Mao finally died on September 9, 1976. Just before he died, in what amounted to his last words, he delivered what was perhaps a verdict on his own rule. However, his last words were not ones of regret, reconsideration, or thoughts of what might have been done differently. Rather, he suggested that the revolution was still unfinished and that it needed to be continued and needed to be moved forward.

After Mao's death, a leadership struggle followed. Deng Xiaoping, who had been purged earlier, and his allies, emerged victorious. He put Mao's wife and her associates, the so-called *Gang of Four*, on trial.

The results, however, were mixed, even in the aftermath. Though the policies of the government turned in more pragmatic directions after Mao's death in 1976, the Communist government was unable to force a break with Mao Tse-tung, and all that he had stood for historically.

The Communist government still hailed, and still hails, "Mao Tse-tung thought," and claimed that his contributions outweighed any mistakes that he might have made later in life. What's clear is this: An honest reckoning with this period, its toll of victims, its triumph of irrationality and pseudo-science has yet to emerge in China in the fullest sense. Slowly, personal accounts, reconsiderations, and criticisms have been emerging, but an open and honest reckoning, in the fullest sense, has not yet come to pass.

Bizarrely, the result is a case of historical amnesia about some of these darkest periods of Chinese history, and, even stranger, in cultural phenomena we can observe today. In today's China, Cultural Revolution propaganda styles are sometimes used for advertisements, for restaurants or for products; these intend to appeal to a nostalgia for the days of revolutionary will and fervor, forgetting their costs.

In our next lecture, we'll consider the regime of Cambodia's Pol Pot and the Khmer Rouge, who sought quite deliberately to overtake and outdo even Mao's Red China.

Lecture Nineteen
Cambodia and Pol Pot's Killing Fields

Scope:

In Southeast Asia, Cambodian Communists led by the mysterious Pol Pot, educated in France, turned their own land into a laboratory for a social experiment, described in this lecture. On coming to power in 1975, the Khmer Rouge declared that they were making a new start in human history. To build their rural utopia, they totally emptied Cambodia's cities in the course of one week, expelling people into the countryside, where they suffered intense privation. The populace was then screened for "enemies of the people," including intellectuals (the wearing of eyeglasses could be a death sentence), who were summarily executed, along with their families. In the three years of their rule, before they were overthrown by an invasion from Vietnam, the Khmer Rouge caused the deaths of some two million people, or more than 25 percent of Cambodians.

Outline

I.   Cambodian prelude.

   A. The past.

     1. The Khmer empire ruled in Indochina from the ninth to the 13th centuries, but then, the country came under Thai rule.

     2. Cambodia was a French protectorate in the 19th century, then was occupied by Japan in World War II. Afterward, it became an independent kingdom in 1955.

   B. In the Cold War.

     1. Though Cambodia declared neutrality in the Vietnam conflict, it was infiltrated by Viet Cong, with sections of the Ho Chi Minh Trail running through its territory.

     2. The Khmer Rouge were the Cambodian Communists, active from 1963.

   C. In 1970, the monarchy was overthrown, and American and South Vietnamese forces intervened secretly.

     1. American bombing raids directed against Communist forces also took a toll on civilians and destabilized the government.

2. When the United States withdrew from Vietnam and South Vietnam collapsed, the Khmer Rouge moved to take control.
3. In April 1975, the Khmer Rouge took the capital, Phnom Penh, and began to put their revolution into action.
4. Cambodia was renamed Democratic Kampuchea.

II. Pol Pot.

   A. Origins.

      1. The man later known as Pol Pot (1925–1998) was born as Saloth Sar to a farmer family along the Thai border. He claimed that he spent two years as a Buddhist monk.

      2. On turning to politics, he cut himself off from his family.

   B. Turn to radicalism.

      1. In the 1940s, he was active in the resistance against the French directed by Ho Chi Minh.

      2. In 1946, he became a member of the Cambodian Communist Party.

      3. In 1949, Pol Pot left to study in France. Though he was supposed to be studying radio electronic engineering, he devoted himself to Communist political activities.

      4. After failing his examinations, he returned to Cambodia in 1953 and taught at a private school at Phnom Penh.

      5. Pol Pot organized the Communist underground in Cambodia. The party was founded in 1960, and in 1963, he became its general secretary.

      6. Pol Pot became prime minister of the new Khmer Rouge regime from 1975 until its overthrow in 1979.

      7. In a contrast to other dictators, Pol Pot remained obscure, and no cult of personality around him was encouraged.

III. The year zero.

   A. Beginning of the regime.

      1. Ordinary Cambodians hoped that, at long last, stability and peace were at hand.

      2. The black-clad Khmer Rouge, however, were obsessively secretive in their actions. Many of their recruits were young (recruited at the age of 12 or younger), adding a generational dimension to the tragedy.

3. The ruling body was a shadowy entity called *Angkar* ("organization"), which was referred to as the "mother-father" of the people.
4. The aim of the enacted policies was not only to imitate Mao's Great Leap Forward in China but to surpass it.

B. Revolutionary violence.
1. In the campaign for ruralization, cities were ordered emptied out in 24 hours. Sixty percent of the population was exiled, and Phnom Penh, the capital city of two million, was deserted.
2. Former citydwellers were labeled "new people" and were segregated from the peasantry. Through repeated deportations, they were decimated.
3. Those who were educated, spoke foreign languages, or wore glasses were slated for execution as enemies of the people. Buddhist monks, as well as members of minority religions (Muslims, Catholics) and ethnic minorities (Chinese, Vietnamese), were also eliminated.
4. Many executions used the blade of a hoe, reminiscent of the French guillotine. Functionaries prided themselves on polite killing.
5. Conditions in the prisons were so bad that many guards died as well.
6. Pits where bodies are thrown were called "killing fields." Hundreds of mass graves, large and small, are scattered throughout the land.
7. An estimated two million (out of a total population of seven million) died as a result of the Khmer Rouge's policies, through killing, hunger, and abuse. Recently, new evidence has prompted higher estimates.

C. The new society.
1. The regime followed radical measures to purify society, while cutting the country off from the world and seeking autarchy.
2. Money was abolished in one week.
3. Total collectivization of land was decreed.
4. On communes, people ate in collective canteens and shared the same thin rice soup.
5. All Cambodians were ordered to wear black clothes.

6. Religion, writing, and education all disappeared.
7. Only arranged marriages approved by the Khmer Rouge were allowed.
8. Individualism was to be overcome. A slogan stated, "Losing you is not a loss; keeping you is not a gain."
9. People were seen as human material for the revolution.

D. Results.
1. Construction and agricultural projects were marked by irrationality and a reliance on will over matter.
2. The collapse of agriculture led to famine and cases of cannibalism.
3. Suspecting sabotage, the Khmer Rouge movement began to purge itself of alleged enemies, and prisons filled with former members.

IV. End of the regime.

A. Intervention.
1. After border clashes, Communist Vietnam invaded in 1978 (in a refutation of Communist solidarity), and the Khmer Rouge government was overthrown by January 1979.
2. The Vietnamese set up a puppet regime that was friendly to Vietnam.

B. Khmer Rouge guerrillas.
1. Even after their overthrow, Khmer Rouge forces continued to fight in border areas and from within Thailand until 1992, when an UN-brokered plan sought to include them in elections.
2. In 1997, Pol Pot was arrested by his associates and condemned for treason. In April 1998, he died in the jungle, in mysterious circumstances, never having been brought to public trial.

C. International responses.
1. In part because of the secrecy of the regime, news of Khmer Rouge activities filtered out only slowly.
2. As part of Cold War politics, Thailand, China, and the United States supported the Khmer Rouge after their overthrow by Vietnam.

D. Memorials.

1. In Cambodia today, the skeletons of the killing fields are displayed in open-air museums.
2. The documentation of executions, including haunting pictures of the condemned, are preserved as eloquent witness to the tragedy.
3. Resistance to trials of surviving Khmer Rouge leaders continues from different quarters in Cambodia and abroad, especially China. Cambodian politicians have suggested burying the past.

Essential Reading:

Elizabeth Becker, *When the War Was Over: Cambodia and the Khmer Rouge Revolution*.

Supplementary Reading:

Samantha Power, *"A Problem From Hell": America and the Age of Genocide*, pp. 87–154.

Questions to Consider:

1. In what specific ways did the Khmer Rouge seek to surpass China's Communists?

2. Why was Pol Pot not the center of a personality cult like that of Hitler or Stalin, with portraits and propaganda appearances?

Lecture Nineteen—Transcript
Cambodia and Pol Pot's Killing Fields

In our previous lecture, we examined the rise of Communist China under Mao's leadership, and the remarkable ways in which Marxist ideology was adopted to Chinese conditions.

In today's lecture, we'll examine a similar case, in fact a linked case, that of Cambodia, and Pol Pot's Khmer Rouge regime. This regime lasted three years. Even by the standards of the dictatorships we've been discussing, it was strange in its nature and distinctive. I think we need to return to that thought that we've brought up several times before. This is the notion that we need to consider the regimes that we've been discussing in relation to one another.

The Khmer Rouge in Cambodia sought to outdo all other revolutionary regimes that had come before. Most immediately, it sought to surpass Mao's China. In Southeast Asia, Cambodian Communist leaders who had been educated in France, and who were led by the mysterious leader Pol Pot, would turn their entire country into a social experiment.

When they came to power in 1975, the Khmer Rouge declared that they were starting a new epoch in human history. They would build a pure racial utopia, and to this end, they emptied the cities, expelled people into the countryside, and purged the population again and again of those who were considered enemies of the people. In the last analysis, they would end up causing the deaths of some two million people in Cambodia, or over a quarter of the population.

We need to consider, first of all, Cambodia's longer history, its past, because although the Khmer Rouge announced that they were building the bright future, in many ways, the idealized rural paradise, which supposedly had existed in some previous age, was a model to be striven after, as well.

In the past, a Khmer empire had ruled in Indochina, from the ninth to the 13th centuries, so there was a glimmer of bygone glories. Then, however, the country had come under the rule of the Thais, from outside. Cambodia then became a French protectorate in the 19th century, and it was occupied by Japan in World War II. Afterward, it would become an independent kingdom, in 1955.

The Cold War conflict, that we've outlined in a previous lecture, would then hit Cambodia very hard, with dire results. Though Cambodia declared neutrality in the Vietnam conflict raging next door, it was, nonetheless, infiltrated by the Vietcong, the Vietnamese Communists, and indeed, sections of the Ho Chi Minh Trail supplying the insurgents ran through Cambodian territory.

Allies of the Vietnamese Communists, at least at this stage, were the Khmer Rouge. They were the Cambodian Communists who were active from 1963. In 1970, the Cambodian monarchy was overthrown, and American and South Vietnamese forces also intervened secretly in the country. American bombing raids, directed against the movement of Communist forces in Cambodia, took a dreadful toll on civilians and destabilized the Cambodian government.

When the United States withdrew from Vietnam, and South Vietnam collapsed, replaced by Communist control of the entire country, the Khmer Rouge now moved to take control in Cambodia as well.

In April of 1975, as the government collapsed, the Khmer Rouge entered the capital, Phnom Penh, and began to put the revolution into action. Their new state was renamed Democratic Kampuchea, and I've sometimes mentioned in lectures that it's especially of a bad sign when a state needs to call itself democratic. That's usually a sign of bad things to come. Yet, many Cambodians felt that surely, after such dislocation, after such turmoil and violence, the Khmer Rouge would be offering a better way of life, and, at least, stability.

The Khmer Rouge were a group about which little was known. When they moved forward to take control of the country, dressed in their distinctive black uniforms, their checkered red and white scarves, and their plain sandals, a very austere uniform, the population waited to see what would happen. Indeed, what happened next, what we'll be describing in the lecture today, was something that, at the time, remained largely unknown to the outside world. Secrecy and shadowy realities would be a hallmark of the Khmer Rouge, and especially, of their mysterious leader, Pol Pot.

The man who would later be known as Pol Pot, which was an assumed, pseudonymous revolutionary name that didn't have any specific meaning, was born as Saloth Sar to a farmer family, apparently undistinguished, along the border of Thailand. The man who became Pol Pot later claimed that he had spent two years as a Buddhist monk before setting out on the route to his new personality. If this is true, it would be an intriguing similarity to other cases of leaders we've seen who have had a religious education, and were perhaps affected by the forms of religious doctrine and belief that they had observed.

Upon turning to politics, the man who became Pol Pot cut himself off entirely from his family and his earlier life. In many ways, this foreshadowed what would happen with Cambodia itself. A radical break would lead to radical isolation and a cutting off from the rest of the outside world. Years later, his family would be stunned to realize that leader of the country was, in fact, a family member.

Pol Pot's turn to radicalism was also intriguing. In the course of the 1940s, he was active in the resistance against the French colonizers, directed by Ho Chi Minh, the leader of the Vietnamese Communists. In 1946, Pol Pot became a member of the Communist Party of Cambodia. In 1949, he left the country to study in France. This was a contrast to Mao's relatively more limited experience.

Pol Pot's years in the West clearly shaped his ideas. While in France, he was supposed to be studying radio electronic engineering, but it seems that he neglected his studies, and instead, devoted himself to Communist political activities. There was a vibrant Communist movement in France at the time. After failing his examinations at university, Pol Pot returned to Cambodia in 1953, and taught at a private school, Phnom Penh. Meanwhile, he began to organize underground and to agitate for the Communist Party in Cambodia.

The Communist Party had been founded in 1960. By 1963, Pol Pot had become its general secretary, a man working underground, and excelling in such activities. Pol Pot became prime minister of the new regime established in Cambodia, from 1975, right up until its overthrow in 1979.

When we consider Pol Pot in the context of some of the other dictators whom we've discussed in our lectures, we see a figure who's really in remarkable contrast to the others. Throughout his rise to power, as well as during the period of his dominance in Cambodia, Pol Pot remained obscure, shadowy, unknown. In contrast to such dictators as Hitler, Stalin, or Mao, no cult of personality was encouraged around Pol Pot. This man, an anonymous comrade, as it were, by his very unknown nature, his shadowy identity, was supposed to be all the more imposing. One sees, here, Pol Pot diverging from the models of some earlier dictatorships, the very dictatorships, in some cases, that he wished to overtake. He was, perhaps, carving out a new path for his new regime.

No statues, no omnipresent portraits, were established to this shadowy leader of the Khmer Rouge. As I mentioned before, his family would later be shocked to discover that this man, whom they knew well from his youth, was, in fact, the leader of the country.

This was perhaps also indicative of the radical break which the Khmer Rouge announced they were bringing to the country itself. This was summed up in the term applied to the beginning of the rule, "The Year Zero." We see here, perhaps, echoes, or references, back to the revolutionary calendar of the French Revolution, marking the beginning of a new regime, a new age in human history. The Khmer Rouge announced that they were bringing something entirely new and unprecedented to Cambodia. Paradoxically, however, they were also returning the country to the sort of rural idyllic conditions it might have known in some bygone age.

As we've mentioned before, many ordinary Cambodians, in fact, were receptive at first to message that at long last, stability, peace, and harmony, could be at hand. It would take awhile before the full scope of the ambitions of the black-clad Khmer Rouge would become known, because they were excessively secretive in their actions. Many of their recruits were young. Young boys and girls were recruited at the age of 12 or younger, and quite deliberately cut off, as Pol Pot himself had cut himself off, from their families, and from the society and the sort of context they had known before.

In the tragedy that would unfold in Cambodia, they would be a marked generational dimension. The young would be turned into killers of the society which they now had been turned against.

The ruling body that was to oversee the transformation of Cambodian society was a shadowy entity. Very little was known about it. It denied aspects of its own existence in its propaganda. This entity was known as the *Angkor*, meaning the "organization."

Even as little was known about it, one thing was stressed in its propaganda, and that was that this organization was all-powerful and would provide for the Cambodian people. In one phrase that was used in propaganda, the Angkor, or "organization," was called the "mother-father" of the people. More than any parent, this government would steer the development of Cambodians.

The aim of the policies that would unfold in Communist Cambodia would be, not only an imitation of aspects of Mao's Great Leap Forward, the attempted mobilization of the countryside, and a great leap into the future of industrialization and productive agriculture, but much more than that. It was an attempt to surpass Mao's model as well. This would be accompanied by ferocious revolutionary violence.

The Khmer Rouge immediately mounted a campaign of what they called ruralization. They viewed cities as "tainted," full of impurities and deviations, full of lapses in those virtues that were associated with the peasantry. In other words, we see here a great deviation that wouldn't have been recognized at the time by these activists from classical Marxism. We'll recall that Marx had emphasized that the workers, especially in the cities, were the vanguard of the future, while the peasants were often denounced as being in the state of "rural idiocy," or "retardation."

Instead, the Khmer Rouge were taking Marx's ideas and changing them to fit their realities, and their vision of the utopian future. The cities, thus, were slated for annihilation. They were ordered to be emptied out in 24 hours. With tremendous dislocation, involving even the evacuation of hospital patients in their beds, the cities were, indeed, turned out, their populations expelled.

Sixty percent of the entire population of the country was exiled from its earlier place of residence, and Phnom Penh, the capital city, a great cosmopolitan city of two million people was deserted in short order, silent, and vacated. The social transformation of Cambodia had begun. What happened to those people who were now exiled to the countryside?

Even this transformation of their circumstances didn't mean that they could escape their former identities. Former city dwellers, now thrust into a new context that many of them had not known before, were labeled, even in their rural exile, as the "new people." As such, they were segregated from the peasantry, who were judged more healthy and virtuous. These "new people" would be uprooted again and again, and deported from one part of the countryside to another. In the process of these repeated deportations, many of them were decimated. They had few supports, or people to draw upon, in unfamiliar regions, as a way of securing survival.

The fury of the revolutionaries also focused on those whom they saw as especially tainted, those who had moved away from their original roots; those, in particular, who had been tainted, as they saw it, through education. What amounted to a manhunt now began. Of those from the earlier Cambodian society who were educated, for instance, those who spoke foreign languages, as French had often been the language of advancement in the colonial period, or of cultivation; all such people were now targeted for persecution or extermination.

The wearing of eyeglasses, in particular, could be the distinguishing feature that would slate one for execution, because such a person, clearly, was one who had need of such corrective lenses for reading, education, or other subversive activities. Such so-called "enemies of the people" faced a dire fate.

Religion was also focused upon as a target. Buddhist monks, as well as members of the minority religions who were represented in Cambodia, including Muslims as well as Catholics, were persecuted and suspected of being enemies of the people.

The fury of the revolutionaries would also begin to target ethnic minorities, and here we see some of the energies of nationalism beginning to, perhaps, combine with a revolutionary ideology. The ethnic minorities of the Chinese and Vietnamese were now also eliminated, viewed as "impure," imperfectly Cambodian. Executions became commonplace.

Many of the executions took place without the benefit, as it were, of modern technology, but instead, were meted out with the most primitive of objects and tools. Agricultural tools, such as the hoe, in particular, would be used in executions where victims would be struck from behind, with a blow aimed at the neck. It's been suggested that, symbolically, this mode of execution was supposed to be reminiscent of the French Revolution's guillotine, and its "hygienic" mode of killing. One thing in particular was an object of pride for the Khmer Rouge functionaries who meted out these revolutionary executions. They prided themselves on being polite as they did so. This was supposed to emphasize that this form of revolutionary justice was not personal, was not motivated by hatred, but rather, by the purity of revolutionary rationality and revolutionary fervor.

Those who were not immediately executed were, instead, sent to prisons strewn throughout the country. Conditions in some of these prisons were so bad, indeed, that many guards are said to have died there as well, from the privations. One riveting record of the terrors of the Khmer Rouge regime are the photographs, which were carefully, bureaucratically recorded, filed, and organized by the Khmer Rouge administrators of these prisons. They show the faces of those who were imprisoned there, or who faced imminent execution. One views picture after picture of such photographs: Men, women, children, mothers and their children. One sees a range of dismaying human emotions: Fear, anxiety, resignation; the faces of people who faced a dreadful fate. These pictures form a riveting and terrifying documentary, the legacy of the Khmer Rouge.

The pits where the bodies of those who were executed were thrown came to be called the "killing fields" of Cambodia. The country was dotted with them. Hundreds of mass graves, both large and small, are scattered throughout the land. Indeed, the newspapers, in recent months, have conveyed reports of ever more such mass graves being discovered today.

It's estimated that some two million died as a result of the Khmer Rouge policies, out of a total population of seven million in Cambodia, as a result of the executions, the killings, hunger, and abuse. Some recent estimates by historians and students of this period in this country range even higher, because of the new evidence emerging in those recently discovered mass graves that I mentioned a moment ago. Thus, some estimates suggest that even that figure of two million might need to be revised significantly upward.

What was this all in aid of? The promise was that the Khmer Rouge, in this brutal fashion, by endorsing revolutionary violence, would create a new society. To make that new society, the regime was to follow radical measures to purify the human material of the people within, while the world would be cut off from the country, so that the country would be isolated, and would form a universe of its own, seeking autarchy, perfect self-sufficiency. The Khmer Rouge felt that they had a chance to create the world anew in Cambodia.

There were symbolic actions that immediately made their resolve clear. Money, currency, was abolished in one week within their coming to power. It was replaced by a new form of economic equality. Total collectivization of land was decreed. These were not the measures of the Soviet Union or China, which had been extensive enough, though they still allowed some private plots to be kept by the peasants. By contrast, the Khmer Rouge demanded total collectivization of land. The communes, as had been the case in Communist China, were also present. People ate in collective canteens, in dining halls, where they were not separated into families, but rather, worked in a collective. There they shared the same thin rice soup that represented the same starvation diet of ordinary Cambodians.

Moreover, all Cambodians were ordered to wear black clothes, on the model of the Khmer Rouge themselves. They were to shed vestiges of individuality, and instead, were to become uniform, to become one in their appearance.

Religion, writing, and education all disappeared. In their places, the Khmer Rouge and Pol Pot argued that revolutionary fervor itself would be able to bring the benefits of higher civilization, medicine, and industrialization, even in the hands of young children. In many senses, this echoes Mao's insistence upon will, and its capacity to achieve remarkable transformations.

Indeed, the Khmer Rouge sought to control even the most intimate parts of people's lives. Only arranged marriages that were approved by Khmer Rouge officials were allowed. Those who engaged in relations outside the bounds of such sanctioned relationships would be punished most harshly.

Individualism was seen as something that needed to be overcome. In chilling propaganda slogans, the Khmer Rouge didn't hide how they viewed human nature, or indeed, the individuals under their own control. Instead, they emphasized their disregard for the individual. One potent slogan stated, "Losing you is not a loss; keeping you is not a gain." The individual was relegated to a revolutionary mass that was to be formed and remade. People were seen as human materiel for the revolution. What were the results of this revolutionary fervor, this determination to create the world anew in the Khmer Rouge?

As one might have predicted, construction and agricultural projects undertaken throughout the country were marked by that same irrationality and pseudo-science, and that reliance on will triumphing over the constraints of matter that we've seen in other regimes, steered by their ideology, rather than by pragmatism, rationality, or compromise.

The collapse of agriculture, as a result of the disastrous policies of the Khmer Rouge, as was also the case in China, or in the terror famine of the Ukraine in the Soviet Union, once again led to instances of famine in Cambodia, and cases of horrifying cannibalism in these crisis situations.

The Khmer Rouge government reacted in ways that might have made sense in terms of their ideology, but which represented yet another ratcheting up of violence against the subject population. These catastrophes in agriculture and other projects led the Khmer Rouge and Pol Pot to suspect sabotage. The movement began to comb through the civilian population even more determinedly and led them to start purging themselves, ever more alleged enemies within the ranks of the party itself. The prisons soon filled with former members, former true believers, in the Khmer Rouge regime itself.

As we've noted before, the revolution "could be a mother that eats her children," as had been the case in the French Revolution, and was a phenomenon being echoed in the Khmer Rouge regime. Now, that regime neared its collapse. However, that collapse came from a surprising quarter. It came precisely at the hands of fellow Communists.

Perhaps out of desperation, the Khmer Rouge began attacking Vietnam and its Communist regime in border clashes. The Vietnamese government invaded in 1978. To many, this came as a surprise, because this had a reputation of international Communist solidarity, until Communist Vietnam invaded Communist Cambodia.

Soon, the Khmer Rouge government was overthrown by the invading Vietnamese in January of 1979, bringing its three years of rule, at long last, to an end. The Vietnamese then set up a Communist puppet regime, which broke with the Khmer Rouge, denounced their crimes, and was friendly to Vietnam.

The Khmer Rouge story did not end there, however. These "Red Cambodians," the Khmer Rouge, continued their fight. Even after their overthrow, their guerrilla forces retreated into the jungles, and continued to fight in the border areas, and even from within Thailand, the neighboring country, until 1992. At long last, a United Nations brokered plan sought to solve this continuing struggle and conflict by including the Khmer Rouge in Cambodian elections for a new state.

What happened to the shadowy leader, Pol Pot? In 1997, under circumstances that are still shrouded with mystery and obscurity to this very day, Pol Pot was arrested by his own associates and allies. Some suggested that his condemnation for treason, and then his subsequent house arrest, were merely a show trial without serious intent on the part of his former allies to hold him responsible for his actions, but was instead intended as a fig leaf for the new respectability that the Khmer Rouge aimed to achieve.

In April of 1998, it was announced the world that Pol Pot had died in the jungle, under mysterious circumstances of natural causes. He was never brought to public trial. In an interview that was held with Pol Pot shortly before he died, he was asked about his legacy. He had what amounted to last words, as well.

In this case, he acknowledged that many looked upon him as a man who was responsible for many deaths, and one whose policies had yielded suffering, but he tearfully announced that he was not to blame. He had trusted subordinates who had done bad things and that this was his legacy. Not a show of remorse, but rather, a shedding of responsibility.

In terms of responsibility and responses, we need to ask: How did the world respond to the unfolding of the Cambodian tragedy? In part, because of the intense secrecy of the regime, its shutting off of the country from the outside world, news of Khmer Rouge activities would filter out only very slowly. However, relief workers in neighboring countries started to observe a horrifying phenomenon: Refugees fleeing the Khmer Rouge regime tended to tell the same stories again and again. Though their stories boggled the imagination, the sheer weight of accumulated witness testimony slowly allowed outside countries to form an impression of what had been unfolding within the country.

Nonetheless, the response of the outside world had been ambivalent, to say the least. As part of Cold War politics, Thailand, China, and United States continued to support the Khmer Rouge long after their overthrow by the Vietnamese Communists, because they saw this group, criminal as they might have been before, as a counterweight to the Vietnamese.

Now the question is, at long last: How will these events be remembered, and how will individuals be held responsible? In Cambodia today, memorials are set up throughout the country. The skeletons and skulls of those who died in the killing fields are displayed in open-air museums. The documentation of the executions, including those haunting pictures of the condemned taken by their executioners that I mentioned, are preserved as an eloquent witness to the tragedy.

Only slowly, however, has movement grown to hold some of those who committed these crimes responsible. Resistance still continues in regard to holding trials for the surviving Khmer Rouge leaders; progress has been very slow. The resistance comes from different quarters, both in Cambodia and abroad. The Chinese government especially has objected to setting up such courts. Some Cambodian politicians suggest that indeed, perhaps it's better to bury the past, to allow bygones to be bygones, and to forget this legacy of killing. Many ordinary Cambodians cannot agree, because they see killers still among them walking free. They raise a question, asking how a country can steer towards a healthy future without dealing with the ghosts of its past.

In our next lecture, we'll consider three other trajectories of Communist rule, in East Germany, the Soviet Union, and North Korea.

Lecture Twenty
East Germany, the Soviet Union, North Korea

Scope:

During the Cold War, different variants of Communist regimes emerged. This lecture considers the development of three such states. The German Democratic Republic from 1949 was considered a success story. Behind the Berlin Wall, "really existing Socialism" was built up under the supervision of the state and the surveillance of the Stasi secret police. In the Soviet Union, the system lurched toward stagnation, repressing dissidents but also steadily losing confidence in the ideology of the ruling party. North Korea, often called the *Hermit Kingdom*, enshrined its militarized isolation from the world in the ideology of *juche*, or "self-reliance," first under Kim Il-Sung, then his son, "Beloved Leader" Kim Jong-Il, who has developed nuclear weapons.

Outline

I.   Varieties of Socialist experience.

    A. Socialism and Communism took markedly different forms in different countries.

    B. In Western Europe, Social Democracy moved toward moderate forms.

        1. Social Democrats stressed reform over revolution, seeking broader appeal.

        2. Emblematic was the German Social Democratic Party's Bad Godesberg Program in 1958, revising Marxist doctrine to avow both economic planning and economic freedom.

    C. By contrast, examining East Germany, the Soviet Union, and North Korea shows diversity and commonalties among hardline regimes.

II. Eastern Germany.

    A. German Democratic Republic (GDR): "State of Workers and Peasants."

        1. After the Berlin Wall was erected in 1961, a grim "stabilization" set in, as citizens saw that they must come to terms with the inevitable.

2. It was commonly said that if anyone could make Communism work, it would be the Germans. The GDR was to become a showcase.

3. In spite of egalitarian claims, party elites enjoyed class privileges: special cars, separate quarters, special stores, and greater access to education and international exchanges.

4. Erich Honecker (1912–1994), leader from 1971 until the eve of collapse, rose through the party's ranks.

5. The Free German Youth organization (FDJ) regimented youth.

6. Churches were harassed, infiltrated, or closed, and religious ritual was replaced with secular traditions, such as "youth confirmation."

B. Coercion and the Stasi secret police.

1. Border troops guarded the wall with orders to shoot to kill. "Flight from the republic" was a crime.

2. Dissidents were kept under surveillance and spied on by informers in their midst.

3. The State Security Police (*Stasi*) established a remarkably intricate repressive apparatus for spying on East Germans. "Unofficial collaborators" denounced coworkers and family.

4. An estimated 274,000 people worked with the Stasi from 1950 to 1989. This included one secret policeman for every 166 citizens; when informers were added, the ratio would be one security person for every 6.5 persons.

5. The Stasi generated 121 miles of files on targets and maintained feared prisons, such as Hohenschönhausen.

6. Activities included bugging apartments, cooperating with international terrorist groups, trafficking in people "bought free" to emigrate to West Germany, and engaging in active cooperation with the Soviet KGB.

7. The Stasi were proud to consider themselves in the lineage of Lenin's Chekists.

C. Seeking legitimacy.

1. Shortcomings were rhetorically justified as "really existing Socialism."

2. Vast resources were spent on the Olympic program and Leipzig's Sports University. Doping was common and led to tragic results.
3. In the 1986 Five-Year Plan, the GDR invested in cybernetics, robots, and computer engineering, but the results disappointed.

D. Visions of the future.
1. In a bizarre utopian vision, planners envisioned making the wall totally mechanized by 2000, a perfect border.
2. In fact, another technology, Western television, undermined GDR slogans.

III. U.S.S.R.

A. Façade of vigor and realities.
1. The Soviet Union projected an image of power and progress, underlined by the 1957 Sputnik and space race successes.
2. Nuclear weapons gave it undisputed superpower status.
3. However, some observers called it "Upper Volta with rockets."
4. In the 1980s, the Soviet Union was spending an estimated quarter of its gross domestic product (GDP) on arms. Added to this were subsidies to Communist satellites worldwide.
5. Widespread winding down of ideological fervor followed de-Stalinization.
6. A privileged elite nicknamed *Apparat* or *Nomenklatura* undermined egalitarian claims.

B. Geriatric leadership and continuing repression.
1. Khrushchev was turned out of office in 1964 and replaced by collective leadership, from which Leonid Brezhnev (1906–1982) emerged as the main leader. Brezhnev announced that the Soviet Union was in the stage of "developed Socialism."
2. Repression of dissidents continued (including psychiatric hospitalization), though without Stalin's mass murder.
3. In Eastern Europe, the *Brezhnev Doctrine* justified intervention in Czechoslovakia in 1968.

C. Economic, technological, and environmental disaster.

  1. Empty stores made economic decline clear, despite falsified official statistics. Stalin's decimation of specialists left damaging gaps in Soviet science.

  2. Crackpot agricultural projects, such as the Virgin Lands, produced environmental disaster (by contrast, private garden plots were productive).

  3. On April 28, 1986 (just before May Day parades), the Chernobyl reactor near Kiev exploded. Costs of this accident and its initial denial by Soviet authorities eroded state credibility.

D. Loss of confidence.

  1. Although loss of political confidence in a ruling elite is difficult to quantify, it is nonetheless important.

  2. Jokes about the lived absurdity of the Soviet system proliferated.

  3. Within the party itself, a mood of crisis grew and led to the elevation of a true believer and reformer, Mikhail Gorbachev.

IV. North Korea.

  A. Establishing the dictatorship.

  1. Korea, earlier a Chinese satellite, was annexed by Japan in 1910.

  2. After World War II, Korea was to become an independent country, but with the Cold War occupation, two separate states were declared in 1948: South Korea, under American patronage, and North Korea, under Soviet patronage.

  3. With Stalin's go-ahead, North Korean leader Kim Il-Sung invaded the south on June 25, 1950. When UN troops advanced, China intervened. The "forgotten war," ending in 1953, claimed three million dead.

  4. Without a peace treaty, a tense standoff has endured for half a century.

  5. North Korea remains a massively militarized state, spending an estimated 30 percent of its GDP on one of the world's largest armies.

  6. At the same time, famine has wracked the land, killing perhaps two million or more in the 1990s.

B. Leaders and ideology.

   1. The first leader was Kim Il-Sung (1912–1994), known as "Great Leader" and installed by Soviet forces.

   2. Born Kim Son Ju near Pyongyang, he became an anti-Japanese guerrilla, was trained and educated in the Soviet Union, and served in the Soviet army during World War II.

   3. He crafted the ideology of *juche,* or "self-reliance," pursuing autarchy and radical isolation for the nation of 22 million.

   4. In 1994, Kim Il-Sung was succeeded by his son, Kim Jong Il (b. 1941), called the "Sun of the Twenty-First Century." Born in Siberia and schooled in East Germany, he has a reputation for being a volatile and cruel playboy.

   5. Elaborate cults of leadership were built up around both leaders, including posthumous veneration of Kim Il-Sung, omnipresent statues, mass parades and calisthenics displays, and flower shows of Kimjongilia blooms.

   6. Like many other dictators, Kim Jong II is an avid film enthusiast, styles himself a director, and has kidnapped actors for his entertainment.

C. Tools of state.

   1. Every household is to have a radio receiver, "the speaker," which broadcasts marches, songs, and proclamations. Like the Soviet *punkt* radio, it cannot be turned off, nor can its stations be changed.

   2. A dozen prison camps resembling the Soviet Gulag hold an estimated million prisoners.

   3. As recently admitted by the government, in the past, there were kidnappings of Japanese to serve as agents.

   4. A former ally, Russia, reported North Korean chemical and biological weapons experimentation.

   5. Sporadic attempts at controlled economic reform yielded only growing economic crises and tens of thousands of refugees trying to flee to China.

D. Continuing policies.

   1. In the new century, North Korea is one of the last surviving Stalinist states and has intensified its threatening stance toward the outside world, perhaps seeking to extort more food and fuel aid.

2. It has kept up arms sales (including sales of Scud rockets and other technology) to the highest bidder and conducts rocket tests.

3. In 2002, North Korea announced, then denied, that it possesses nuclear weapons.

V. The role of confidence in utopian futures.

A. Ideological dictatorships need powerful visions of the future to sustain their momentum and compel awe from believers, as well as foes.

B. In the absence of such confidence in the future vision, regimes can stall and begin to disintegrate.

Essential Reading:

Loren R. Graham, *Ghost of the Executed Engineer: Technology and the Fall of the Soviet Union*, pp. 67–106.

John O. Koehler, *Stasi: The Untold Story of the East German Secret Police.*

Supplementary Reading:

Kang Chol-Hwan and Pierre Rigoulot, *The Aquariums of Pyongyang: Ten Years in the North Korean Gulag.*

Mary Fulbrook, *Anatomy of a Dictatorship: Inside the GDR, 1949–1989.*

Questions to Consider:

1. What were the crucial turning points in each of the three regimes, leading to a decline of political confidence?

2. Why has the North Korean regime been more durable than that of East Germany or the Soviet Union?

Lecture Twenty—Transcript
East Germany, the Soviet Union, North Korea

In our previous lectures, we've considered the different forms that Communist regimes in China and in Cambodia could assume, though still claiming loyalty to the same ideology. In our lecture today, we'll examine how, in the age of the Cold War, many different routes to socialism could exist. In particular, we'll focus on the regimes of East Germany, the Soviet Union, and North Korea.

The varieties of socialist experience, however, would be even wider than those of the Communist East. Socialism and Communism could take markedly different forms in different countries. In Western Europe, a vibrant social democratic movement, espousing social democracy, steadily moved towards more moderate forms. Social democrats increasingly stressed reform over revolution. This would have been a heresy to Lenin and to other Communists.

They sought a broader appeal, across classes, for the notion of the amelioration of social problems. Emblematic of this development was the fortunes of the largest, and earlier, one of the best-known, highly reputed social democratic movements, that of Germany's Social Democratic Party. In its Bad Godesberg Program in 1958, the SPD revised its Marxist doctrines, to instead avow both economic planning and economic freedom as cardinal parts of its program.

By contrast, however, in today's lecture, we'll move our focus to the case of three hard-line states, which showed, not this reform, but rather a movement towards radical models of transformation. These will be East Germany, the Soviet Union, and North Korea, and I hope what will emerge from today's lecture is a sense of both the diversity and the commonalities among these hard-line regimes.

In the case of East Germany, the German Democratic Republic was declared to be the "State of the Workers and Peasants." After the wall had been erected in 1961, closing off the possibility of voting with one's feet, a grim "stabilization" began to set in East Germany. Many citizens saw that they must now come to terms with the inevitable and find their peace with the regime that ruled over them.

However, there was another element that certainly gave a sense of optimism to East Germany in its earliest years. It was a certain sense of pride that Marxism, its official ideology had certainly been a product growing out of German culture and German experience. Indeed, in what otherwise might be considered almost a nationalist statement, it was commonly said, or joked, that if anyone in the world could make Communism work, it would be the Germans. The Germans were said to have the requisite virtues of hard work, discipline, and industry. The German Democratic Republic was to become a worldwide showcase, showing how this model of government and social organization would move toward success. At the same time, however, there were internal contradictions.

In spite of the claims that were being made by the regime to an equality among its citizens, in fact, one could see the emergence of certain groups with privileges. The party elites enjoyed what they themselves would not have called class privilege, but whose special favors could certainly appear in that way to the population. This included access to special cars, special quarters and districts where the party elites would live, special stores that were not open to ordinary citizens of the Republic, greater access for their children to education, to movement up in their careers, as well as to those highly prized international exchanges.

One member of the party elite who rose steadily through the ranks, and who would be the leader of the East German state from 1971 right until the eve of its collapse, was Eric Honecker, who had risen through the party's ranks, and was quite clearly a product of the system that he ruled over.

In ways that are reminiscent of other dictatorial regimes we've discussed, the East German state concentrated on making sure that its message was passed along to the youth. The Free German Youth organization, the FDJ, regimented youth, sent them marching, singing patriotic songs, hailing the advance of socialism. To the critics of this organization, in many ways it bore haunting resemblances to the Hitler Youth.

The churches in East Germany were harassed, infiltrated, or closed. Increasingly religious ritual, traditional ritual, was replaced with secular, newly created, newly invented traditions like "youth confirmation," replacing earlier confirmation in the Christian right with a pledge of one's loyalty to socialist ideals.

The flip side of attempting to indoctrinate and win loyalty through propaganda was an atmosphere of coercion, control of the East

German state by the secret police, known as the *Stasi*. Stasi was a bureaucratic acronym that stood for the *Ministerium für Statessicherheit*, or the "State Security Service." The coercive forces of the police also manned the borders. Border troops guarded the Wall in Berlin itself, as well as stretching down across the German/German border, and these troops had orders to shoot to kill.

"Flight from the republic" was an official crime. In this case, one could pay for that crime with one's life. Dissidents and others who protested against the regime within were kept under constant surveillance, and were spied upon by a remarkably extensive web of stool pigeons and informers in their midst. Taken altogether, the state security police, the Stasi, established a remarkably intricate repressive apparatus for spying on East Germans. There were not only the regular secret police, but also those informers who were called "unofficial collaborators." They were rewarded, encouraged to denounce and to spy upon co-workers and families. When this was later revealed after the collapse of the East German regime, its results, obviously, could be shattering on those who had been thus betrayed by family members and friends.

The numbers of those who were tied into this web of complicity were enormous. An estimated 250,000 people worked for the Stasi from 1950 to 1989. When one breaks down the figures, this included one secret policeman for every 166 citizens. When informers were added, this increased to one security person for every 6.5 persons. I point out in my classes on German history that the implication for a classroom students such as the one listening to a lecture would be that, almost certainly, within their number, there would be a significant number of informers.

The Stasi generated enormous amounts of paperwork in the process of spying on its own citizens. It's been estimated that this included 121 miles of files on targets. The Stasi also maintained feared prisons, like Hohenschönhausen. Their activities included bugging apartments, collaboration with international terrorist groups, trafficking in people, in fact, as older individuals could be "bought free" by relatives in West Germany, and allowed to emigrate, as was also sometimes the case for some dissidents.

The Stasi was especially proud of its active, fraternal collaboration with the Soviet KGB. The Stasi thought of themselves as being in that lineage. They were proud of being descendants of Lenin's Cheka, the secret police that had been established right at the beginning of the Bolshevik Revolution.

East German state would also seek to win a sense of legitimacy for itself, a sense of the agreement of its population pertaining to the legitimacy of its own rule. At the same time, there were difficulties. There were inequalities in terms of how people were treated, the party elites versus ordinary citizens; these were all too patent. It was quite clear that there were failures in terms of providing a higher standard of living for most. At the same time, rhetorically, the shortcomings would be justified in an elegant term of phrase as "really existing Socialism." It was claimed that the East German state had achieved the closest advance to socialism that had yet been achieved. Thus, the "promised land" was but a hand's breadth away.

Legitimacy was also sought in other ways. In part, it was sought by showing, quite literally, that the new man and new woman had been built in this revolutionary regime, in the sports programs of the East German state. Vast resources were spent on the Olympic program and on Leipzig Sport University. Vast sums were pumped into the sports programs, and, as is now clear, vast amounts of drugs were also pumped into the veins of athletes who were competing for the honor of the East German state in the Olympics, as well.

This was a reality that was hidden, in many cases, from the athletes themselves. This doping, this drugging of athletes in order to achieve superhuman performance was common, and often led to tragic results. Now, one reads about women athletes who had been given so many drugs that, in fact, they had physically turned into men; their health has been damaged and perhaps destroyed, all in the interests of a state that was willing to sacrifice them on the altars of Olympic success. I recall, how, at the Olympic competitions, one would see nearly superhuman figures of great muscular bulk, men as well as women, standing in the competition for the East German state.

In the Five-Year Plan of 1986, the East German state further announced that it was surging ahead in technology. This was to be German genius and efficiency deployed, to show what socialism could achieve in a German context. This Five-Year Plan promised investments in cutting-edge technology: Cybernetics, robots, and computer engineering. The results, however, were intensely disappointing, in fact. Their rhetoric of the view of the future and the desire to move towards it was there, but the resources for it were already lagging, in fact. The East German state was not delivering on its promises.

Nevertheless, we might pause for a moment to consider some of the visions of the future that were offered to the people of this state. They included the promise that soon the standards of living in the West would be outstripped and overtaken. Clearly, however, these results were lagging.

In a bizarre utopian vision that was not shared with the population at large, government planners envisioned making the wall between the Germanys, the "anti-Fascist protection Wall," as it was termed, a perfect border, a perfect barrier. In retrospect, this seems to have been a very odd thing to have devoted so many resources towards, and seems a particularly ignoble utopian vision.

The hope was that by the year 2000, a year that the East German state didn't live to see, this border would have been perfectly mechanized, perfectly technologically coordinated, with automatic guns that didn't even need border guards, and with surveillance devices that would make it impermeable, a perfect border. In fact, another technology was steadily undermining the East German state, and its claims to holding a plausible vision of the future. That other technology was television.

The location of the East German state, cheek-by-jowl with the West Germany, the Federal Republic of Germany, meant that Western television, with its popular entertainment, news broadcasts, including also in its programming those advertisements for all sorts of consumer goods that just had to be had, were also being beamed into East German territory, and being picked up on the television screens of East Germans. In fact, this was, as it turned out, a feature of East German life that was tolerated, at least, by the East German state, because it was seen as a perhaps harmless outlet for citizens' curiosity. Nonetheless, the subversive message that life was otherwise in the rest of the world, was making headway in the East German state, in ways that are difficult to quantify.

East Germans used to joke about those members of their own East German territory who were out of the range of West German television. They were considered to be living in the "valley of the clueless." They were the people who didn't have a clue about what was going on outside.

We return to a theme that we've seen again and again in this course. That is that means of communication and technology could be a double-edged sword. They could propagate a message effectively, beaming it to the masses, as in the radio of the Nazi regime. On the other hand, as in this case, technology could also subvert the government's message.

We turn next to the case of the "Big Brother," the founding state of the Communist project, the Soviet Union. It had a façade of vigor, with disappointing realities lurking behind. The Soviet Union managed to project a remarkably attractive image, to many, of power and progress after World War II. This was underlined by its technological achievements, such as the launching of atomic weapons, and that of the Sputnik satellite in 1957, which panicked Western societies with the prospect of being left behind in the "Space Race." The Soviets would then go on to achieve remarkable successes.

In this context, nuclear weapons were an especially important feature of the technological prowess of the Soviet Union. Nuclear weapons would give it undisputed superpower status, even in a time when its economic performance was lagging. Even Western intelligence agencies were slow to understand the depths of the Soviet Union's systemic crisis in its planned economies; this was also true of other Eastern European states. However, some observers, who had already noted the lack of consumer goods, the statistical unreliabilities, the outrageous claims made in propaganda about advances in economics, considered the Soviet Union to be little better than, as one put it, "Upper Volta with rockets." Upper Volta is a Third World country, in essence, whose claim to status was its military machine.

That military machine clearly exacted an enormous price, and was an enormous drag on the economy of the Soviet Union. We might mention parenthetically that the Cold War was expensive for both sides. It was an enormous expense in the Soviet case. It was estimated that perhaps a quarter of its Gross Domestic Product was spent on the arms race. Economic historians have pointed out that, in fact, it's difficult to be precise about these estimates, because the entire economy of the Soviet Union was remarkably militarized. Added to these expenses were further subsidies to Communist satellites and Communist movements worldwide, who had to be encouraged, given the ideological commitment to revolution.

Yet, observers of the Soviet system noticed a certain "winding down" of the ideological fervor that had characterized the Soviet Union earlier, under Lenin and Stalin. This was especially true after the impact of de-Stalinization, and Khrushchev's revelation of Stalin's crimes, in which crimes against the party were emphasized. This turning away from revolutionary fervor and fanaticism raised the question of how the system could yet continue to exist, given its ideological mission.

What's clear is that within the ranks of the party itself, groups of people who had worked their way up the system, perhaps with ideological conviction, but also with careerist goals, grew into a privileged elite that came to be called the *Apparat*, meaning the "machine," or the *Nomenklatura*, meaning those whose names mattered in the nomenclature of lists of the party elite. This phenomenon undermined the egalitarian claims of the "classless society" of the Soviet Union. The leadership itself also seemed to be stumbling.

The leadership grew old; some historians of the regime in its later stages speak of a "geriatric leadership," which had not passed the torch to a younger generation. This undermined the image of the Communist ideology's vitality. This problem was coupled with continuing repression.

Khrushchev had angered some of his own allies within the movement because of his unsparing revelation of Stalin's crimes. In part because of this, he was turned out of office in 1964, and was replaced by a collective leadership. From the ranks of that collective leadership, one man emerged as main leader: Leonid Brezhnev.

Leonid Brezhnev announced that the Soviet Union was on course, and that it would stay that course. He said that it was in the stage of "developed Socialism," a theoretical phrase that was supposed to inspire confidence, though it probably didn't. He said that this was the stage that "indicated the approach of the perfection of Communism." Brezhnev's own appearance was stolid, heavy, and increasingly aging. In his last years in office, it seemed a perfect expression of the immobility and the lack of will for reform or consideration of new ideas that burdened Soviet Union toward the end of its time.

The repression of dissidents continued, without Stalin's emphasis on mass murder and the Gulag, but it could include such brutal measures as psychiatric hospitalization. The reasoning was that anyone who dissented, or was unhappy with the state of affairs, must clearly, ipso facto, be mentally ill.

In Eastern Europe and elsewhere in the world, the *Brezhnev Doctrine* was coined as a rationale for intervention. The Brezhnev Doctrine argued that Communist advance was inevitable, and was not to be rolled back. Once a socialist revolution had been achieved, the Soviet Union would intervene, if necessary, to stop it from going back. Thus, intervention in Czechoslovakia in 1968 was justified by the Brezhnev Doctrine, as was the disastrous invasion of Afghanistan in 1979.

At the same time, however, there was a mounting bill to be paid in terms of economic, technological, and environmental disasters, in what appeared to be the mighty Soviet Union.

Visitors to the Soviet Union, and I had a chance myself to visit, in these times, would be shocked by the sites of empty stores, selling, perhaps, enormous jugs of vinegar, though I never really understood what that was for, but otherwise with bare shelves, with little in the way of consumer goods. This made economic decline clear, despite falsified official statistics.

In the long term, Stalin's decimation of generations of specialists had left damaging gaps in Soviet science, which now were evident. The crackpot agricultural projects championed by people like Trofin Lysenko, including the "Virgin Lands" project, to plow up enormous plains in central Asia and central Russia, produced environmental disaster, with the soil blowing away, as Americans could probably have predicted from their own experiences with the Dust Bowl. By contrast, the private garden plots that farmers had still been allowed to have as a small concession, perhaps temporary, were enormously productive in comparison to the state-owned farms. This was already an indication of where things might be headed.

Then came perhaps an archetypal environmental disaster. In April of 1986, just before the Mayday parades celebrated by the Soviet Union, the Chernobyl reactor near Kiev exploded. The costs of this accident, and Soviet authorities' initial denial of it, eroded state credibility.

One needs to hear the voices of parents whose children were sent out to cheer and to march in the Mayday parades, while a cloud of atomic debris floated overhead, to hear their fury and disgust with their government, to sense the loss of confidence that had ensued.

This loss of confidence in the ruling elite is difficult to quantify, but nonetheless, was important. Jokes about the absurdity of the Soviet regime proliferated, making that loss of confidence clear. Within the party itself, a mood of crisis led a true believer and reformer, Gorbachev, to take leadership by 1985. His attempt to save the system would bring about its end.

A final regime that we'll consider is North Korea. North Korea had earlier been a Chinese satellite that was annexed by Japan in 1910. After World War II, it was to become an independent country. In the Cold War, however, it was divided into two states, the South Korean under American patronage, and the North Korean under the Soviets.

With Stalin's go-ahead, the North Korean leader, Kim Il-Sung, invaded the South in 1950. China then intervened when the Americans counterattacked. The "forgotten war," as it's been called, ending in 1953, claimed three million dead. Without a peace treaty, the tense standoff has endured for half a century. North Korea remains a massively militarized and isolated hermit kingdom, spending an estimated third on its Gross Domestic Product on one of the world's largest armies. At the same time, famine has stalked the land, killing, perhaps, over two million, in the 1990s.

The leaders of the North Korean state are significant. The first leader was Kim Il-Sung, called the "Great Leader," installed by Soviet forces. He was born as Kim Song Ju near Pyongyang, later became an anti-Japanese guerrilla, and was trained and educated in the Soviet Union. He then served in the Soviet army. Later, he was made leader of the North Korean state, and crafted the ideology of *juche*, or "self-reliance," preaching autarchy and radical isolation.

In 1984, upon his death, he was succeeded by his son, Kim Jong Il. In the propaganda, he was called the "Sun of the Twenty-First Century." This man was born in Siberia, was schooled in East Germany, and has the reputation of being a volatile and cruel, narcissistic playboy. He's said to be enormously vain, is apparently only five foot three inches in height, but has a high hairdo and platform shoes, to emphasize his prominent status.

Elaborate cults of leadership were built up around both leaders, including the declaration of Kim Il-Sung, even after his death, as "president for eternity." There are omnipresent statues, mass parades, songs with titles like "The Leader will Always be With Us," or "My Country Under the Sunshine of the Party," and flower shows featuring blooms dedicated to the leaders are common.

Like many other dictators we've surveyed in this course, Kim Jong Il is an avid enthusiast of film. He said to have the largest collection of Daffy Duck films in the world. In fact, he's even kidnapped actors for his entertainment. His own lifestyle is enormously self-indulgent and luxurious.

The tools of state that are deployed in enforcing the ideology and the authority of the state are also significant, and in many ways, mimic ones that we've seen before. Every household in North Korea is said to have a radio receiver, called "the speaker," which broadcasts marches, songs, speeches, and proclamations. Like the Soviet *punkt* radio, it cannot be turned off, nor the stations changed. It is always on, always speaking to the masses.

As a repressive apparatus of the state, a dozen prison camps resembling the Soviet Gulag in their brutality are said to hold an estimated million prisoners. The state is isolated from the outside world. There's no access to the Internet, and the people are shielded from outside influences. Yet, there is an energetic foreign policy, often disastrously irrational its approach, that is taken to be characteristic of this North Korean state. As was recently admitted by the North Korean government, in the past, Japanese citizens were kidnapped, to serve as agents in the spreading of North Korean ideology. A former ally, Russia, has in fact reported that North Korea had been experimenting with chemical and biological weapons.

Sporadic and often disorganized attempts at controlled economic reform have yielded only more economic crisis. Tens of thousands of desperate North Korean refugees have tried to flee to China. Sometimes they're turned back and face execution.

Moreover, these are policies that continue into our own day, into the new century. In the new century, North Korea is one of the last surviving Stalinist states. It recently has taken on an intensified, threatening stance toward the outside world. This is perhaps an expression of its interior paranoia, or perhaps, some have argued, a rational attempt to show its danger, in order to extort more food or fuel aid from the international community.

It has kept up arms sales, including those of Scud rockets and other military technology, to the highest bidder, and has undertaken reckless rocket tests. It has also been suggested that North Korea has a sideline in the international drug trade. Recently, a ship with North Korean officials, carrying massive amounts of drugs, was seized on the high seas.

In 2002, North Korea also shocked the world with an announcement that it had nuclear weapons. Shortly thereafter, it denied its own announcement that it had nuclear weapons. In a brief space after that, it once again re-announced that it had nuclear weapons. The question of what's going on in this isolated, North Korean state, is one of urgent importance to the wider world.

I want to conclude with a note on the role of confidence in these regimes. The role of confidence in utopian futures is difficult to quantify, but clearly is an enormously important ideological and political factor. The kinds of dictatorships that we've discussed so far need compelling visions of a future that is said to be inevitable and unstoppable, to both sustain their own inner momentum, and to compel awe from believers as well as foes, to convince them that resistance is not possible.

These are visions of the future that have been propagated with greater or lesser success by the regimes that we've discussed in today's lecture. In the absence of this confidence in the future vision, with the erosion of that utopian horizon, such regimes can easily stall out and begin to disintegrate.

That's precisely the phenomenon we'll be discussing in our next lecture, on the democratic revolutions of 1989, which could either yield democratic stability, or even greater turmoil, as we'll see next time.

Lecture Twenty-One
From the Berlin Wall to the Balkans

Scope:

As the 20th century neared its end, the spirit of the times seemed to be sending mixed signals. On the one hand, from 1989 to 1991, Communist regimes in Eastern Europe and the Soviet Union fell with astonishing speed, and hopes for a transition to democracy abounded. Yet at the same juncture, Europe saw a reversion to the crimes that had marked World War II in the troubled Balkans. As Yugoslavia began to crumble, the Serbian leader Slobodan Milosevic came to power with the ideology of establishing a "Greater Serbia," ethnically cleansed of minorities. Radio propaganda and even pop music incited ethnic hatreds. In Bosnia and Kosovo, Serbian paramilitary groups and government forces cooperated in mass terror and expulsions, also setting up concentration camps before belated intervention by the international community.

Outline

I. The democratic wave.

    A. An epoch ends.

        1. For most of the Cold War, an estimated third of the world's population lived under Communist regimes.

        2. The remarkable self-liberation of societies made the century's close a hopeful time.

    B. Simultaneously, however, certain events suggested that millenarian expectations were premature.

II. The hopes of 1989.

    A. Figures.

        1. Remarkable individuals, many more than can be described here, challenged authoritarian states, and their demands converged around 1989.

        2. The 1975 Helsinki Acts on human rights gave dissidents a foundation for argument.

        3. A rich literature of dissidence circulated in *samizdat* ("underground press") form, including Solzhenitsyn's works.

        4. Czechoslovakian playright Vaclav Havel (b. 1936), later president, was imprisoned for his human rights activism.

His ideas on "civil society" seemed a prescription for recovery from totalitarianism.

5. Pope John Paul II (b. 1920), born Karol Wojtyla, the first non-Italian pontiff since 1522, was shaped by his experience of Nazi and Communist control of Poland and influenced Eastern European transition.

B. Perceptions of the future.

1. Economic failure and political repression eroded confidence in future visions of Communist regimes.

2. American and Western European economic progress contrasted starkly.

3. Movement toward European unification also created fear of being left out.

C. Technology.

1. Technology's role was ambiguous: It enabled surveillance and jamming, but television, radio (Radio Free Europe and Voice of America), and movies also had the opposite effect, opening societies.

2. Fax machines were used by opposition movements.

3. The S.D.I. program of space defenses proposed by American president Ronald Reagan raised the prospect of another unsustainable arms race.

D. Peaceful revolt.

1. The revolutions of Central and Eastern Europe were remarkably peaceful, given that the potential for violence seemed so high.

2. An important catalyst and model for change came earlier, with the Polish trade union Solidarity (Solidarnosc) in Gdansk in the 1970s, led by Lech Walesa. Even after being banned in 1982, it was an open conspiracy including a quarter of the population.

3. After Brezhnev's death in 1982, the Soviet leadership moved to reform. In 1985, Mikhail Sergeyevich Gorbachev (b.1931) became the party's general secretary, charged with saving Communism.

4. Born to a peasant family in southwestern Russia, he rose in the Komsomol and party and, in 1985, was the Politburo's youngest member.

5. His *Perestroika* movement sought reform of economics. *Glasnost* encouraged constructive criticism.

6. Too radical for hardliners yet too limited for democrats, Gorbachev's reforms both raised popular expectations and disappointed them. In the West, he was lionized but misunderstood.

7. Gorbachev sought to cut expensive subsidies and improve relations with the West by shedding the "outer empire."

8. In East Germany, after refugee outflows and internal conflict among the elite, the Berlin Wall fell on November 9, 1989. Scenes of celebration broadcast live worldwide set off chain reactions, and German unification followed in 1990.

9. Communist regimes elsewhere in Eastern and Central Europe were simultaneously liberalizing, abolishing Communist monopoly: Poland, Hungary, and Czechoslovakia (the fall of Romanian dictator Nicolae Ceausescu [1918–1989] was violent).

10. The chain reaction also spread to the Soviet Union. National liberation movements, such as Sajudis in Lithuania, rallied populations, even after violence by Soviet special-forces troops in 1991.

11. In August 1991, Gorbachev's hardliner allies attempted a coup, which failed, leading to the Soviet Union's final breakup.

E. General observations.

1. Such total collapse, without conflagration, was astonishing.

2. The opposition movements leading the revolutions of 1989–1991, in spite of high expectations, were not utopian.

3. The process of escaping the mindsets created by these ideological regimes was not quick and is still ongoing.

4. Surveys of damage done to Central and Eastern European societies are still underway. Bitter Russian observers describe a century's "negative selection."

5. This underlines the need in such societies to confront the past, accounting for history's blank spots. Recovery of the past is crucial to this reckoning.

III. Chastened expectations.

    A. Democratic euphoria.

        1. Some observers believed that a democratic millennium had arrived.

        2. American political scientist Francis Fukuyama speculated that this was the "end of history."

        3. In fact, the democratic wave was not irresistible, as contemporary events made clear.

    B. Tiananmen Square massacre.

        1. Chinese student demonstrations in favor of democratic reforms massed in Beijing.

        2. On June 4, 1989, the army moved in, killing, it was estimated, several hundred students and arresting about 10,000 more.

IV. The agony of Yugoslavia: Bosnia and Kosovo.

    A. General observations.

        1. The breakup of unitary Yugoslavia, earlier held together by Josef Tito (1892–1980), involved mass violence and genocide.

        2. Although in 1948 the United Nations proscribed genocide, these atrocities at first met with international inaction.

        3. Notions of "the international community" were used to evade responsibility.

    B. Yugoslavia.

        1. Yugoslavia ("State of the South Slavs") united Serbs, Croats, Bosnian Muslims, and Slovenes. Bosnia's Sarajevo showcased peaceful coexistence.

        2. With Communist collapse in Europe, an ideological vacuum opened.

        3. Serbian Communist leader Slobodan Milosevic (b. 1941) exploited this situation with a Nationalist ideology of "Greater Serbia."

        4. Milosevic was born to a Montenegrin family in Serbia.

        5. Joining the Communist Party at 18, he rose swiftly, betraying his own patron.

6. In 1987, Milosevic spoke at Kosovo's ancient battlefield, a prime example of abuse of history to mobilize present-day grievances.

7. Other nationalities grew anxious, and, in 1991, Slovenia and Croatia seceded and became independent after a brief war.

8. In the new aggressively Nationalist climate, radio and television broadcast propaganda and songs of the Turbo-folk genre.

C. Bosnia.

1. When Bosnia tried to secede in 1992, Milosevic mobilized paramilitaries to seize territory. Mortars and snipers targeted Sarajevo.

2. Paramilitaries, such as Arkan's Tigers, engaged in "ethnic cleansing," terrorizing, raping, and killing to expel. Stages of ethnic cleansing were systematized and became routine.

3. In concentration camps, such as Omarska, non-Serbs were abused, tortured, and killed.

4. When Srebrenica, declared a UN "safe area," was overrun by Serb forces in July 1995, Muslim men and boys were separated from their families, and some 7,000 were killed.

5. International inaction, blaming "age-old hatreds," allowed ethnic cleansing to continue. European diplomats declared this a European problem but did not intervene.

6. In a brutal cycle, ethnic Serbs were likewise driven out of areas where Milosevic was not in control.

7. NATO air war against Serb forces in August 1995 helped end the war, leading to the Dayton negotiations in November 1995, with de facto partition of Bosnia and no return for refugees.

8. In four years of fighting, some 200,000 died and two million were left homeless.

D. Kosovo.

1. Brutal repression of the majority ethnic Albanians in Serbia's Kosovo province led to a guerrilla movement. In the summer of 1998, Serbian police actions of

increasing ferocity took place, including killings in Racak in January 1999.

2. As NATO forces began bombing the Yugoslav army in March 1999 (without UN approval), Milosevic sped up ethnic cleansing already underway (Operation Horseshoe).

3. Television showed scenes of railcars of Albanians being expelled. Nearly a million Kosovar refugees were forced from their homes.

4. On June 3, 1999, Yugoslavia surrendered, losing control of Kosovo.

E. After losing presidential elections in 2000, Milosevic was handed over by Serbia to the Hague to stand trial for war crimes.

V. The future legacy of the past.

A. A crucial point comes into focus: The past does not dictate present or future actions.

B. However, the past is often manipulated for visions of a desired future.

C. This fact highlights the importance of knowledge of the past and a critical perspective.

Essential Reading:

Jan Willem Honig and Norbert Both, *Srebrenica: Record of a War Crime.*

Tim Judah, *The Serbs: History, Myth and the Destruction of Yugoslavia.*

Samantha Power, *"A Problem From Hell": America and the Age of Genocide*, pp. 247–327 and 391–473.

Supplementary Reading:

Rezak Hukanovic, *The Tenth Circle of Hell: A Memoir of Life in the Death Camps of Bosnia.*

Questions to Consider:

1. What are the main reasons that the Soviet Union's collapse took place largely without explosions of mass violence, as many had predicted?

2. Why did China's democratic movement fail while opposition movements in Eastern and Central Europe succeeded?

Lecture Twenty-One—Transcript
From the Berlin Wall to the Balkans

In our last lectures, we've considered a whole series of regimes close to our own times, whose ideologies, and whose atrocities in the name of their ideas have done much to shape the violent course of the 20th century.

In today's lecture, however, we want to observe a remarkable transition, what many felt at the time was a turning point. As the 20th century neared its end, the spirit of the times seemed to be sending mixed signals. On the one hand, there seemed to be a message of hope, and on the other hand, a suggestion that, perhaps, a whole new round of ideological conflict might yet emerge.

From 1989 to 1991, truly remarkable years in modern historical experience, a whole series of Communist regimes in Eastern Europe, and then the Soviet Union itself, fell apart with astonishing, unexpected speed. In this context, hopes for transition to democracy abounded in these newly liberated countries.

Yet, at precisely the same juncture, in the Balkans, Europe saw reversion to crimes that many had hoped would not occur again. These were crimes resembling those of the Second World War. As the formerly unified state of Yugoslavia began to come apart and crumble, new leaders emerged, who proclaimed new nationalist ideologies with the aim of ethnic cleansing to produce states on the basis of national unification and identity.

Radio, television, and even pop music were deployed to incite ethnic hatreds. In Bosnia and Kosovo, atrocities were seen that reflected, all too well, the experiences of bygone generations.

In today's lecture, we want to consider, in other words, both the causes of these remarkable phenomena, and to consider the reasons for the belated intervention by the international community, as things went wrong in the Balkans.

First, we'll consider the democratic wave centered around the year 1989. Clearly, 1989 marked the end of an epoch. For most of the Cold War, it's estimated that about a third of the world's population had lived under Communist regimes. In 1989, and in the few years that followed, this state of affairs would be remarkably overturned. The self-liberation of societies in Eastern Europe and Russia thus made the century's close a hopeful time. However, at the same time, there were certain events that suggested even to contemporaries, that millenarian expectations of a democratic utopia being just over the horizon were premature.

Let's speak, then, first, to the hopes of 1989. There were certain remarkable figures, who had been active before this year, and who now came into their own and were recognized as models for civic behavior.

These were remarkable individuals. Indeed, there were many more of them than can be described in our lecture today. They had in common the fact that they challenged authoritarian states, held up the standard of human rights, and their demands tended to converge around 1989.

An event years previous had given many of these dissidents a foundation for argument. This was the 1975 signing of the Helsinki Accords on human rights. These Helsinki acts, which were treated by the Soviet Union, essentially, as a formality or a dead letter, would turn out to have remarkable significance, because their rhetoric, their promises of human rights, would now be a commitment the governments would be held to by their dissidents.

At the same time, in previous decades, a rich literature of dissidence had circulated underground. It was given a name, indeed, from the Russian language that entered into the English language and other languages: *samizdat*, meaning, "to publish yourself." It meant, in essence, the "underground press." Novels and political works were circulated in the underground, in the samizdat form, including the works of Solzhenitsyn.

There were other examples of such dissidence in writers, in other Eastern European countries. A prominent example of one whose trajectory was remarkable and significant for our purposes, was the Czechoslovakian playwright, Vaclav Havel. He wrote absurdist, surrealist plays. Some have argued that only the form of surrealism could actually be a realistic depiction of the sort of society in which he and others were living. This man later would become president of his country. In this period, however, he was imprisoned for his human rights activism.

He articulated ideas that others were also proposing at this time, ideas summed up in the phrase, "civil society." Civil society was the notion that a buffer zone should exist between the isolated individual and the state. There should be a zone of protection between the great power of the government and the naked, sole individual. Civil society, in other words, encapsulated all of those private, nongovernmental, relationships, as well as ties that existed between people in families, churches, and independent organizations. This notion seemed especially attractive, because it seemed to offer a prescription for recovery from totalitarianism of the sort that Hannah Arendt had analyzed.

Another man whose role would be important, though a subtle one, in this period, was the pope of the Roman Catholic Church, John Paul II. He was born Karol Wojtyla, and as a Pole, was the first non-Italian pontiff since 1522. As a young man, he had been shaped by his experiences in a series of occupations of Poland. There was first Nazi and then Communist control. His championing of human rights, with a religious message, influenced the Eastern European transition in important ways.

Yet, there still remains something about this remarkable set of democratic revolutions in 1989 that evades the close, quantifiable analysis that historians might like to achieve. I'd argue that one element, which is very difficult to even recover, at this distance from those events, and which played a crucial role in these transformations, was the anticipation of the actors' futures, their perceptions of what lay beyond the horizon, and what the future likely held. These changing perceptions of the future tended to give more confidence to dissidents, while they eroded the ideological confidence, once so strong, in the Communist parties of the regime.

In particular, there were concrete reasons for this. There was economic failure, which was now undeniable, as well as political repression. These eroded confidence in those earlier future visions presented by the Communist regimes. Indeed, jokes circulated in this period, which made clear that the sort of popular sense that this was where the future lay, had seriously deteriorated. There was a joke, for instance, which asked, "Is Communism truly a viable form of government?" In this joke, the answer is, "Of course Communism is a viable form of government, because if this kind of mess existed under capitalism, it would have collapsed long ago." Another joke suggested that Communism was like the horizon. It always receded into the future.

The sort of bitter irony already testified to the sense of a loss of confidence in the future utopian visions being presented by a once vital ideology. In this context, the apparent economic progress of the United States or Western Europe was a stark contrast to those who lived under other regimes.

Around the 1980's, another intangible element was important, but difficult to trace exactly. The movement taking place in the richer, more prosperous countries of Western Europe towards European unification, also had a subtle effect on dissidents in Eastern Europe. While this European unification was taking place in the West, they felt that they might be left out, that the doors, in some sense, might be closing on their European identity; this was part of a project that they wanted to share in. This sense of urgency, that there was no time to lose, I think, demonstrably hurried along the revolutionary events of 1989.

Further, technology played an important role in speeding up the revolutions of 1989 to 1991. We need to note a recurring phenomenon here, one that we've tried to emphasize in our lectures. That's the ambiguous role of technology in both the functioning of repressive regimes and in the resistance to those regimes.

On the one hand, technology could certainly enable governments to perform remarkably extensive surveillance, and to jam foreign radio transmissions, in order to keep their populations isolated.

On the other hand, technology could also play a subversive role. Television and radio broadcasts, for instance, from the Radio Free Europe or Voice of America broadcasting systems, as well as, perhaps more insidiously and slowly, Western movies that were imported into the Soviet Union or Communist societies. These also could have the opposite effect of seeming to open the societies' eyes, those subject to their influences, to the notion of broader horizons. The role of technology also includes the way in which fax machines could be used by opposition movements in order to keep communication with one another while these democratic revolutions were in process.

Technology also played a very important role in creating a sense of crisis in the leadership elites of the Soviet Union in particular. The so-called "SDI Program," or "Strategic Defense Initiative," often jokingly nicknamed "Star Wars," was a program of space defenses that had been proposed by the American president, Ronald Reagan. They raised the prospect of another unsustainable arms race that might be just around the corner. Debate still continues about whether this program would even have been technologically viable. Nonetheless, we have testimony from Soviet generals as well as politicians that the very prospect of a whole new round of escalating arms competition was one that many leaders felt was not sustainable.

Yet, the hopes of 1989 and of these democratic revolutions would issue in remarkably peaceful revolt, rather than elemental, violent revolutions. This is an abiding mystery. Why were the revolutions of Central and Eastern Europe, around 1989 to 1991, so remarkably peaceful, when the potential for violence seemed so very, very high? It's a question that we need to deal with.

An important catalyst and model for change had come earlier, in nonviolent resistance, in particular in Poland, which had a centuries-old tradition of social organization to resist foreign occupiers. In Poland, a true workers' trade union, known as Solidarity, or Solidarnosc, in Gdansk in the 1970s, had arisen, led by an electrician, not a committed, ideological revolutionary, by name of Lech Walesa. Even after this organization was banned in 1982, it continued as an open conspiracy, including about a quarter of the Polish population and the mobilization of civil society from below.

At the same time, a sense of crisis was building in the Soviet Union. I would argue that it sapped the confidence of the leadership elites. There was a joke that was current during this period about the pass at which the Soviet Union had arrived. The Soviet Union was depicted as a once very formidable symbol of industrialization, a train. This symbol of the train was deployed to show the way in which it had ground down and finally stalled out. The joke was that the Soviet Union's train had been hurtling towards the future, and then Stalin had taken over. Stalin had suspected that the engineer driving the train was a traitor, and he had him shot. Now the train had completely ground to a halt.

When Khrushchev took over, this joke continued, Khrushchev denounced Stalin's actions, and rehabilitated the engineer. The train wasn't moving forward any faster, because the engineer was still dead.

When Brezhnev, the geriatric leader of the Soviet Union, took over, he hit upon a new tactic. That was to declare that the train was moving forward. He ordered the passengers to pull the shades down over the windows, and everyone had to sway from side to side and make the noises of a train surging forward. The reality hadn't changed, and everyone knew it was a lie, but nonetheless, the system trundled forward for a while longer.

After Brezhnev's death in 1982, the Soviet leadership, in this mood of crisis, of having arrived at a moment of decision, now gambled on reform. In 1985, the remarkably young Mikhail Sergeyevich Gorbachev became the party's general secretary, with a mission. He was charged with saving Communism.

Gorbachev had been born to a peasant family in southwestern Russia. He was a young man who had grown up within the Soviet Union. He had risen in the Komsomol youth organization, and then in the party. In 1985, he was the Politburo's youngest member, even as he was placed in control.

He announced that his mission was to break with totalitarianism. This had been a taboo word earlier, but now it was being used by the leader of the Soviet Union. They were to break with Stalin's abuses and go back to a purer form of Communism from Lenin's times.

To this purpose, he deployed the *Perestroika* movement, which meant, "restructuring," to seek economical reform. In terms of social life, *Glasnost*, or "openness," was encouraged to promote constructive criticism. Gorbachev himself was probably surprised by the tidal wave of not only constructive criticism, but also very radically critical expressions that could now be heard from society. Soon, these programs were out of control.

His reform programs were too radical for hard-liners, yet too limited for democrats who wanted to push forward. Gorbachev's reforms raised popular expectations, and also disappointed them. In the West, and in the United States, Gorbachev was often lionized, but often misunderstood as well, in his real aims.

Gorbachev sought to save the system. In particular, he sought to cut expensive subsidies to Communist movements in other countries, and to improve relations with the West by shedding the "outer empire" of satellite states. In East Germany, one of the most important satellites, after refugee outflows, and conflict within the ruling elite itself, the Berlin Wall fell on November 9, 1989, as ordinary Eastern Germans pounded it down.

The scenes of celebration, those mind-boggling pictures of crowds of people celebrating on top of the Wall, or smashing away at it with sledgehammers, were broadcast worldwide, and had a decisive impact on other political systems as well. In Eastern Europe, they set off chain reactions emulating those scenes of liberation. German unification followed in 1990.

Communist regimes elsewhere in Eastern and Central Europe were also simultaneously liberalizing, and abolishing the Communist monopolies that had earlier been the rule. In Poland, Hungary, and Czechoslovakia, new governments took power. In the case of Romania, its notorious dictator, Nikolae Ceausescu, met a violent end at the hands of some of his former allies, who sought to hijack the democratic transition.

This chain reaction, uncontrollable now, spread to the Soviet Union itself. In one after another of the national republics of the Soviet Union, liberation movements, like Sajudis in Lithuania, rallied their populations, even after violence by Soviet special-forces troops in 1991 showed that Gorbachev was now taking a harder line.

In August of 1991, Gorbachev's hardliner allies attempted a coup, which failed, and ultimately led to the Soviet Union's final breakup. The lack of confidence on the part of the hard-liners was crucial, in this context. One can recall the news reports of these days, as the coup plotters, who had Gorbachev under house arrest, announced that they were now in control of the country. One of the coup plotters was obviously falling-down drunk. The man who was reading the bulletin announcing the seizure of power was laughed at by the journalists who were covering it, because very obviously, as he was reading these comments, his hands were shaking.

This didn't inspire confidence in the plotters themselves, and made clear that the determination to quell resistance, which might earlier have existed under a hard-line regime, was lacking in this case.

Such total collapse, without conflagration, of the Soviet Union, was, and still remains, an astonishing feature. However, the opposition movements in Eastern Europe as well as Russia, which led to the revolutions of 1989, in spite of their high expectations for fundamental change, were not utopian in nature. One might even argue that they were anti-utopian, in the sense that what they were promising was not a resolution of all social problems, and not a moving forward into a perfect society. Rather, their plaintive request was for the ability, finally, to live in a "normal" society, as they put it.

At the same time, the process of getting out of the mindsets that had been cultivated by the ideological regimes that had ruled over these liberated countries was not quick; arguably, it's still ongoing, at this remove.

The surveys of the damage done to Central and Eastern European societies, in terms of economic and environmental damage, as well as in pure human terms, are still underway. Many bitter and keen Russian observers of their own society describe sadly what some of them call a century-long "negative selection," in which those who showed the most initiative, most creativity, most imagination, and most decency were mowed down again and again by despotic regimes.

This very fact underlines a recurring and important point: The need in such societies to confront the past, when that past has been brought to a close, because otherwise, its ghosts will continue to haunt. History's blank spots, in other words, need to be filled in for these societies, in an important psychological sense. The recovery of the past, and an estimate, objectively, of what that past involved, is crucial to a reckoning and a healthy beginning for such shaken societies.

At the same time, even in such a hopeful mood, expectations were chastened. While the leaders of the movements in Eastern Europe were not utopians themselves, some observers, especially in the West, felt what was almost a utopian euphoria about the future of democracy.

Some observers were led to believe that a democratic millennium had arrived. To give but one example, the American political scientist, Francis Fukuyama, speculated that we were living through the "end of history," not in the sense that the clocks would now end, or that events would stop taking place, but in the sense that the great debates over how to live politically had been resolved and that liberal democracy had won.

In fact, as was being demonstrated even at that time, the democratic wave was not irresistible. Contemporary events were making clear that there were other, alternative futures on offer as well.

One case came in 1989 with the Tiananmen Square massacre in China. Chinese student demonstrations in favor of democratic reforms had gathered in Beijing, in Tiananmen Square. Then, however, on June 4, 1989, as a horrified world looked on, the Chinese army moved in, and killed an estimated several hundred students, while arresting 10,000 more. It was clear that this elite, the Chinese Communist Party, had not lacked the confidence to intervene.

The agony of Yugoslavia, in the Balkans, and events in Bosnia and Kosovo would also make clear that democracy was not foreordained, but could, in fact, be hijacked. The breakup of an earlier, unified Yugoslavia, earlier held together by the charismatic Communist leader Josef Tito, who died in 1980, involved mass violence and genocide. The international community's record was not a positive one on this score. Though the United Nations had prescribed the crime of genocide in 1948, the atrocities that were taking place, even at this time of democratic transition elsewhere, at first largely met with international inaction.

The very notion of the "international community" could be used by some countries to evade the sense of their own responsibility. Yugoslavia, the so-called "State of the South Slavs," had united disparate groups: Serbs, Croats, Bosnian Muslims, and Slovenes. These were groups that managed, for a time, to live together in relative harmony. Bosnia's capital of Sarajevo, which we've already remarked upon as the starting place of the First World War, a historically resonant spot, for a time showcased peaceful coexistence, in the mixing of populations of different ethnic groups and religions in the cafes of that once-beautiful city.

With Communist collapse in Europe, however, an ideological vacuum opened up, and it was ready to be exploited by cynical leaders, and in particular, the Serbian Communist leader, Slobodan Milosevic. He exploited the situation, announcing a nationalist ideology of "Greater Serbia." He would exploit pre-existing ethnic frictions, in order to create the appearance of a spontaneous ethnic war, to serve his ideological purposes.

Milosevic himself was, in some sense, an outsider. He was born to a Montenegrin family in Serbia itself. He joined the Communist Party at the age of 18, and rose swiftly, in the process very cynically betraying his own patron in the Communist Party, a man by the name of Stambolic, who, it's now being suggested, was killed by Milosevic later, and whose body was recently found.

In the year 1987, a crucial turning point in these events, Milosevic spoke to a crowd of Serbians at Kosovo's ancient battlefield. This was a prime example of the abuse of ancient history to mobilize as present-day grievances, as he promised the Serbs that they would never be victims again.

Other nationalities grew anxious at this sort of nationalist ambition. In 1991, Slovenia and Croatia seceded from the earlier Yugoslavia, and became independent after a brief war.

In this new, aggressively nationalistic climate, radio and television were used by Milosevic to spread his message. The television stations broadcast historical messages, calling the Muslim minority in Bosnia "the Turks," using historical references to Ottoman oppression, pointing to the Second World War and its cruelties as a situation that might be just around the corner. At the same time, a popular genre of music, so-called "turbo folk," which is a blend of folk music and electronic dance music, announced an aggressive nationalist message as well.

We see in this use of technology and communications a remarkable phenomenon. We tend to hope that as communications spread around the world, that mutual understanding becomes more common. In this case, television, which some have considered to be more immune to the sort of manipulative message that the Nazis might have passed along with their radio stations before, was used to devastating effect. One trembles at the notion of what the Nazis might have been able to achieve with this modern medium.

Bosnia was the first to fall victim, in the largest sense. When Bosnia tried to secede in 1992, Milosevic mobilized paramilitary groups, to seize territory. Mortars and snipers targeted the once-beautiful city of Sarajevo and besieged it. They practiced the "big lie" in their relationship with Western media, and announced with remarkable cynicism that they were merely observing the city from the hills around Sarajevo, while "those people" within were bombarding themselves and killing their own people, in an attempt to manipulate Western opinion. This was the "big lie" practiced to an enormous degree.

Paramilitaries, like Arkan's Tigers, private armies, in essence, engaged in ethnic cleansing at Milosevic's direction. Ethnic cleansing, a term developed to describe this particular period in our own times, though the phenomenon had certainly existed over previous centuries, involved an almost sickening regularity of pattern: The terrorizing of civilians, men, women, and children, the raping of women in order to terrorize, and then killing, to force mass expulsions. The stages of ethnic cleansing were systematized and became a horrifying routine.

Its estimated that some 10,000 to 20,000 rapes took place, and involved not only the humiliation of those were subjected to this mistreatment, but was also a symbolic attempt to destroy the culture of the Bosnian Muslims, which also became clear in the dynamiting of mosques and other cultural monuments.

In concentration camps, such as those at Omarska, non-Serbs were abused, tortured, and killed. When Srebrenica, a town that had been declared a United Nations' "safe area," was overrun by Serbian forces in July 1995, Muslim men and boys were separated from their families under the very eyes of UN peacekeepers, and some 7000 of them were killed and thrown into mass graves.

International inaction, however, followed. The international community found it easy to fall back on the notion of "age-old hatreds" in the Balkans, the notion that "those people" had always been killing one another, and what could one do? It was very nearly a sort of ethnic stereotyping, and an element of racism was involved, the notion that, unlike the civilized West, it was simply to be expected of such people that the sort of behavior would be common. European diplomats declared that this was a European problem, but did not intervene. Then, in a brutal cycle, ethnic Serbs, who lived as minorities in other areas, were likewise driven out from those territories where Milosevic was not in control.

At long last, out of shame, perhaps, at this constant television reporting of scenes that seemed to be from documentaries of the Second World War, the international community, at last, did intervene. NATO air war against Serb forces in August of 1995 helped end the war, leading to the Dayton negotiations in November, with de facto partition of Bosnia, there was no return for refugees, essentially a ratification of ethnic cleansing.

In those four years of fighting, some 200,000 were killed and two million were left homeless. Then, these scenes repeated themselves once again, close to the end of the 20th century, in Kosovo.

Milosevic now turned his energies to this region. Brutal repression of the majority ethnic Albanians in Serbia's Kosovo province led to an Albanian guerrilla movement. In the summer of 1998, Serbian police actions of increasing ferocity took place and culminated in a mass killing in Racak, in January of 1999.

As NATO forces, now without UN approval, began bombing the Yugoslav army in March of 1999, Milosevic sped up an ethnic cleansing, which was presented as being in response to the NATO bombing, but actually, clearly, as a massive, logistical operation, had been planned before. Operation Horseshoe was put into effect.

Television once again showed scenes of railcars of Albanians being expelled. Nearly one million Kosovo refugees were forced from their homes. After a long bombing, on June 3, 1999, Yugoslavia at long last surrendered, losing control of Kosovo.

After losing presidential elections in the year 2000, in part because of a disastrous series of defeats that Milosevic's ideology had led Serbia to, Milosevic was handed over by Serbia to The Hague to stand trial for war crimes.

I want to close with an observation on the way in which the past does affect the future and yields a legacy. A crucial point now comes into focus. The past, those archetypal and stereotypical ancient hatreds, do not, in fact, always dictate present or future actions. However, the past can be and often is manipulated for visions of a desired future by cynical politicians like the Milosevic. It's precisely this fact that makes knowledge of the past, and a critical perspective on the past, so very important to our present day.

In our next lecture, we'll consider yet another case of genocide that the world wished to keep at a distance, and to ignore, but that nonetheless, of necessity, pressed its image upon the world's attention.

Lecture Twenty-Two
Rwanda

Scope:

In 1994, as the world looked on, horrific events unfolded in the central African country of Rwanda. Tension between two social groups erupted into genocide, encouraged by the state. The Hutu-dominated government organized the mass murder of the Tutsi minority. The state provided machetes for the killers, directed their movements through radio broadcasts and lists of intended victims, and enflamed them with propaganda, including hate-filled songs and quasi-religious Hutu commandments preaching the destruction of the enemy Tutsis. In the course of 100 days, 800,000 people were slaughtered, while the international community failed to intervene to prevent this recent genocide.

Outline

I. Background.
   A. Hutu and Tutsi.
      1. The Hutus and Tutsis of the central African country of Rwanda speak the same language and have the same religious background.
      2. Traditionally, the minority Tutsis were herders and landowners, while the majority Hutus were farmers.
      3. In the past, the Tutsi minority had been dominant.
      4. Some scholars argue that the lines of division between the groups were initially fluid and based on class and occupation, not ethnic difference. Intermarriage was common.
   B. Colonial legacies.
      1. Rwanda became a German colony in 1885 and, after World War I, was transferred to Belgian rule.
      2. Belgian administrators invented a "nasal index" to measure Tutsis and to scientifically categorize people on identification documents.
      3. Colonial administrative division of Rwandans led to an increasingly strict separation of the groups, which had earlier intermingled.
   C. Independence.

1. Rwanda became independent in 1962.
2. The majority Hutu dominated the new republic. Discrimination compelled many Tutsis to flee Rwanda.
3. Fighting continued between Tutsi rebel groups and the Hutu-led Rwandan government, which was supported by France and Belgium.
4. The Arusha Peace Accords of 1993 called for a new government to include the Tutsi rebel groups, such as the Rwandan Patriotic Front (RPF). UN peacekeepers, coordinated by Kofi Annan (later UN secretary general), were sent in to observe.

II. Unleashing "Hutu power."
   A. Origins.
      1. Some Hutu political leaders, championing "Hutu power," began to cultivate a racial hatred of the Tutsi, and their publications referred to the Tutsi as cockroaches, dehumanizing their opponents.
      2. At the head of the movement was Juvenal Habyarimana, leader of the National Revolutionary Movement for Development and Democracy (MRND).
      3. A clear aspect of a political religion, the official newspaper published in 1990 a document called "The Hutu Ten Commandments," which praised Hutu ideology, Hutu purity through separation, and a merciless approach toward the Tutsis.
      4. Hutu activists organized a militia called the *Interahamwe* ("those who work together").
      5. The militia gathered weapons and more than half a million machetes, one for every third Hutu man.
   B. Inspirations.
      1. A government document found after the genocide quoted Lenin and Josef Goebbels on the uses of propaganda.
      2. Films about the Nazis were later found at the home of President Habyarimana.
      3. In an echo of the Reign of Terror of the French Revolution, local killing units were called Public Safety Committees.
   C. Language.

1. A phraseology was invented to cloak preparations for massacre, referred to as "work," in ideological terms. The genocide was called *umuganda*, "public work."
2. Weapons were called "tools." The overall killing plan was called, in imitation of the Nazis, the "final solution."

D. Propagating the message.
1. The government used newspapers and radio to spread its message.
2. The government provided free radios to expand its reach.
3. Songs of hate against Tutsis were played on radio stations that would later relay orders for killing.
4. Weekly propaganda meetings featured arts performances with messages of hate.
5. Images of President Habyarimana were posted ubiquitously and worn as buttons.

E. The flashpoint.
1. On April 6, 1994, Hutu President Juvenal Habyarimana was assassinated under mysterious circumstances. The moderate vice president and Belgian peacekeepers were murdered immediately after.
2. The United Nations withdrew troops and observers on April 21, 1994.

III. Genocide.
A. The campaign.
1. Most killings took place in April 1994.
2. The massacres claimed 800,000 lives over the course of 100 days.
3. Although organized by the government, the killers included a remarkably broad section of Rwandan society, whether eager, enticed, or coerced. Neighbors turned on neighbors.
4. The massacres grew more radical as they continued, increasingly including women and children and even spouses.
5. Churches were not able to offer effective sanctuary. In some cases, pastors betrayed their parishioners.
6. Religious affiliation was trumped by the power of political religion.

7. Radio broadcasts coordinated the killings and read out lists of names of targets.

8. The popular singer Simon Bikindi was accused of writing songs inciting killings and participating in massacres.

9. The Rwandan minister for family and women's affairs, Pauline Nyiramasuhuko, was accused of encouraging the rape of Tutsi women.

10. There were, however, many cases of heroic saviors who hid and sheltered intended victims.

B. Ending.

1. In July 1994, the Tutsi-led RPF took control in Rwanda.

2. Killers mixed in with the two million refugees fleeing the fighting.

IV. Aftermath.

A. International passivity.

1. Reasons for international inaction were complex, including stereotypes of Africa, lack of interest, and the remoteness of Rwanda, which meant that visual images took longer to reach an international audience.

2. While the killings were taking place, diplomats in the United Nations and in the United States deliberately avoided calling the events *genocide*, because doing so would obligate them to take action.

3. In November 1994, the UN Security Council approved a resolution for an international court to try crimes of genocide in Rwanda.

4. In March 1998, U.S. President Clinton visited Rwanda and apologized for international inaction.

B. Reckoning.

1. In 1995, the United Nations set up an International Criminal Tribunal for Rwanda in Arusha, Tanzania.

2. Genocide trials are still ongoing in other jurisdictions as well.

Essential Reading:

Samantha Power, *"A Problem From Hell": America and the Age of Genocide*, pp. 329–389.

Supplementary Reading:

Philip Gourevitch, *We Wish to Inform You That Tomorrow We Will Be Killed with Our Families: Stories from Rwanda.*

Questions to Consider:

1. What action by the international community could have been most effective in forestalling the full tragedy (a) before the killings began and (b) after they had begun?

2. What role did religion play in the massacres in Rwanda?

Lecture Twenty-Two—Transcript
Rwanda

In our previous lecture, we had considered the international context of the end of the 20th century. We'd considered the remarkable democratic revolutions of 1989 to 1991, with their surprising lack of violence, but we'd also considered the darker portent of turmoil in the Balkans, in Bosnia and Kosovo, with the repetition of scenes of horrors that many had hoped would now be distinguished from the European continent, after World War II, replaying themselves before the world's eyes.

In today's lecture, we want to consider an event that happened roughly at the same time, towards the end of the 20th century, which the world very much wanted to look away from and to ignore. That is the genocide in Rwanda.

In 1994, as the world looked on, truly horrific events unfolded in central African country of Rwanda, where tension between two different social groups erupted into genocide. This was a genocide that, in spite of the way it was presented by the media or in newscasts, was not spontaneous, predetermined, inevitable, and not simply native to that region. Rather, it was encouraged by the state. This is really one of the central points of the lecture today.

The Hutu-dominated government of Rwanda organized the mass murder of the Tutsi minority. It organized it with preparation, calculation, and malice of forethought. As with so many of the other genocides we've discussed, this was not simply an elemental outbreak of human hatred, but rather, it was prepared well in advance. The state provided weapons, particularly machetes, for the killers. It directed their movements through radio broadcasts and lists of those who were to be killed. Propaganda in the form of songs, as well as written commandments preached destruction. In the course of 100 days, in a ferocious pace of slaughter, 800,000 people were killed, while the international community tried to look away.

First of all, we need to consider the context, the earlier background of Rwanda. Rwanda, a central African nation the size of Vermont, was celebrated in earlier decades as very nearly a "Switzerland" of Africa. It was called "the land of thousand hills." It was felt to be idyllic because of the order, the development that had been obtained there, and for the relative tranquility that was hoped would continue.

There was trouble underneath, however. In this densely populated country of eight million people, land was at a premium, and was perhaps being overworked. The competition for land could exacerbate existing ethnic tensions. These were tensions that had a longer history between the two groups of the country, the Hutus and the Tutsis.

Some question is even raised as to what the principles of division are between these two groups, the Hutus and the Tutsis. They speak the same language, and have roughly the same religious background, thus, the differences between them are subtle. Traditionally, the minority Tutsis were herders and landowners, while the majority Hutus were farmers.

Certainly, there were stereotypes about the physical appearance of the Hutus and the Tutsi. The Tutsi were said to be tall and thin; the Hutus were said to be lower in stature and more heavyset. However, these were stereotypes that often had no correspondence to the reality of the people being talked about. In many cases, it was hard for people themselves to know which group someone should be ascribed to.

In the past, the Tutsi minority had been dominant. Some scholars have advanced the argument that the lines of division between these groups were in fact not set in stone, or ethnic in nature, but that rather, in bygone centuries the groups had been fluid, and that the designations of Tutsi versus Hutu had, in fact, been based more on class, on one's wealth and standing in society, and occupation, herding versus agricultural, not on ethnic difference.

In reality, intermarriage between these groups was common, further exacerbating the difficulty of making clear ethnic divisions. It was at this point that another factor intervened. It's one that Hannah Arendt, in analysis of the 20th century's course in totalitarianism, had stressed as a crucial element in shaping the fortunes of the century: Imperialism.

The colonial legacy of Rwanda, as Europeans intervened to seize the territory, and to influence it, would set a new framework for these differences and divisions in Rwandan society. Rwanda became a German colony in 1885, and then after World War I was transferred to Belgian rule. Belgian administrators set about, as they felt, administering the country "in an enlightened way." One of their cornerstone tactics in administration was to discern, "scientifically," they thought, the dividing lines in Rwandan society.

What had earlier been a fluid division, a shifting set of identifications between Tutsi and Hutu, was now, indeed, bureaucratically set in stone. In fact, in an expression of the sort of racist "science" that was proposed by colonial administrations in many places around the world, the Belgian administrators invented what was called "a nasal index," to measure the noses of Tutsis and Hutus, feeling that this was a scientifically irreproachable way to categorize and measure who belonged to which group. Then, these designations, arbitrary as they were in practice, were then imposed and imprinted in identification documents, which became compulsory.

The colonial administration had divided the population along lines that had been far more shifting. Now, the groups were increasingly strictly divided, though they had earlier been intermingled. This was part of a policy of "divide and rule," in that the colonial powers favored one or another group, in order to consolidate and "outsource" its control of the territory. Even so, in spite of these bureaucratic divisions, the human reality of intermarriage, interdependence, and interrelationships continued, nonetheless.

A new page opened in Rwandan history when, in the process of decolonization that swept the world in the course of the 1960s also brought independence to Rwanda in 1962. Now, the majority Hutu, who had been ruled over earlier by the Tutsi minority, dominated the new republic. The shoe was now on the other foot, and discrimination against the Tutsis became a common occurrence.

There were also periodic waves of massacres of the Tutsi minority by the Hutu majority. Thus, many thousands of Tutsis were compelled to flee Rwanda, but hoped, someday, to return to their homes. Fighting continued in the '60s, '70s, and '80s, between rebel groups of the Tutsis. In some cases, some of these Tutsi fighters had never, in fact, visited their homeland that they aimed to return to, on the one hand, and then the Hutu-led Rwandan government, which enjoyed support from former colonial powers France and Belgium, in Europe.

A new stage in these political and military confrontations, however, occurred in 1993, when the Arusha Peace Accords were put together through the mediation of the Tanzanian government. These peace accords of 1993 called for setting down arms, and a new beginning of a new cooperative government, which would include power-sharing with the Tutsi rebel groups outside of the country. This included the RPF, the Rwandan Patriotic Front, led by Tutsi leaders.

United Nations peacekeepers, coordinated by Kofi Annan, who later became UN Secretary-General, were sent in with a specific mission: To observe, and, at the pleasure of the Rwandan government, to provide a sense of stability. In reality, however, the Hutu-dominated government of Rwanda had other plans.

It was determined not to share its power. It feared that returning Tutsi minority members to power might enable them to exact vengeance or justice for the acts that had been committed in previous periodic massacres. Thus, we need to observe the underground plotting of the government, as it laid its careful plans for the reality of genocide. This was referred to as "the unleashing of Hutu power," and it was an organized process, a well-planned venture indeed. What were the origins of this Hutu power movement?

Some Hutu political leaders championed the notion of Hutu power in order to consolidate their own rule. There were also certainly many moderate Hutus who did not, in fact, cleave to this message of hatred. This minority, however, was an important one, as a catalyst to stir society and to move it in a particular direction.

These political leaders, these elites championing Hutu power, began to carefully and deliberately cultivate a widespread racial hatred of the Tutsi. Frictions had been there before, but now, this hatred was to be inflamed further. The publications that were subsidized by the government dehumanized the Tutsi minority by referring to them in demonic terms. They were labeled *inyenzi*, or "cockroaches." They were dehumanized by being referred to in these terms, but then, paradoxically, they were also dehumanized by being referred to as "devils in human form," not human, but in fact, implacable opponents.

Here we see that much of the stereotyped demonizing of different ethnic groups, that has been unfortunately all too common throughout the 20th century, has often been this sort of compound of irrational, irreconcilable opposites. On the one hand, the minorities are said to be powerless and subhuman, but on the other hand, nearly superhuman in their allegedly malevolent force. These were exactly the same terms in which the Nazis had cultivated their hatred of the Jewish minority.

At the very head of this movement, was the president, Juvénal Habyarimana. He was the leader of the dominant party, the MRND, which stood for the National Revolutionary Movement for Development and Democracy. These were noble words hiding a genocidal reality.

In a clear aspect of a turn towards political religion, the harnessing of religious impulses, but turned towards politics, the official government newspaper, published in 1990, well before the genocide itself, published a document that was called, sonorously enough, the "Hutu Ten Commandments." The Hutu Ten Commandments praised Hutu ideology, preached Hutu purity through separation, with no intermixing with the Tutsis, and a merciless approach toward the Tutsis.

To mention just a few of these commandments: The military forces were to be under Hutu control. Any Hutu who was not with the Hutu power movement, who was a moderate, and might object to this preaching of ethnic hatred, was ipso facto a traitor to the Hutu cause, and, for all practical purposes, would be treated like the Tutsi would be treated; in addition, in a sentence that would speak volumes about what was to follow, it was commanded that "Hutu should stop having mercy on the Tutsi."

Hutu activists now began to organize a militia of paramilitary forces throughout the country, who were prepared to initiate mass murderer at the proper time. This militia was called, in a term that obfuscated their task, *Interahamwe*. This has been translated as either "those who work together," or "those who attack together." They would work at murder; they would attack the Tutsi minority and their Hutu friends.

The militia began to gather weapons. Indeed, the government bought weapons abroad. It ordered machetes on a massive scale. More than 500,000 machetes were bought, which represented one machete for every third Hutu man.

Even children were recruited into the militias, young people who had not, as yet, assimilated some of the social norms that might otherwise have been inculcated, and were readied for the task of mass murder.

What were the inspirations for this sort of movement? They were many, and in fact many of them will go back to some of our earlier lectures, in which we considered similar ideological movements. A fundamental point of our lectures has been many of these ideological movements have not existed in a vacuum or been isolated from broader trends, but have looked to other despotisms, other ideological regimes, even ones they were ideologically opposed to, for examples of how to rule or how to attack.

Vivid evidence of this was given in a government document that was found after the genocide, in government offices, which quoted Lenin and Josef Goebbels, the Nazi propaganda minister, on the uses of propaganda. These were two men who were ideologically opposed, but who were now linked together, in that they were emulated by the government and its activists.

Films about the Nazi reign of terror and its genocide were later found at the home of President Habyarimana. In an echo of the long-gone days of the French Revolution's Reign of Terror, the local killing units even called themselves "public safety committees." They were drawing on a wide range of references. They also, as has been the case with other movements we've seen, perverted the language to their purposes. That insightful analyst of the Nazi perversion of the German language, Viktor Klemperer, who had analyzed Nazi vocabulary, would not have been surprised at any of this.

A phraseology was invented to cloak in ideological terms, to veil them in euphemism, preparations for massacre. The massacre itself was called "work." The genocide was called *umuganda*, or "public work," a project in social engineering, in other words. The weapons for this destruction were referred to as "tools of work." In addition, the overall killing plan was called, in an obvious imitation of the Nazis, the "final solution."

The message of hatred still needed to be propagated and spread to the wide masses, to implicate ordinary Rwandans of Hutu descent in this project. For this purpose, the government used modern media, newspapers, and radio, with television less evident, to spread its message.

Indeed, the government provided free radios in the countryside, to expand the reach of its message. On a special radio station, government-controlled, which came to be nicknamed "radio hate," songs of hatred against the Tutsis were played. These same radio stations would later relay precise orders for coordinated killing throughout the country.

Well before the genocide itself, weekly propaganda meetings in the countryside featured arts performances, plays, all communicating the messages of hate against the Tutsi minority. Images of President Habyarimana, about whom there was a cult of personality, were posted ubiquitously around the country, and were even worn as buttons by the activists themselves.

In their propaganda, the government also drew upon earlier phenomena. The propaganda argued that not only that the Tutsi were evil or subhuman, but they also argued that the Tutsi were about to unleash genocide upon the Hutus. In fact, they referred to the RPF, the Tutsi guerrillas, as "the black Khmer Rouge," who were about to wreak the sort of violence upon the Hutu group as had been seen in Cambodia.

This was a case of a phenomenon that we've seen many times before, a projection onto one's intended victims of one's own intentions, as was clearly the case in Rwanda. However, some flashpoint was still needed, and that flashpoint came as a surprise.

On April 6, 1994, the Hutu president, Habyarimana, who, with his allies, had been promoting this program, was assassinated under mysterious circumstances. Many analysts believe that his own allies assassinated him in order to provide the spark for this event. The moderate prime minister and the Belgian UN peacekeepers, who were protecting her, were murdered immediately thereafter.

The expectation of the plotters had been, as we now know, that a strike against Western peacekeeping forces would soon provide the impetus for a withdrawal of those forces, fearing greater casualties. In this respect, they were right.

The United Nations withdrew its troops and observers on April 21, 1994, in spite of the pleas of the UN peacekeeping commander on the ground, a French-Canadian, who argued that thousands of lives could be saved from what was impending, if only more troops were sent. Now, the genocide unfolded.

The campaign raged, with most killings taking place in a concentrated period, in April of 1994. During the peak of the killing, it's estimated that one murder was taking place every two seconds around the country. In total, the massacres would claim 800,000 lives, over the course of 100 days. These massacres were conducted, not spontaneously at first, though they certainly took on a momentum of their own later, but from careful lists that had been compiled by the government.

While the government organized, the killers included a remarkably broad section of Rwandan society, from a variety of motives. Some were eager, some were enticed into the killing in the interests of gain, while others were coerced and forced to share the complicity by being ordered to kill. Neighbors turned on neighbors. In an echo of the Cambodian killing fields, those with eyeglasses were hunted down as intellectuals who were dangerous.

The killing was done with machetes, with guns, and with the most primitive of tools as well, such as sharpened car springs, clubs with nails driven through their heads, even screwdrivers. The massacres grew more radical as they continued. At first, elites had been targeted, and men, then increasingly, women and children, and even spouses of Tutsis were targeted in this killing.

Churches were not able to offer effective sanctuary, and in some dreadful cases, pastors betrayed their parishioners, who were killed in the places of worship. These pastors included religious leaders of different denominations: Catholics, Anglicans, as well as Seventh-day Adventists. In one horrendous exchange, which later provided the title for a powerful book on the Rwandan massacres, a group of parishioners wrote to their minister with this plea: "We wish to inform you that tomorrow, we will be killed with our families," pleading for some intercession on the part of their Hutu minister. That minister replied, in a chilling abdication of fellow human feeling with these words: "There is nothing I can do for you. All you can do is prepare to die, for your time has come." Religion clearly was being trumped by ethnic hatreds and by the atrocities now ongoing.

Radio broadcasts throughout this genocide coordinated the killings, and read out the lists of targets' names, including their addresses, the license plate numbers of those who were trying to flee, as well as the hiding places where some might be trying to seek refuge.

The killers, it has been reported, went about their task of mass murder with a machete in one hand and a radio in the other, for the radios were relaying orders. Afterwards, some killers told reporters that they had killed because the radio had told them to kill. Disembodied voices had been directing this genocide from above. At the start of the genocide, the radio announced that "the time for the harvest was ready," and that the harvest needed to be taken in, that the work needed to be done. Afterward, the radio also still commented that the graves were not yet full and needed to be filled.

The radios also played songs. In a dreadful case of an artist's reported complicity, the popular singer Simon Bikindi, who is now standing trial, was accused of writing songs that incited the killings, and participating in the massacres themselves. Simon Bikindi, who had been hired by the government's Ministry of Youth and Sports, was a popular artist. He had been called the "Michael Jackson of Rwanda." His songs certainly showed a flair for powerful rap, as well as rhythm. The songs, however, which denounced Hutu and showed sympathy for the Tutsi, and otherwise incited ethnic hatred, were played throughout the massacres over the radio. It's been reported that the killers themselves sang these popular songs as they went about their business of murder.

Another official implicated in this was the Rwandan Minister for Family and Women's Affairs, a woman by the name of Pauline Nyiramasuhuko. She was accused of actually encouraging the rapes of Tutsi women and their massacres.

These were not the absolute rule, however. There were many other cases of heroic saviors who hid the Tutsi victims, and otherwise sheltered the intended targets of this killing.

At long last, a decisive result was brought about by the force of arms. The genocide was ended when the Tutsi-led RPF finally took control of Rwanda, in July of 1994. In a certain sense, however, the drama still continued with paradoxes yet to follow.

Two million Hutu refugees fled the fighting, across the borders of the country, to refugee camps. The killers mixed in among them. In a great paradox, international aid flowed then. It flowed not to the Tutsi victims within the country, rather, to these refugee camps, where humanitarian aid workers themselves began to understand that in a cruel paradox, the camps themselves were a continuing spot of domination by the Hutu elites, who were preparing for revenge because of their expulsion from the country, against those who had earlier been there victims, in the months previous.

This was a dreadful paradox. Humanitarian aid had come too late, and was, in some cases, furthering the ends of those who were the guilty.

What can we speak of in terms of the aftermath, the moral reckoning that would follow afterward? The record needs to be dealt with, of international passivity. The reasons for international inaction were complex. They included stereotypes of Africa, in many cases verging on racism, of "those people" simply being the kinds of people who were prone, supposedly, to tribal violence, which was a reality from time immemorial, supposedly.

They also included the reality that many nations seemed to decide that they simply weren't interested. Their national interests seemed not to be involved. Furthermore, the very remoteness of Rwanda meant that visual images, the horrific images now imprinted on international consciousness, took much longer to reach a world audience. Some journalists have pointed out that footage of the genocide itself, or still photographs of the killings as they were taking place, were few and far between.

Moreover, the harsh verdict is that many in the outside world simply just didn't believe that these events, or the Rwandan situation, were important enough to merit international intervention. In the case of some countries, such as France, its government continued to support the Hutu regime until late in the day. Indeed, the record was, in many ways, an even darker one, in terms of international inaction.

While the killings were taking place, and as it was becoming increasingly clear what the vast reach of this atrocity was, diplomats in the United Nations and in the United States government, cynically and very deliberately and calculatedly avoided using the word *genocide* to describe these events. The "G" word was avoided, because this terming, this naming, of what was going on as "genocide" would thus obligate them to take action against what had been agreed to be an international crime.

In November of 1994, the UN Security Council approved a resolution for an international court to try the crimes of genocide that it was belatedly recognizing had taken place in Rwanda. Afterwards, in March of 1998, U.S. President Clinton visited Rwanda and apologized for international inaction.

The reckoning also continues in Rwanda itself today. A fragmented, tattered, bloodied society needs to find a way forward. In 1995, the United Nations was helpful in setting up an international criminal tribunal for Rwanda across the border in Arusha, Tanzania. There, trials of the accused are still ongoing, as they are in other jurisdictions elsewhere, in the Western world as well. Thousands of potential defendants are yet to be brought to trial. Ultimately, the world found that its inaction did not enable it to look away from these horrors entirely.

In our next lecture, we'll consider the case of another regime, the Iraqi government, whose ideological actions and behavior would draw international attention to it, of necessity, and would thus lead to the regime's overthrow, as well.

Lecture Twenty-Three
Saddam Hussein's Iraq

Scope:

In the lands of ancient Mesopotamia, there arose a movement proclaiming a new secular ideology of Arab unity, Ba'athism. The Ba'ath Party came to power in a coup in 1968, and by 1979, Saddam Hussein had become president. This lecture traces how Hussein established his personal dictatorship, modeling himself on long-ago despots and surrounded by elite Republican Guards. He launched a war against Iran that lasted eight years, resembling World War I in its ferocity, and followed this with chemical attacks against Iraq's Kurdish minority. Even after the failed invasion of Kuwait and the Gulf War in 1991, the regime endured until 2003.

Outline

I. Ba'athism: Nationalism and Socialism.
   A. Origins.
      1. The Ba'ath Arab Socialist Rebirth Party grew out of 1930s pan-Arabism, synthesizing Marxist Socialism with Arab Nationalism.
      2. The first organizers in the 1940s were educated at the Sorbonne in Paris: Michel Aflaq and Salah al-Din Bitar.
      3. Their origins reflected the ideology's secular nature; Aflaq was Greek Orthodox and al-Din Bitar was a Sunni Muslim.
      4. The mystical ideology aimed to revive "one Arab nation with an eternal mission," shedding tradition and religion and uniting Arabs into a modern civilization, following the slogan "Unity, Freedom, and Socialism."
      5. Observers claim affinities of Ba'athism to Nazism, as well as Stalinism.
   B. Ideology in power.
      1. The Ba'ath Party, split between branches, came to power in Syria in 1963 and Iraq in 1968.
      2. Ideological consistency took second place to establishment of personal dictatorships.
      3. Iraq, site of ancient Mesopotamia, was established after World War I as a British mandate.

4. Its diversity of populations and faiths often made it unstable.

II. Saddam Hussein: "Great Son of the Arabs."

A. Background.

1. Saddam Hussein was born in 1937, near Tikrit on the Tigris, into a poor peasant family. Though poor, Tikrit is notable as the birthplace of Saladin the Great, 12th-century conqueror of Jerusalem.
2. One translation of Saddam's name is "He who confronts."
3. Young Saddam was abused by his stepfather and fled to live with an uncle of radical racist views.
4. Saddam became notorious as a street thug.
5. He joined a Ba'athist coup attempt in 1959, fleeing to Egypt after its failure.
6. While exiled in the 1960s, Saddam reportedly became fascinated with Stalin and later imitated his show trials.

B. Rise to power.

1. Saddam returned to Iraq in 1963 after the Ba'ath Party came to power. When it was overthrown, he spent two years in prison.
2. The Ba'ath Party retook control in 1968, and Saddam rose to prominence.
3. In July 1979, Saddam took over leadership.
4. He gathered relatives and friends from Tikrit, including his brutal sons Uday and Qusay, into an inner circle often compared to the Mafia.
5. Republican Guards were core troops, while Special Republican Guards were his trusted elite.
6. Like Stalin, Saddam purged his following repeatedly.
7. Mukhabarat security services terrorized and spied on the population.
8. Saddam held many offices, including president, commander-in-chief, chairman of the Revolutionary Command Council, and general secretary of the Ba'ath Party.

C. Cult of personality.

    1. His portraits were ubiquitous, in different poses and costumes.

    2. Like Stalin, Saddam used propaganda to rewrite his past exploits.

    3. He rarely appeared in public, however.

    4. The newspaper *Babel* (run by his son Uday), radio, and television spread propaganda celebrating the image of the leader.

D. Paranoia.

    1. Even Saddam's own elite was suspected.

    2. He reportedly had eight body-doubles standing in for him to avoid assassination.

    3. He is said to have had an intense fear of germs and infection.

III. Armed action.

A. The Iran-Iraq War: clash of revolutionary ideologies.

    1. After Iran's 1979 Islamic Revolution, Saddam attacked. The war strikingly resembled World War I and cost a million lives.

    2. The United States saw Iraq as a useful counterweight to Iran.

B. War on the Kurds.

    1. Kurds are about a quarter of the population, and Kurdish rebels challenged Saddam.

    2. In the Anfal campaign, launched in 1988, thousands of Kurdish villages were wiped out to remake society and concentrate Kurds in new "victory cities." Some 100,000 Kurds were killed, mostly in mass executions.

    3. From 1987, chemical weapons were used against Kurds by "Chemical Ali" Hassan al-Majid, a cousin of Saddam.

    4. In March 1988, the Kurdish town of Halabja was gassed using mustard gas, nerve gasses, and perhaps, biological agents. Some 5000 were killed, with thousands more hurt.

IV. Saddam's regime and ambitions.

    A. Ancient and recent models.

        1. Saddam emulated great past rulers, including Babylon's Nebuchadnezzar of the sixth century B.C. and Hammurabi of the 18th century B.C. Symbols link their destinies.

        2. In Tikrit, a mural showed twin armies, modern and ancient: Saladin's and Saddam's, headed for Jerusalem.

        3. Buildings of Babylon (where ancient bricks bore Nebuchadnezzar's name) were rebuilt, using bricks with Saddam's name.

    B. Strategic aims.

        1. Saddam presented himself as leader of the Arab world.

        2. He aimed for hegemony in the Middle East, evidenced by repeated wars of aggression.

        3. He sought to build nuclear weapons but was impeded by a 1981 Israeli airstrike on a nuclear plant built with French help.

    C. Lunge for hegemony.

        1. In 1990, Saddam invaded Kuwait with the world's fourth largest army. As "Province no. 19," Kuwait was annexed and pillaged.

        2. In the 1991 Gulf War, the United States led a UN force against Iraq, winning after 90 hours of land war.

        3. After six weeks, Iraq was expelled from Kuwait, but Saddam was allowed to remain in power and quell rebellions by Kurds and Shi'ites.

        4. Afterward, Saddam allegedly said that his true mistake was to invade without nuclear weapons.

V. Repression, the religious turn, and dynamics of the regime.

    A. Torture.

        1. Reports from Iraqi prisons included extreme instances of torture, as well as "cleansing" of jails through mass killings.

        2. Relatives of targeted people were also jailed, tortured, and killed to deter others.

        3. Rape was used as a tool of coercion.

  4. Hussein's son Uday reportedly used his Olympic program building to torture athletes for disappointing performances.

B. The religious gloss.

  1. After defeat in the Gulf War, Hussein's regime took on a new religious coloration despite the Ba'ath secularism, recalling Stalin's tactical alliance with the Russian Orthodox Church in World War II.

  2. The words "God is great" were added to Iraq's flag.

  3. In 1999, the Ahlamlalamaniyah campaign, "Enhancement of Islamic Belief," was launched, banning drinking and gambling. A radio broadcasting the Quran was set up.

  4. Accusations of prostitution against women mistrusted by the regime led to public executions.

  5. Hussein claimed to champion the Palestinian cause and Muslim control over Jerusalem, organizing an "Army of Jerusalem" for propaganda effect.

  6. Hussein reportedly donated $15 million in support for families of suicide bombers attacking Israel. Saddam decided on specific cash payments for specific actions.

  7. Propaganda showed Hussein in traditional clothes and at prayer and claimed his descent from the prophet Muhammad.

C. Mosques and palaces.

  1. In spite of UN sanctions, which the regime blamed for numerous civilian deaths, Hussein built magnificent new palaces, mosques, and amusement parks.

  2. After the Gulf War, about 50 presidential palaces were built at an estimated outlay of $2.5 billion a year.

  3. In 2002, 30 mosques were built in Baghdad.

  4. The Mother of Battles Mosque was opened in 2001. Saturated with symbolism, it featured minarets made of missiles, details recalling Saddam's background, and a Quran said to be written in his blood.

  5. Under construction was the Mosque of Saddam the Great, intended as the second largest Muslim worship center after Mecca.

D. Bolstering the personality cult.

   1. On October 2002, a referendum on his presidency was held, with nearly unanimous results reported.

   2. In 2002, the government issued a little white book (reminiscent of Mao's *Little Red Book*), *Saddam Hussein: Great Lessons, Commandments to Strugglers, the Patient and Holy Warriors*, containing 57 commandments.

   3. These sayings were also displayed in public places, repeated at schools, and read after prayers five times daily.

   4. In private, Saddam's habits were reportedly indulgent, including Cuban cigars and rosé wine. His narcissism was reflected in his appearance and retinue.

VI. Steering toward conflict.

   A. In November 1998, Hussein ended cooperation with UN inspectors after systematic, long-standing subterfuges. Defectors revealed details of weapons programs, including weapons of mass destruction (chemical, biological, and nuclear).

   B. Observers described one of Saddam's central weaknesses as miscalculation in international politics because of the closed circle around him.

   C. By 2003, with the United Nations unable to enforce its resolutions on disarming Iraq, confrontation with the United States intensified.

   1. American and British forces went to war with Iraq in March 2003, a conflict that lasted about a month.

   2. The Iraqi regime melted away quickly; Saddam and his sons vanished. Hannah Arendt would not have been surprised by this rapid collapse.

   3. Before the war began, Saddam's son Qusay took $1 billion from the Central Bank, a return to the mobster role so common in such regimes.

   4. Mass graves have since been uncovered in Iraq.

Essential Reading:

Sandra Mackey, *The Reckoning: Iraq and the Legacy of Saddam Hussein.*

Supplementary Reading:

Con Coughlin, *Saddam: King of Terror.*

Questions to Consider:

1. Which lessons has Saddam seemingly learned in his emulation of leaders of the past?

2. Is the religious turn in the propaganda of the regime a genuine change or a ploy? What arguments speak for either position?

Lecture Twenty-Three—Transcript
Saddam Hussein's Iraq

In our previous lectures, we've examined cases of ideological regimes, and their actions that the international community tried to look away from. In today's lecture, we'll examine the case of a regime that pressed itself upon the world's attention at the very close of the 20th century, and beyond. That was Saddam Hussein's Iraq.

In the lands of ancient Mesopotamia, a movement came to power announcing a new secular ideology of Arab unity called Ba'athism. The Ba'ath Party came to power in a coup 1968, and by 1979, Saddam Hussein had become president. In this lecture, we'll trace his rise to personal dictatorship, and the way in which he modeled himself on long-ago despots, as well as more recent ideological movements. We'll examine the wars that he unleashed, and we'll examine his atrocities against the people of Iraq as well.

First, we need to examine the set of ideas Saddam Hussein would champion, at the same time, identifying his own personal power, his ideology. Ba'athism was, in essence, a combination of nationalism and socialism. Its origins lay in what we've described as the "dark decade" of the 1930s. The Ba'ath Arab Socialist Rebirth Party, to give its full name, grew out of the pan-Arabism of the 1930s. The argument was that Arab peoples should not be divided along the lines of artificial national boundaries of states that have been carved out in the postwar settlement, after World War I, but that they, rather, should be unified. This was added to Marxist socialism, fused with the Arab nationalism of the pan-Arabists. Some historians have considered this blending of nationalism and socialism, arising in the 1930s and '40s, to bear resemblances to the Nazi National Socialism.

The first organizers of the Ba'ath movement, in 1940, were educated abroad in the West, at the Sorbonne in Paris. They were Michel Aflaq, and Salah al-Din Bitar. Their origins reflected the ideology's secular nature, its turn away from traditional religion, as they were of mixed origins. Aflaq was Greek Orthodox, Salah al-Din Bitar was Sunni Muslim.

Religious differences were to be bridged by commitment, now, to a mystical, nationalist ideology, one which aimed to revive "one Arab nation with an eternal mission across time," shedding old traditions, shedding traditional religion, and uniting Arabs into one modern civilization. Not a look backwards, but the promise of a modern civilization for Arabs united slogan of "Unity, freedom, and Socialism."

Observers locating Ba'athism in its time and place in the ideological currents of the day have seen affinities to Nazism as well as to Stalinism, in this movement that arose at roughly the same time. The ideology would come to power.

The Ba'ath Party split between two branches. One came to power in Syria in 1963, and the other later in Iraq, in 1968. In spite of their pledges to Arab unity, however, the ideological consistency of unifying, which didn't take place, took second place to the establishment of personal dictatorships in those countries.

In many senses, Iraq was an artificial creation. It was certainly the site of the ancient Mesopotamian civilization, but it had gained its borders and establishment after World War I as a British mandate, as a colonial territory. As the British would discover, its diversity of populations and faiths: The Kurds, the Sunni, the Shia, often made it unstable. Saddam Hussein would step forward as the master of this diversity. He would be proclaimed as the "Great Son of the Arabs," bringing the Ba'athist ideology to realization.

As we've seen in the case of other would-be dictators, such as Hitler, Stalin, or Mao, his beginnings were not auspicious. His origins were lowly. Saddam Hussein was said to have been born in 1937. There some doubt about this date itself. Some historians have suggested that while his official biography records 1937 as the year of his birth, in fact, he was born later, but assumed an earlier date, in sort of an act of self-fashioning, to make himself appear older, and thus more worthy of respect in his society. Thus, some historians have underlined that there's a certain malleability about Saddam's own stories about himself, and the sense of self-fashioning, creating a persona for oneself, may be something shared with the other dictators who we've examined in this course.

Thus, Saddam Hussein was born around 1937, in a small, muddy village close to the larger town of Tikrit, on the Tigris River, into a poor peasant family. His father disappeared mysteriously; his fate is unknown. Tikrit itself is notable, though it's poor, as the birthplace of another famous man, Saladin the Great, the 12th-century Arab conqueror of Jerusalem.

Saddam Hussein, however, born into lowly origins, could look back on what he felt were portents of his own future greatness. Such portents were also there in his very name. One translation of Saddam's name is "He who confronts," and this was a telling verdict on his later career.

Young Saddam suffered at the hands of classmates, precisely because he didn't have a father. It was sometimes suggested that he was illegitimate, and his childhood was an unhappy one.

When his mother remarried, he was abused by his stepfather, and would flee to live with an uncle of radical, racist views, indeed, a Nazi sympathizer, in Tikrit, and later in Baghdad. His uncle looked to the Nazi regime and to Hitler as a heroic regime that might rescue the Arabs from domination by colonial powers like the British.

Saddam was entranced by his uncle's nationalist enthusiasm and fervor, but also became notorious as a street thug and a bully. We spoke earlier in our lectures about the "mobster outlook" and mentality of many of the totalitarian regime elites. Saddam Hussein's origins were located in just this sociological group.

As a result of the first political murder that he committed, Hussein was invited to join a Ba'athist coup attempt against the current leader of Iraq in 1959. However, it's suggested by historians that this botched assassination was, in fact, due to Saddam's own ineptitude. He started shooting too early, and was wounded himself, in what amounted to a clumsy attempt. He fled to Egypt after its failure. There, in a formative period, he rethought some of his political ideas, and changed his political notions.

While in exile in the 1960s, Saddam reportedly became fascinated with another leader of stature from an earlier period, Josef Stalin. He was intrigued by Stalin's one-man rule, his seemingly absolute control. Later, once in power, Hussein would imitate Stalin's show trials, in particular. A few years later, Hussein reportedly became intrigued with Adolf Hitler, the dictator of Nazi Germany, as well, not out of a great feeling of sympathy for his particular ideas, but certainly out of an admiration for Hitler's devious maintenance of his own control.

Hussein's rise to power would be brisk, after this period in exile. He returned to Iraq in 1963, after the Ba'ath party came to power. However, it was soon overthrown once again, and Saddam would spend two years in prison. The Ba'ath party retook control again, in 1968. This gives us a clear image of the turmoil that was current at the time. Saddam would soon rise to prominence.

In July of 1979, Saddam took over leadership. Perhaps from those days when he was abused by classmates and fellow villagers in his town of origin, Hussein seemed to have learned a lesson, that he could trust only his very closest relatives, in particular blood relatives. He gathered some of his friends, and especially relatives from Tikrit, to his center of power. They constituted an inner circle, one that included his sons, who are famous for their brutality, Uday and Qusay.

This group of relatives and friends, hailing many of them from Tikrit, formed a circle that was often compared to the Mafia, because they amounted to mobsters in control of the country. Hussein would continue to build a formidable base of control around himself, including, in particular, not just the regular army, but the Republican Guards as well, who were elite corps troops. The army's loyalty might be suspected, the republican guard's loyalty perhaps trusted a little more. However, even they were objects of Saddam's paranoid suspicion. And elite within the elite had to be established, as so-called Special Republican Guards within the Republican Guard were a trusted elite unit.

Like Stalin, Hussein purged his following repeatedly, and he seemed to relish public meetings, at which he lured forth independent thought, and then crushed it. These were meetings at which people were invited to speak their minds, and then afterwards, they were demonstrably executed for having done so, at Hussein's invitation.

The security services, the so-called Mukhabarat, terrorized and spied on the population. In addition to the Mukhabarat, there were also a proliferation of other groups and units who were supposed to uphold Saddam's rule. Most recently, these included the establishment of a group of fanatical enforcers, who on occasion have been compared to the SS, the so-called Fedayeen Saddam, meaning "the men of sacrifice for Saddam."

They were said to have numbered some 25,000, and were known for their brutality, and for their lording of it over the subject population. They were distinctive in their black uniforms, and their black balaclava helmets and ski masks, which hid their identities while they went about their missions of terror. In their black uniforms, they seemed to resemble the SS enforcers of Nazi Germany. Many of them were recruited from orphanages, without ties to society, bound to Saddam Hussein, he hoped, in total loyalty.

Children's organizations, the so-called "lion cubs" of Saddam, were also established, to breed loyalty at the very youngest ages, for Saddam's regime. It was said that these children were trained in cruelty against animals, in order to deaden their human feelings, and to make them pliant servants of the regime.

Hussein himself held many offices within his regime. These offices simply proliferated. He was president, commander-in-chief, chairman of the revolutionary command council, and general secretary of the Ba'ath party. As we'd already seen with Benito Mussolini's proliferation of title, this was a vivid example of an aspiration to total control.

A cultive personality was also developed around this formidable person, including his own stature. He stood six feet two inches tall, which made him a very tall man in Iraqi culture. Thus, the task of celebrating him was perhaps made easier, with ubiquitous portraits in different poses, of him firing a shotgun or riding on horseback, at prayer, in costumes of the Bedouin, in modern Western costume, resembling a gangster outfit in some cases, with a fedora and double-breasted suit, as well as old costumes of bygone ages. All served to develop this cultive personality.

In a break with the traditional disapproval for figurative art in Islamic tradition, Saddam Hussein's statues became ubiquitous as well. Like Stalin, Hussein also used propaganda to rewrite his past exploits, and to make his revolutionary role in his coming to power even more prominent than it, in fact, had been.

Like Stalin, Hussein also watched films about himself, and on occasion, criticized them for not being sufficiently realistic in appreciating his heroic roles. Hussein would rarely appear in public, however, perhaps testimony to a distrust of the population.

The newspapers, including the newspaper *Babel*, named after the tower of Babel, run by his son Uday, radio, and television broadcast propaganda, all celebrated the image of the all-powerful leader. Yet, he was consumed with paranoia, much as his erstwhile model, Stalin, had been. Even his own elite was suspected, and reportedly purged, again and again. Hussein reportedly had eight body doubles to stand in for him at public events were in the routine of his day, so that he might avoid assassination. His paranoia also extended to an intense fear, reportedly, of germs and infection.

He might, perhaps, have been working out some of these anxieties in his relentlessly aggressive armed action and approach to the outside world. This was first truly evidenced in the Iran-Iraq War, a clash of revolutionary ideologies in the Middle East, which in many ways resembled the Great War, the First World War, in its ferocity, a replay of this event.

After Iran's radical Islamic revolution in 1979, Saddam felt that the country had been weakened, and was ripe for the picking. Thus, he attacked. This war, which featured chemical weapons, trench warfare, human waves of fanatical frontal attacks, resembled World War I in our own times, and cost a million lives.

In this international context, the United States often saw Iraq as a useful counterweight to Iran, in the balance of power in that region. Thus, on occasion, the United States encouraged this role.

Hussein also waged war on minorities within his own borders whom he suspected of disloyalty, in particular, the minority of the Kurds. The Kurds make up about 25 percent of Iraq's population, and Kurdish rebels challenged Saddam, trying to win independence, a long-sought goal for their territories.

Hussein reacted with crushing force. In the Anfal campaign, launched in 1988, thousands of Kurdish villages were wiped out, in order to fundamentally remake the landscape, to change society, eliminate a distinctive Kurdish identity, and to concentrate the Kurds into new centers where they'd be kept under control, euphemistically called "victory cities." This was yet another species of that movement of populations, forced population movement as social engineering, as we've seen before in our lectures.

In the process of this campaign, some 100,000 Kurds were killed, mostly in mass executions of the men, and those suspected of resistance. We also see, in some of these related campaigns, that Hussein did not shy away from radical weapons.

From 1987, chemical weapons were used against the Kurds, by a man named Ali Hassan al-Majid, a cousin of Saddam's. His use of chemical weapons earned him the nickname "chemical Ali."

Notoriously, in March of 1988, the Kurdish town of Halabja was gassed in one these campaigns, using mustard gases, nerve gases, and perhaps biological agents as well. Some 5000 men, women, and children were killed, with thousands more wounded in the village of Halabja. Images began to filter out, ones that still haunt us today, of those who had fallen prey to these weapons, including a mother cradling her child, both dead in the street. In his ambitions, Hussein didn't shy away even from these most radical of arms.

In aid of what? For what purpose? Saddam's regime and ambitions had much to do with both ancient models of greatness, as well as more recent models of control. He quite explicitly emulated, in his propaganda and in his own thinking, great past rulers. These included Saladin, the Arab leader from whose area Saddam also hailed, as well as more remote leaders such as Babylon's emperor Nebuchadnezzar, of the sixth century B.C., and Hammurabi, of the 18th century B.C. His propaganda sought to link their destinies, in symbolic form.

The busts of Hussein that were set up around his palace would show, on occasion, Saddam himself wearing the helmet of Saladin the Great. In his hometown of Tikrit, a mural showed two armies advancing on Jerusalem, armies both modern and ancient: Saladin's army of medieval times, and Saddam's modern army, engaged in a common struggle.

On the archeological sites of Babylon's bygone greatness, new buildings were built so that Babylon's greatness could be reconstructed. Ancient bricks unearthed in the archaeological digs there bore the name of Nebuchadnezzar, who had immortalized his memory in this fashion. Thus, when the new buildings were rebuilt, bricks using Saddam's name were used to show that this had been built in his reign, greatness reachieved.

What were his larger strategic gains? Saddam presented himself as the Ba'athist ideology suggested, as the leader of the Arab world, the leader of an emergent unity just in the future. Thus, he aimed for hegemony in the Middle East, evidenced by repeated wars of aggression.

Moreover, he sought to win that coin of the realm, that of great power status in the present day, nuclear weapons, as well. However, in this project, he was impeded by airstrike from Israeli air forces in 1981, which hit a nuclear plant that had been built up with French help. According to many experts, this set his program for nuclear power and arms back considerably. However, he shared a gambler's nature with the other dictators we've discussed in these lectures. Thus, he would lunge for hegemony repeatedly towards the end of the 20th century.

In 1990, Hussein invaded Kuwait, a neighboring small country whose territory had long been claimed by the Iraqis, with his armed forces that had been built up into the world's fourth-largest army. Kuwait was now occupied, annexed as Iran's "Province no. 19," and pillaged relentlessly.

In the war that followed, the 1991 Gulf War, United States led a UN-sanctioned force against Iraq, and won its battle after 90 hours of land war. After six weeks, Iraq was finally expelled from Kuwait, but Saddam was allowed by the coalition forces to remain in power. He was not overthrown, and thus, he was able to turn his energies to the quelling of rebellions by Kurds and Shi'ites in his own country, who had risen up to challenge him.

Afterwards, Saddam felt that he learned a lesson from his failure in the first Gulf War. He allegedly commented that his true mistake had been to invade Kuwait without nuclear weapons, with which he may have held the other outside forces at bay.

Next, we want to consider how the regime operated its repressive apparatus, it's strange religious turn, and some of the dynamics of the regime's inner functioning. Torture was endemic throughout Hussein's regime. Reports from Iraqi prisons included extreme instances of torture, as well as the occasional "cleansing" of jails in order to make room, through mass killings of those currently in the cells.

Relatives of targeted people were also jailed, suspected of disloyalty. They were tortured and killed to deter others. Rape was commonly used as a tool of coercion, as a way of bringing relatives of those suspected of resistance in line. Hussein's brutal son Uday reportedly used the building in which his Olympic program was housed to torture athletes for disappointing performances.

After defeat in the Gulf War, Saddam's regime, which otherwise had been typically secular in its Ba'athist ideology, now took a turn toward a new religious emphasis. In many ways, this new emphasis of religion recalled Stalin's tactical alliance during World War II, with the traditional Russian Orthodox Church. In many different ways, the religious gloss was added to the regime's ideology. The words "God is great" were added to Iraq's flag. In 1999, in the so-called Ahlamlalamaniyah campaign, which stood for "the enhancement of Islamic belief," drinking was banned, gambling was banned, and a radio broadcasting the Quran was set up, emphasizing the regime's religious turn. Accusations of prostitution against women who were distrusted by the regime led to public executions by the Fedeine, taking place in the street.

Hussein also tried to identify himself with larger causes by claiming to champion the Palestinian cause, and the idea of Muslim control over Jerusalem, by organizing a so-called "Army of Jerusalem," for propaganda effect within Iraq. He also reportedly donated 15 million dollars in support, for families of Palestinian suicide bombers attacking Israel. He micromanaged this incentive program by deciding on specific cash payments for specific actions, or other forms of martyrdom.

With this religious turn, propaganda also showed Hussein in traditional Arab garb, and prayer, and emphasized his claimed descent from the Prophet Mohammed. A so-called "program for the rewriting of history" also sought to rewrite schoolbooks, as well as the official history of the land, to emphasize the regime's accomplishments.

Mosques and palaces were also built up, as a remarkable testimony to the might of the regime. In spite of United Nations' sanctions, except for an "oil-for-food" program, which the regime blamed for numerous civilian deaths by closing off imports and exports, he nonetheless built up magnificent new palaces, mosques, and amusement parks.

After the Gulf War, in spite of the sanctions, about 50 presidential palaces were built at an estimated outlay of 2.5 billion dollars a year. One American general later joked that had been so much an "oil-for-food" program as an "oil-for-palaces" program.

At the same time, in 2002, 30 mosques were built in Baghdad, underlining the religious self-identification of the regime. On the outskirts of Baghdad, in 2001, one particularly potent symbolic site was opened, the "Mother of All Battles Mosque." This was a religious site, saturated with symbolism. Its towers, or minarets, surrounding the mosque, and are made up of scud missiles. The details of the mosque's fountains and minarets all recall certain important dates or numbers of Saddam's background, such as his alleged birthday. Within the mosque, a Quran, said to be written in his own donated blood, was put on display.

Under ongoing construction is the mosque of "Saddam the Great," not a very modest title. It was intended as the second-largest center of worship in the Muslim world, after Mecca.

Saddam's personality cult was also to be bolstered. In October of 2002, a plebiscite, a referendum on his presidency was held, which yielded nearly unanimous results, in a cowed population.

In 2002, the government also issued an important, symbolic little booklet, a little white book of Hussein's sayings. In some sense, this is reminiscent of Mao's little red book that had played such an important symbolic role in the cultural revolution of China. This little white book was given the not very modest title, *Saddam Hussein: Great Lessons, Commandments, Strugglers, the Patient and Holy Warriors.*

As we've seen other cases, there are "commandments" listed for this ideological movement, playing on a religious motif. In this case, instead of a mere Ten Commandments, as we've seen in other cases, there were 57 commandments. The sayings were also displayed in public places, incorporated into the curriculum at schools, read after prayers five times daily, and were meant to indoctrinate the population.

In private, this image of Saddam Hussein as an austere and pious man was contradicted by the reality of his habits, which were reportedly enormously indulgent, including the "good life" of Cuban cigars, and a special predilection for rosé wine. Friends of mine who are connoisseurs of wine to me that this particular favoring of rosé wine is good evidence of insanity.

Hussein's narcissism was reflected in his appearance, his vast retinue, and his private habits. However, his gambling nature also steered him towards renewed conflict. In November of 1998, Hussein ended cooperation with United Nations inspectors, after systematic long-standing subterfuges, and hiding his programs for weapon development. Defectors from the regime later revealed details of weapons programs, including weapons of mass destruction, chemical, biological, and nuclear weapons programs that had eluded the inspectors from the United Nations.

Observers of Saddam describe one of his central weaknesses as a propensity to miscalculate in international affairs, in part due to the fact that his closed circle, surrounding him, are loathe to give him accurate information about the true balance of power. Having "yes" men around him, in this case, would ultimately be a liability to the regime.

By 2003, confrontation with the United States loomed. The United Nations was unable to enforce its resolutions on disarming Iraq. Thus, confrontation intensified. American, British, and other coalition forces went to war against Iraq in mid-March of 2003, in a conflict that lasted about a month. The speed with which their military operations unfolded undercut what seems to have been the expectation of Saddam's regime, of being able, in a protracted conflict, to manipulate world media. They've been successful in this regard before. After the war, CNN revealed that it had neglected to report many details that it knew about the regime's brutality, for fear of losing access, and of being punished for these revelations. Saddam's regime had been capable of manipulating even Western media.

As the war unfolded, the minister of information for the regime, Mohammed Saeed al-Sahaf, became something of a cult figure for people who followed the media, as he brazenly reported his lies that the regime was still standing proud, that the Allies, on their way into Iraq, were being held at bay, even as split screen televisions showed American and British forces already occupying the country. His last known remark, an epitaph for a regime, was, "I now inform you," he said to the reporters, "that you are too far from reality." He perhaps had believed his own propaganda, as Saddam had.

The regime melted away. Saddam and his sons vanished. Hannah Arendt, that student of totalitarian regimes, would not have been surprised at the totality of the collapse. The interior world, the utopian mindset of an ideological regime came crashing down with shocking rapidity.

Before the war began in earnest, it's now reported that a son of Saddam Hussein's, Qusay, engaged in what is probably the largest bank heist in history by taking one billion dollars from Iraq's central bank. In this case, it seems that the regime came full circle, back to its mobster origins, which it shared with other ideological regimes. Now in Iraq, a reckoning is being made, as mass graves are being uncovered, and as a shattered society will, of necessity, try to find its way towards a healthier model.

In our next lecture, we'll consider the verdict, and the lessons to be learned from these many cases of the brutality of ideological utopias.

Lecture Twenty-Four
The Future of Terror

Scope:

Ultimately, what are the lessons of the 20th century's linked experiences of the promise of utopia and the reality of terror? This lecture poses the urgent question of how to be vigilant against the revival of movements such as those surveyed and how they can best be resisted. It examines the phenomenon of terrorism in the world today, attempts at international justice, and strivings for the effective proscription of genocide. Among other present-day developments, this lecture examines the growing appeal of Islamist radicalism, transmuting religion into ideology, and the mission of such groups as Osama bin Laden's al Qaeda, along with other groups spreading politicized religious messages. The question of whether these global trends are likely to continue and intensify is of vital importance to the future.

Outline

I. Terror today.

   A. After the rise of "political religions" in the 20th century, today we see more explicit syntheses of politics, religion, and ideology emerging.

   B. Aum Shinri Kyo.
      1. On March 20, 1995, Japan's *Aum Shinri Kyo* ("Supreme Truth") cult released sarin gas in Tokyo's subways, leaving 12 dead and thousands injured.
      2. Teachings of their spiritual master, Shoko Asahara, drew on Buddhism but turned to predictions of apocalypse.
      3. Rather than simply await it, they tried to accelerate the apocalypse, also seeking an "earthquake machine."

   C. Suicide bombers.
      1. Palestinian suicide bombers, young men and women called *shahid*, or "martyrs," are increasingly common in the Israeli-Palestinian conflict, exploding themselves among civilians.
      2. Polls indicate they enjoy wide popularity in their communities.

3. Most are from religiously oriented groups, Hamas and Islamic Jihad, and alter long-standing prohibitions against suicide in Islam. However, secular groups have also adopted this tactic.

D. Radical Islamist ideology.

1. Islamism, as distinct from traditional Islam, synthesizes religious impulses and modern ideology.
2. Radical Islamists view themselves as carriers of a total ideology that supersedes modern Western ideologies.
3. In a population of a billion Muslims worldwide, radical Islamists are a small group.
4. In spite of expressing longings for restoration of the caliphate of the seventh century, Islamists often break with traditional Islam in significant ways: altering traditions, identifying Islam with state power in new ways, and hardening prescriptions for personal faith into political dogmas.
5. Introduction of the concept of progress is also an important contrast with traditional Islam.
6. Adherents are often from prosperous backgrounds and may be students of science or engineering. The movement's use of technology, whether the Internet or modern weapons, is characteristic.
7. In spite of denunciations of the West and the preaching of armed *jihad*, Islamist thinking is heavily influenced by Western ideologies it has appropriated.
8. A key thinker, the Egyptian Sayyid Qutb (1906–1966) of the Muslim Brotherhood, who studied in the United States, accepted Marx's timeline of historical stages, adding a final one after Communism, the triumph of Islamism.
9. His writings called for a unitary state and classless society, achieved through violent means.
10. Similar trends can be seen in other schools of Islamist thought, including that of revolutionary Iran under Ayatollah Khomeini (1900–1989) after 1979.
11. Islamism is not a throwback but, rather, a modern ideological form.

II. September 11th and al Qaeda.

    A. On September 11, 2001, New York's World Trade Center Towers were destroyed by al Qaeda terrorists, coordinated by Osama bin Laden.

        1. The attack was also intended as an act of propaganda.

        2. In al Qaeda texts found later in Afghanistan, suicide missions were praised in a booklet entitled "The Solution."

    B. Osama bin Laden.

        1. Bin Laden (b. 1957) was born into a prosperous family in Saudi Arabia; when his father died, he inherited millions from his father's construction empire.

        2. He studied in Saudi Arabia, without finishing school, and was drawn to radical activists in Central Asia near Afghanistan, including the Egyptian Ayman al-Zawahiri.

        3. In 1989, bin Laden became leader of a group that became al Qaeda, "the base," with a worldwide network.

        4. In 1996, bin Laden made a declaration of *jihad* against the West.

        5. In February 1998, bin Laden and Zawahiri declared a *World Islamic Front*, reminiscent of ideas of Socialist and Communist internationals, and issued a *fatwa* ruling against "Crusaders" (Westerners) and "Zionists," ordering the killing of Americans, whether civilian or military.

    C. Terror and ideological visions.

        1. Of the September 11 attacks, bin Laden said, "It is what we instigated, for a while, in self-defense... Every time they kill us, we kill them so a balance of terror can be achieved."

        2. In a tape released in December 2001, bin Laden spoke of "blessed terror."

        3. Videos and other documents found in Afghanistan in 2002, after the defeat of the group's Taliban hosts, showed experiments with chemical weapons.

    D. Such instances show that terror and utopia are still dynamic and active as the 21st century begins.

III. Why, then, did it all happen?

    A. The 20th century's violent record requires explanation, at least in broad outline.

    B. Indisputable improvements in sciences and material progress opened up new horizons of what seemed possible in other areas of life, including social organization.

        1. Paradoxically, optimism about utopian possibilities led to frustration with obstacles to their realization (whether material limits or people).

        2. Glorious ends were used to justify any means, including violence, coercion, and terror.

    C. Modern popular politics, whether in the form of democracy or totalitarian attempts to orchestrate the masses, injected new forces into the international and domestic political arenas.

    D. Decline of traditional religions left a hunger for meaning to be filled by political faiths.

    E. Ultimately, readiness to undertake both utopian experiment and terror depended on views of man's nature.

        1. Mao's musing on the beauty of humans as "blank pages" to be written on captures one view.

        2. The resistance or dissent of the witnesses of the century we have discussed hinged on a different view of mankind, as intrinsically inviolable and durable in individual dignity.

IV. Institutional solutions?

    A. The United Nations.

        1. From its founding, the United Nations is a collection of states, not a world government.

        2. As an arena that includes democracies and dictatorships, it has not been immune from the contradictions of politics and ideology.

        3. In 2002, Libya, a state sponsoring terrorism, chaired the Human Rights Committee, illuminating these contradictions.

4. In such crises as those that took place in Bosnia, Kosovo, or Rwanda, appeals to an "international community" often released nations from responsibility for action.

B. The International Criminal Court.

    1. In 2002, a new International Criminal Court was established, with claims to universal jurisdiction.

    2. Some nations, including the United States (which declined to participate), are concerned about the implications for national sovereignty, the basis of democratic responsibility.

C. A level even deeper than that of institutions is that of the individual and how the individual's human rights and being are regarded in politics and by ourselves.

V. The question of human nature.

A. Much of the confrontation with utopias, their hopes, disappointments, and terrors, centered on the issue of human nature and whether it can be changed: Is there one essential human nature that is enduring and durable, or is man a product of environment, education, and social influence (what Steven Pinker calls the "blank slate")?

B. Isaiah Berlin.

    1. The late historian of ideas Isaiah Berlin (1909–1997) took as a central motto for his work a quote by philosopher Immanuel Kant on the "crooked timber of humanity."

    2. Kant's aphorism suggested that man is made of material so complex, organic, and "crooked" in its individuality that "nothing entirely straight" can be carved from it.

    3. A central paradox is this: Is it in human nature to imagine utopias in which that human nature is overcome?

C. A new threshold?

    1. Is the utopian dream of changing human nature now to be accomplished by other means—technology?

    2. Advances in genetic engineering and pharmacology accelerate at such a dizzying pace that consideration of long-term implications lags behind.

3. Aldous Huxley's surmise in fiction that cloning would yield a new human condition is perhaps about to be tested in reality.
4. Is a "posthuman" future in store?

VI. Lessons.
A. What lessons emerge from studying the century's record of utopia and terror?
B. Returning to the key elements.
1. In terms of the role played by the masses, one sees the importance of individuality, embedded in true, everyday human community, rather than given over to loneliness in crowds. Genuine individuals resist the "marching impulse" of organized crowds.
2. Although machines of control were important to tyrannies, technology itself is clearly neither a curse nor an answer, given its surprising potential for liberating effects or enslavement.
3. The role of a mobster mentality in elites seeking power in disordered societies urges cultivation of the virtues an active citizenry needs to build responsible states and societies.
4. The fraudulent splendor of total master plans is abundantly clear in the historical record.
C. Amnesia as a danger.
1. The very fact that the ideological dictatorships of the century did not exist in vacuums but interacted, fought, learned from, and occasionally imitated one another carries a crucial implication: It is dangerous to be unaware of their records.
2. There is special danger in forgetting these phenomena and crimes of the 20th century, which could lead to revivals.
3. After Communism's collapse in Eastern Europe and the Soviet Union, scarcely any leaders were held accountable or put on trial. The same is true in the case of other regimes worldwide, such as the Khmer Rouge.
4. Such amnesia, though perhaps initially comfortable, poisons responsible politics and distorts the mature historical consciousness of societies.

5. In Russia today, Communist symbols have returned, while newly discovered mass graves are ignored, in spite of the efforts of such organizations as Memorial. In a poll conducted throughout Russia in 2003, on the 50th anniversary of Stalin's death, 53 percent of all those asked approved of Stalin, while only 33 percent disapproved.
6. In Germany in 2003, an East German Communist theme park is planned by a Berlin company.

D. A basis for cautious optimism.
1. Philosophers continue to debate whether utopias are indispensable to human beings, a precondition of any progress.
2. Our survey of the historical record of the last century urges vigilance against revivals and new forms of the total ideologies, as well as humility and caution in utopian thought experiments.
3. The heroism and humanity of the witnesses to the century we considered, as well as countless other unknown people who confronted terror regardless of their own fates, provide an example that is not utopian, but historically and existentially very real.

Essential Reading:

Daniel Benjamin and Steven Simon, *The Age of Sacred Terror.*

Isaiah Berlin, *The Crooked Timber of Humanity: Chapters in the History of Ideas.*

Steven Pinker, *The Blank Slate: The Modern Denial of Human Nature.*

Daniel Pipes, *Militant Islam Reaches America.*

Supplementary Reading:

Walter Laqueur, *The New Terrorism: Fanaticism and the Arms of Mass Destruction.*

Questions to Consider:

1. Why did suicide attacks become much more frequent as forms of terrorism in the last 10 years?

2. Does an essential human nature exist, or is humanity a material that can be formed and shaped?

Lecture Twenty-Four—Transcript
The Future of Terror

In our previous lectures, we've brought our course of study right up to the end of the 20th century. In our lecture today, we'd like to consider the future of terror.

In the course of our lectures, we've not been able to mention all of the cases of despotic regimes, or of turmoil, or of ideological conflict in the 20th century, such Vietnam, Sudan, Iran, Ethiopia, Cuba, Sierra Leone, or South Africa; the list could go on and on. However, we have sought to indicate cases that spoke to the very largest issues, and suggested what some of the trajectories for the future might be.

In this lecture, we'd like to examine terror today, ideological claims of movements that are abroad in the world, and, not so much predict the future, as to suggest what lessons we might draw from the experience of the 20th century.

In our other lectures, we've commented about the rise of "political religions," in the form of modern ideologies of the 20th century. Today, however, we see a new variation, even more explicit syntheses of politics, religion, and ideology, the use of traditional religious imagery or ideas, fused with political energies, promising a perfect world.

I'd like to consider some cases of this from a Japanese cult, to suicide bombers, to radical Islamist ideologies, as well.

On March 20, 1995, an attack took place in Tokyo. The *Aum Shinri Kyo*, or the "Supreme Truth" cult released sarin gas in Tokyo subways, leaving 12 dead, and thousands injured in an attack that seemed to be entirely irrational, seemed to serve no conceivable purpose. Yet, within the ideological mindset of this group, their aim had been to bring along, or hurry along, a religious apocalypse.

They were driven by the teachings of their spiritual master, Shoko Asahara, who drew on traditional Buddhism, but then had gone far afield, turning to predictions of apocalypse, and the nearing end of civilization as we knew it, a message, perhaps, of renewal through violence.

Rather than simply await the end of the world, however, this cult tried to accelerate the coming of apocalypse. They had at first sought to develop a scientific "earthquake machine" that could produce natural disasters, and then had fallen back on the idea of use of poison sarin.

Another case of the use of technology for murder ends comes with suicide bombers at work in the world today. Palestinian suicide bombers, both young men and young women, called *shahid*, or "martyrs," are increasingly common in the Israeli-Palestinian conflict, exploding themselves among civilians. Polls indicate, moreover, that such bombers enjoy wide popularity in their own communities. Most are from religiously oriented groups, including Hamas, an Islamic jihad. In the process of preaching such suicide with a military purpose, they're altering long-standing traditional Islamic belief against suicide.

At the same time, secular groupings have also tried to adopt this tactic, as it were, not wanting to be left behind. A particularly prominent instance of the fusion of religion and ideology is radical Islamism. We need to stress here the word itself: Islamism, as distinct from traditional Islamic belief. Islamism synthesizes religious impulses and modern ideology with a political agenda.

Radical Islamists view themselves as the carriers of a total ideology, with total answers and solutions to the world's problems, superseding the modern Western ideologies that we've discussed, in part, in our lectures.

In a worldwide population of one billion Muslims, radical Islamists are only a very small group, and yet they've made up for their small numbers by the fervor of espousing their cause. In spite of an occasional expression of a utopian vision of restoring the caliphate of the seventh century, when there was one rule uniting Muslims, the modern Islamists often, in fact, break with traditional Islam in very significant ways.

They alter established traditions by identifying Islam with state power and government authority, in ways that earlier Islamic thinkers would have considered to be unorthodox, and they have offered hardened the prescriptions for personal faith and personal conviction into political dogmas, and rules that must be enforced, however harshly. In particular, there's also one very telling innovation of the Islamists, which is in stark contrast to traditional Islam. That is the incorporation into modern Islamist thought the concept of progress.

As we've seen with the modern Western ideologies that set the 20th century's violence course on its way, progress was a key notion. It was the notion that a bright future awaited, that things were getting better all the time, perhaps inevitably, but especially if one had the key to history. This is a notion that was not familiar to traditional Islamic belief. The notion of traditional Islam had been in the days of the prophet, in the days of the revelation. One had enjoyed, as it were, a golden age, and later generations had deviated from it. Rather, the Islamists suggested that one could, instead, imagine a perfected future. This was something quite new, incorporating some Western ideas.

The adherents of Islamism are often from prosperous backgrounds, and often students of science or engineering. The movement's use of technology for its ends, its embrace of the machinery of technology, even as it might reject some of its Western context, whether the Internet or the use of modern weapons, is characteristic of this blend of the modern with religious ideology.

We also see here something that runs counter to commonly perceived notions about the roots of terrorism. We're often prone to understand terrorism as a reaction to desperation, to a lack of hope in the future, but the prosperous backgrounds of many terrorists, as well as their own professed determination to live and die for particular ideas, should suggest to us that we need to take their professed beliefs seriously.

In spite of denunciations of the West, and the preaching of the arms struggle of *jihad* as a holy war, Islamist thinking is often very heavily influenced by Western ideologies that it has appropriated, even though those debts might not be recognized.

An excellent example is a key thinker of Islamist thought, the Egyptian Sayyid Qutb, of the Muslim brotherhood. He studied in the United States, and then reacted very violently against the civilization that he had encountered there. He did so borrowing terms and ideas from Western civilization, but giving some of these ideologies a distinctive twist.

In particular, Qutb accepted the Marxist timeline of historical stages: Feudalism, capitalism, and Communism, but then did something interesting. He added one more stage after Communism, after the dictatorship of the proletariat, and this was to be the triumph of

Islamism as an ideology. This was to restore the spiritual dimension that he felt had been neglected in Communist ideology, bringing about, finally, a utopian harmony of human existence. Qutb's writings called for a unitary state, consolidation of political control, and a classless society based upon shared belief, that would be achieved through violent means. Similar trends could also be seen in other schools of Islamist thought developing in this period, including revolutionary Iran, under Ayatollah Khomeini, from 1979.

It's crucial to keep this in mind, that Islamism is it is not a throwback, not a revival. Rather, it is a modern ideological form, and its ideas need to be considered in this context, as well as its actions.

We now turn to consider a prominent case of such motivated terrorism, the September 11th attacks of 2001, and the role of Al Qaeda. On September 11, 2001, New York's World Trade Center towers were destroyed by Al Qaeda terrorists, coordinated by their leader, Osama bin Laden. Another attack was launched on Washington, D.C.

The attack, in and of itself, was not merely to do damage to the economy. It was also intended as an act of propaganda through terror, "propaganda of the deed," as revolutionaries and anarchists at the start of the 20th century would have called it. It was intended to spread fear, to cripple the society, and to impress upon the rest of the world that the enemies of the Islamists were on the run.

In Al Qaeda texts that were later found in Afghanistan, after the Taliban hosts of Al Qaeda there were defeated, suicide missions, such as the one of September 11th, were praised, in a booklet which was significantly titled, "The Solution," but was offered here, as terrorism, as a solution.

Osama bin Laden, a shadowy figure, was of great importance in stage managing, or choreographing, these very carefully planned attacks. Who was he?

Bin Laden was not of humble origins, but rather was born into a prosperous family in Saudi Arabia. When his father died, he inherited millions from the family's construction empire. He studied in Saudi Arabia, without finishing school. Some contemporaries have suggested that he wasn't particularly drawn to a fundamentalist version of religion.

Then, over time, he seemed to be attracted by radical activists in central Asia, near Afghanistan, including a man who would become an important ideological ally, the Egyptian, Ayman al-Zawahiri.

In 1989, bin Laden became the leader of an important group. His, by all accounts, in some respects, charismatic personality helped him achieve this leadership role. He's a tall man, looming over others from his culture, as he stands six feet five inches tall, very quiet, soft-spoken, but man who is said to have a particular talent as a stage manager, or as an impresario of the framing of these attacks for propaganda, and public relations effect.

The group that he headed came to be called Al Qaeda, which means "the base." The base of operations, with a worldwide network. It's significant to consider how this Al Qaeda group thinks of itself in ideological terms. One word that is used to describe their self-understanding is one that we've seen before in the context of radical ideological movements, the word "vanguard." They see themselves as being in the very forefront of a larger ideological wave, which they are showing the way for. We'll recall Lenin's ideas of the Bolsheviks, as the "vanguard" of the workers, showing the way. There are clearly resonances here.

In 1996, bin Laden, as an impresario, made a public declaration of *jihad* against the West, a "holy struggle." In 1997, he further added that his plans that he was in the process of organizing would be shown in the future by the media. I think this wasn't simply an announcement to tell us to stay tuned, suggesting that people keep their eyes open for what he would be affecting. I think that the very notion of media attention to these acts is crucial to understanding how a small group uses such actions to effect, it hopes, worldwide change.

In February of 1998, bin Laden and his ally al-Zawahiri declared, in sonorous terms, "a world Islamic front." They argued that they would have global reach.

In many ways, this attempt to muster an international world organization is remarkably reminiscent of ideas we've seen before, of Socialist and Communist internationals, the organizations that would seek to further a global idea of change.

They also issued a *fatwa*, a religious ruling against those they called "Crusaders," particularly the Westerners, and Americans in particular, and "Zionists," meaning Israelis or Jews in general. They ordered the killing of Americans, whether civilian or military, as acts that would further their ideology.

Here we see a fusion of terror, and ideological visions, the proposal of a utopia to follow.

Of the September 11th attacks, in one of recordings that circulated afterwards to further this propaganda, bin Laden is quoted as saying that these attacks were what they instigated, for awhile, in self-defense. "Every time they kill us, we kill them so a balance of terror can be achieved."

The very term "balance of terror" I think is significant. Terror is being endorsed as a tool of politics. Bin Laden followed upon this, in a tape that was released in December of 2001. In it, he deliberately spoke of the idea of "blessed terror," the inspiring of fear, and crippling anxiety, in order to tear down one's enemies and their societies as a cornerstone notion of Al Qaeda and Osama bin Laden.

Videos and other documents that were found in Afghanistan in 2002, after the defeat of the group's Taliban hosts, showed experiments with chemical weapons, proposals for really vast projects like balloons that would carry poisons to rain down upon the enemy, as well as other planning for terrorist acts.

The instances we've just discussed, of the fusion of religion and ideology, suicide bombings, and the Al Qaeda network and Islamism, clearly show instances where terror and utopia are still dynamic and active as they were in the 20th century, as the 21st century begins.

We want to ask a fundamental question: Why, then, did all of this happen in the 20th century, and what can we learn from it?

The 20th century's long and violent record clearly requires explanation, at least in broad outline. There are paradoxes aplenty here. The indisputable improvements in the sciences, and in the material progress that did so much to improve the lives of ordinary people in the 20th century, also opened up new horizons of what seemed possible in other areas of life, in terms of physical change, in terms of changing the landscape and the environment, and decisively, including social organization, as well.

This was, in a way, a killing paradox, because that optimism about utopian possibilities would then inevitably lead to frustration with the obstacles that stood in the way of realizing those hopes. Whether those obstacles were the material limits of one's reality and physical obstacles, or the limits of rationality, or whether, in this case, fatally, they were people who stood in the way of ideological realizations. Again and again, as we've seen, glorious ends, the best of intentions were used to justify any means, including violence, coercion, and terror.

The shape of modern politics, with its mass and popular nature, had a lot to do with this intensity of political confrontation. Modern popular politics, whether in the form democracy, or the form of totalitarian attempts to orchestrate the masses, and set them marching off towards the brave future, all injected new, mass forces into the international and domestic political arenas, and gave new power and potency to politics.

Furthermore, ideas and beliefs played an important role as well, one that's difficult to measure. The decline of traditional religious beliefs might have left a hunger for meaning in modern man that was to be filled by political faith. Ultimately, the readiness to undertake both utopian experiments and terror, however, depended on what I think is the bottom line of these questions: The views that were held about human nature, and what it was, and what could be done.

Hannah Arendt, in her stunning dissection of the trends of the 20th century, quotes a haunting phrase, and that epigram is that normal people do not know that anything is possible. What she meant by that was that civilization at its best, in some sense, places limits on what human beings can do to human beings. Totalitarian societies eliminate those limits, feeling that the nature of man is something to be manipulated, rather than respected.

We think back to our discussion of how Chairman Mao had mused on "the beauty of human beings" precisely because they were "blank pages" on which one could write whatever one wanted, "new and wonderful things." I think that really captures one view.

Another view human nature is captured by those people we've discussed who have dissented, or resisted against such regimes, people who were witnesses to the century's violence and despotism. They had a different view of mankind, a different view of human nature, which saw the human being not as something to be manipulated, or pushed around in population movements and displacements, but rather, as something intrinsically inviolable, and durable, something with a human dignity of the individual that should not be violated.

In particular, we've noted again and again in our lectures and in our discussion of despotic regimes, the jokes that even people under the repressive grasp of these regimes have told time and again, about their regime's shortcomings. These regimes, were, perhaps, not ultimately threatened by them, but these jokes on the part of the suppressed population that I've tried to weave into our discussion now and again, suggest that these regimes all, ultimately, didn't manage to finally quell that last spark of resistance, that sense of irony, or in this case, dark humor that would still be an abiding part of human reality.

Institutions in the form of governments played a very large role in setting the 20th century on its course. We might ask whether institutions might also offer some solutions to these problems, for the future. Many have looked to the United Nations as an embodiment of those ideals which the League of Nations had sought to embody earlier. From its founding however, the United Nations was a collection of states, not a world government with sovereign power. Rather, it has often very usefully been an arena for discussion, but one that has included states whose interests, as well as their conceptions of the world, have sometimes been irreconcilable, and including democracies as well as dictatorships.

Thus, the United Nations has not been immune to the contradictions of politics and ideology. To give one example, in 2002, Libya, a state that has been declared is sponsoring terrorism, chaired the human rights committee of the United Nations and illuminating these contradictions.

During the time of the Rwandan genocide, the Rwandan government was a member of the rotating Security Council.

In crises like Bosnia, Kosovo, or Rwanda, as we've seen, appeals to an "international community" have sometimes, paradoxically, served precisely to release individual nations from taking responsibility for their actions.

There is some hope that the international criminal court, established in 2002, might change this picture with claims to universal jurisdiction. However, there are some anxieties by some nations, like the United States, which declined to participate, and are concerned about implications for national sovereignty, which is the basis for democratic responsibility and accountability.

A level that's even deeper than that of institutions and governments is one that I'd like to consider, as well: The baseline level of the individual, and how the individual's human rights, and human being, are regarded in politics and by ourselves. In other words, this is the question in regard to how we think about human nature. This is an old debate in philosophy, and one that's likely to continue. It's key in our context.

Much of the confrontation in the 20th century with utopias, their hopes, disappointments, and terrors, centered on issues of human nature, and whether that nature can be changed. The fundamental, abiding question was this: Is there one essential human nature, which is enduring, endurable, and can be folded, spindled, and mutilated, but which will bounce back, or is man something different? A product of environment, education, social influence, perhaps infinitely changeable, and open to influence? This is a model which MIT psychologist Stephen Pinker has referred to as the "blank slate" theory.

One notable and respected historian of ideas, the late Isaiah Berlin, spoke very eloquently, I think, to this abiding question of human nature. In his entire work on the history of modern ideas, he himself being a remarkable witness to 20th century in his own work and thinking, took as the central motto for his own work a quote from the German philosopher Immanuel Kant. He talked about the "crooked timber of humanity." Kant's aphorism of the " crooked timber" of humanity suggested that human beings are that crooked timber. They're made up of a material that's so complex, organic, grown, and "crooked," in the sense of being distinctive, individual, and unique, that "nothing entirely straight," as this aphorism continues, "can be carved, or shaped, or molded from human nature."

What was meant by that was that human individuality doesn't fit, according to Isaiah Berlin, the neat schemes and utopian frameworks that are suggested by the ideologies we've discussed. A central paradox, however, is this: Perhaps it is in human nature to imagine utopias in which that human nature is overcome. People need visions of the future. We need the notion of a better tomorrow in order to get up in the morning, and to set about, with some hope and vitality, our everyday business.

Technology might play a role here as well. Perhaps we're nearing a new threshold in our debate on human nature. Is the utopian dream of changing human nature, and manipulating it, about to be accomplished by technology?

In our times, advances in genetic engineering and pharmacology are accelerating such a dizzying pace that some social critics are worrying that the consideration, the thinking through of the long-term implications of this technological change might yet be lagging behind.

Aldous Huxley surmised in his fictional work, *Brave New World,* that cloning would someday yield a new human condition and a new human nature. This is perhaps about to be tested in reality. Is a post-human future in store for us? That's a question well worth considering.

In conclusion, let's ask what lessons one might learn from the long and violent record of the 20th century. What lessons might emerge from studying its record of utopian terror?

We might return to the key elements that made up the regimes we've considered, in order to consider their lessons. Those key elements were: Masses, machines, mobsters, and master plans.

In terms of the role that masses played, one sees the importance, by contrast, of emphasizing for a healthy model of society, the value of individuality. This is not in the sense of being a lonely, atomized individual, but rather, individuals who unfold their own characters, and are still embedded in true, everyday, human community, civic society, and not given over to the loneliness of crowds. Genuine individuals are likely to be better able to resist that "marching impulse" of organized crowds that ideological regimes sought to create.

While machines were important for tyrannies, technology itself, as we've seen, is clearly neither unequivocally a curse nor an unproblematic answer, given its potential for liberating effects, or enslavement. This urges us to think about technology, and to use and be affected by it consciously.

The role of mobster mentality, with elites seeking power over disordered or shaken societies urges us, by contrast, to cultivate the virtues of an active citizenry, which is what is truly necessary to build responsible states and democratic societies.

Finally, the fraudulent splendor of those total master plans, those utopian blueprints, is abundantly clear in the historical record. We must keep in mind that those ideas had consequences. Thus, ideas need to be taken seriously.

Moreover, there is another caution, about amnesia as a danger. The very fact that the ideological dictatorships of the 20th century did not exist in vacuums, but, as we've tried to emphasize, interacted, fought with one another, learned from one another, and occasionally imitated one another, carries a crucial implication: It's dangerous to be unaware of their record, if that record continues. There's a special danger in forgetting these phenomena, crimes of the 20th century, which could lead to revivals.

The signs are not all that positive right now. After Communism's collapse in Eastern Europe, and that of the Soviet Union, scarcely any leaders were held accountable or put on trial for their crimes. The same is true in the cases of other regimes worldwide, such as the Khmer Rouge. Though such amnesia is perhaps initially comfortable, it poisons responsible politics in the long run, and distorts the mature historical consciousness that a society needs.

In Russia, today, for instance, and I've found this even in discussions with Russians whom I've met, Communist symbols have returned, while newly discovered mass graves in Russia are ignored by the public at large, in spite of the efforts of brave organizations like Memorial, who seek to keep the memory of these atrocities alive.

In a poll that was conducted throughout Russia in 2003, on the 50th anniversary of Stalin's death, 53 percent of those who were asked approved of Stalin. Only 33 percent disapproved. Amnesia, indeed.

In Germany in 2003, an East German Communist theme park is being planned by a Berlin company, to allow people to "go back" in time, and to experience those days of fervor. Here, kitsch being produced through the experiences of suffering is a way of adding insult to injury.

I'd like to close on a note of cautious optimism. Philosophers continue to debate whether utopias are indispensable to human beings as we really are, and is perhaps the precondition for any kind of progress. Our survey of the historical record of the last century urges us to be vigilant against revivals, and against new forms of the total ideologies, as well as encouraging us to take on a certain humility and caution, even as we engage in utopian thought experiments.

Finally, the heroism and humanity of the witnesses to century that we've considered, as well as countless other unknown people who confronted terror regardless of their own fates, and often paid the ultimate price, provide an example that's not utopian or imagined, but historically and existentially very real. Their courage and humanity are causes for hope for us, in our new century.

Timeline

1917	February Revolution in Russia, followed by Bolshevik seizure of power in October Revolution.
1917	Cheka secret police formed in Russia.
1918	Germany forces Russia to sign Treaty of Brest-Litovsk.
1918	Bolsheviks shoot tsar and his family. Red Terror declared.
1918–1921	Russian Civil War.
1919	Fascist movement founded in Italy.
1919	Versailles Treaty written; Germany signs under protest.
1919	Radical Socialist revolt in Germany suppressed.
1919	Communist Bavaria and Soviet Hungary suppressed.
1920	Yevgeny Zamyatin writes dystopian novel *We*.
1921	Kronstadt revolt crushed by Bolsheviks.
1921	Lenin introduces NEP.
1921	Hitler becomes leader of the Nazis.
1922	Mussolini becomes prime minister of Italy after March on Rome.
1922	Founding of Soviet Union (U.S.S.R.).
1923	Treaty of Lausanne agrees on "population transfer" between Greece and Turkey.
1923	Hitler's Beer Hall *putsch* fails.

1923	Italian journalist coins term *totalitarian* to denounce Fascists.
1924	Lenin dies.
1927	Stalin dominates government in Soviet Union.
1928	Soviet First Five-Year Plan launched.
1929	Stalin orders collectivization.
1929	Great Depression worldwide.
1930	Breakthrough election for Nazis in Germany.
1932	Socialist Realism made official style in Soviet Union.
1932	Aldous Huxley publishes *Brave New World*.
1932–1933	Terror Famine in Ukraine and elsewhere in Soviet Union.
1933	On January 30, Hitler becomes chancellor of Germany.
1933	Concentration camps established.
1934	Reichstag fire and Enabling Act in Germany. SA purged in Night of Long Knives.
1934–1935	Chinese Communist Long March establishes Mao leadership.
1935	Mussolini invades Ethiopia.
1935	Nuremberg Laws strip German Jews of rights.
1936	Rome-Berlin Axis formed.
1936–1938	Stalin's Great Purge in the Soviet Union.
1936–1939	Spanish Civil War.

1937 .... Rape of Nanking by Japanese troops.

1937 .... Terror bombing of Guernica in Spain.

1938 .... Munich Conference.

1938 .... Kristallnacht in Germany.

1939 .... Nazi-Soviet Pact.

1939 .... Hitler invades Poland, beginning World War II.

1939–1945 .... World War II.

1940 .... Stalin annexes Baltic Republics.

1941 .... Hitler invades Soviet ally in Operation Barbarossa.

1941 .... SS Einsatzgruppen begin mass murder of Eastern European Jews.

1941 .... Japan attacks Pearl Harbor; America enters the war.

1942 .... Wannsee Conference ratifies "final solution" plans.

1942 .... Nazi death camps operating.

1944–1950 .... Stalin's deportations of "punished peoples."

1945 .... Hitler commits suicide; Germany surrenders.

1945 .... United States drops atomic bombs on Japan; Japan surrenders.

1945 .... At Potsdam Conference, Allies agree to "transfer" of ethnic Germans.

1945 .... United Nations founded.

1945–1947 .... Nuremberg war crimes trials.

1945–1947	Cold War tensions rising into open.
1948	Universal Declaration of Human Rights.
1948	United Nations proscribes the international crime of genocide.
1948	George Orwell writes his dystopian classic *1984*.
1949	Communists victorious in China, declare People's Republic.
1950–1953	Korean War.
1953	Stalin dies.
1956	Nikita Khrushchev's "Secret Speech" denounces Stalin.
1958–1961	Mao's "Great Leap Forward."
1960	Famine in China.
1961	East Germans build Berlin Wall.
1962	Cuban missile crisis.
1966–1976	Chinese Cultural Revolution.
1975	Khmer Rouge take power in Cambodia.
1976	Mao dies.
1979	Iranian Islamic Revolution.
1979	Saddam Hussein takes control in Iraq.
1979	Khmer Rouge overthrown by Vietnamese invasion.
1982	Polish union Solidarity banned.
1985	Mikhail Sergeyevich Gorbachev becomes leader of Soviet Union.
1986	Chernobyl nuclear disaster in Soviet Union.

1988	Saddam Hussein's campaign against Kurds uses chemical weapons; Halabja gassed.
1989	Fall of Berlin Wall, collapse of Communist regimes in Central and Eastern Europe.
1989	Chinese government crushes democracy protests in Beijing.
1989	Osama bin Laden becomes head of a group that will become al Qaeda.
1990	Iraq invades Kuwait.
1991	Gulf War expels Saddam Hussein from Kuwait.
1991	Collapse of Soviet Union.
1992–1995	War and ethnic cleansing in Bosnia (former Yugoslavia).
1994	Rwandan genocide.
1995	Aum Shinri Kyo cult stages poison attack on Tokyo subway.
1996	Bin Laden declaration of *jihad* against West.
1999	Kosovo War.
2001	September 11th attacks by al Qaeda on American targets.
2002	International Criminal Court established.
2003	United States confronts Iraq over disarmament.

Glossary

Al Qaeda: Islamist terrorist group, "the base," with networks across the Middle East, Asia, Africa, Europe, and the United States. Led by Osama bin Laden, the group was responsible for attacks against the United States on September 11, 2001.

Aum Shin Rikyu: Originally a Japanese cult, led by Shoko Asahara, combining Buddhist inspiration with apocalyptic predictions. In 1995, cult members tried to hurry along the final crisis by releasing poison gas in the Tokyo subway system.

Autarchy: Self-sufficiency and economic independence of a state from the outside world, theorized by geopolitical thinkers of the 1920s and 1930s and aimed at by many ideological regimes.

Ba'athism: An ideology originating in the 1940s that fused pan-Arab Nationalism with Socialism. This secular ideology came to power under separate leaders in Syria in 1963 and in Iraq in 1968.

Blitzkrieg: Nazi tactic for "lightning war" to avoid the trench stalemate of World War I, using massed tanks and planes to smash and encircle enemy forces. It was used to stunning effect in 1939–1940 in Poland, Scandinavia, and France, but failed against the Soviet Union in 1941.

Bolsheviks: The "majority" radical faction of Russian Democrats that split off from the mainstream in 1903 under Lenin, who remade them into a disciplined organization of professional revolutionaries and led their seizure of power in Russia in 1917.

Cheka: Acronym for Cherezvechainaya Kommisiya, the "All-Russian Extraordinary Commission for the Suppression of Counter-Revolution and Sabotage," formed by the Bolsheviks in 1917 as their secret police and executors of Red Terror, at first under Felix Dzerzhinsky. Later successively called the OGPU, NKVD, and KGB.

Civil society: The idea popularized by Vaclav Havel and other Eastern European dissidents of a buffer zone or safety zone between the individual and the state, made up of private organizations, churches, the family, and other relationships that do not run through the state center (precisely what had been eliminated in total regimes). It was hailed as a route to recovery from totalitarianism.

Collectivization: The elimination of private property (the term usually refers to land) and productive resources, centralized in the hands of the state under Communist and Socialist systems in the form of communes or collective farms. Stalin's collectivization in the 1930s led to famine, as did similar campaigns by Mao, the Khmer Rouge in Cambodia, and others.

Comintern: The Third or Communist International, founded in 1919 by the Bolsheviks to steer Communist movements worldwide and encourage global revolution. It spurned cooperation with moderate Social Democrats. Stalin ended it in 1943 in the interest of cooperation with the Western democracies to defeat Hitler.

Communism: The most advanced stage of Socialism in Marxist theories, eliminating private property in favor of collective ownership of the means of production.

Concentration camps: A perennial feature of the century, these prison centers were first established in the 1896 Spanish suppression of revolt in Cuba and by the British in the 1899–1902 Boer War. They took far more radical and murderous form in the Nazi death camps and the Soviet Gulag.

Cultural Revolution: Formally titled the Great Proletarian Cultural Revolution, this campaign ordered by Mao raged in China from 1966–1976 as Red Guard gangs terrorized society to purge it of alleged counter-revolutionary tendencies, wrecked the educational system, and "reeducated" victims.

Dystopia: A "negative utopia" or utopia as nightmare. In literature, this includes the worlds imagined by Yevgeny Zamyatin, Aldous Huxley, and George Orwell.

Einsatzgruppen: Specially trained SS killing squads sent into Poland in 1939 and the Soviet Union in 1941 to eliminate targeted groups behind the front. In 1941, they murdered a million Jews in Eastern Europe.

Ethnic cleansing: A term that gained currency in the 1990s in the Balkan Wars in Bosnia and Kosovo to describe an age-old practice of intimidation, terror, and violence to drive out different ethnic groups. Ethnic cleansing can easily tip over into genocide.

Eugenics: The doctrine of encouraging "good births," popular throughout the world in the first half of the 20th century under the impact of Social Darwinism and evolutionary theory. In the hands of the Nazis, who largely discredited the school of thought, it would be used to justify euthanasia.

Euthanasia: Related to eugenics, this term means "the good death" or "mercy killing" to eliminate those who are judged unfit. The Nazi euthanasia programs from 1939 killed some 100,000 in medicalized mass murder for the aim of a racial utopia.

Fascism: The Italian Fascist movement (taking its name from the Roman symbol of bundled sticks) was founded in 1919 and came to power under Mussolini in 1922. The movement espoused state power, anti-liberal ideas, discipline, the cult of the leader, technology, and war. Many other similar movements are also sometimes labeled Fascist, less precisely.

Final solution: The bureaucratic euphemism used by the Nazis to refer to their planned extermination of European Jews, as laid out in the 1942 Wannsee Conference.

Freikorps: German mercenary and paramilitary movements arising in 1918 and 1919 in the aftermath of defeat in World War I. The famously brutal and murderous units fought against revolutionaries in German cities and against Poles and Baltic peoples in Eastern Europe.

Führer: Hitler's title as "leader" in the Nazi movement from 1925 and of Germany from 1934. The title expressed the Nazis' mystical cult of the leader.

G.D.R.: The German Democratic Republic, established in 1949 in the Soviet zone of East Germany. The regime was based on repressive rule by the Stasi secret police and the population was confined by the Berlin Wall built in 1962. The state collapsed in 1989.

Genocide: A term invented by Polish jurist Raphael Lemkin for the phenomenon of the extermination of a group on ethnic or religious grounds, in whole or in part. The 1948 Genocide Convention adopted by the UN made it an international crime, but debates continue about the definition and application of the term.

Gestapo: The Geheime Staatspolizei (Secret State Police) was the Nazi secret police established in 1933, an integral part of the machinery of terror.

Glasnost': The policy of "openness" announced by Gorbachev in 1985 to allow constructive criticism to reform the Soviet Union, along with *perestroika*. The process quickly escaped Gorbachev's control.

Gleichschaltung: The "coordination" or Nazification process by which the Nazis used their first years in power to bring German society and the state into line and under their control. Afterward, organized resistance became much more difficult.

Great Leap Forward: From 1958–1961, Mao ordered a battle for collectivization and industrialization to overtake all other societies. The campaign was riddled with failures and produced famine in which millions died.

Great Terror: Also called the Great Purge of 1936–1938, in which Stalin purged the party and society in the Soviet Union. It included staged show trials, mass denunciations, and the expansion of the Gulag camp system.

Greater Serbia: The ideology used by Slobodan Milosevic from 1987 to replace Communist ideology as Yugoslavia fractured and used to justify ethnic cleansing. All Serbs were to be united into an ethnically pure state in the Balkans.

Gulag: The acronym for the "Main Administration of Corrective Labor Camps," a vast network of camps and prisons throughout the Soviet Union, mainly in Siberia. Millions of prisoners provided slave labor during the Stalinist period, working in deadly conditions.

Hutu: The majority ethnic group in Rwanda, traditionally farmers subservient to the Tutsi group. "Hutu power" was the slogan of killers in the 1994 Rwandan genocide.

Interahamwe: "Those who work together," the Hutu militia organized before the Rwandan genocide under the slogan "Hutu power."

International Criminal Court (I.C.C.): Founded in 2002, the court claims universal jurisdiction to try war crimes and crimes against humanity. Some nations, including the United States, express worries about the implications for national sovereignty and have not joined.

Islamism: As distinct from traditional Islamic belief, Islamism is a political ideology with religious forms. Key thinkers, such as Sayyid Qutb (1906–1966), altered traditional religious precepts, calling for a religious state. The Iranian Islamic Revolution of 1979 sought to enact these ideas.

Juche: The North Korean ideology of autarchy.

Khmer Rouge: The Cambodian Communist movement led by Pol Pot that ruled Cambodia from 1975–1979, organizing genocide against its own people.

Kommunalka: The cramped "communal apartments" of the Soviet Union, a distinctive element of Soviet civilization.

Kronstadt: An uprising of sailors at the Kronstadt garrison in 1921, calling for an end to Bolshevik dictatorship, was brutally suppressed by Bolshevik forces.

Kulak: The term of abuse, meaning "tight-fisted," used to single out more successful farmers in Stalin's 1931–1933 collectivization drive. They were to be eliminated as a class and were targeted in the Terror Famine or sent to the Gulag.

Lebensraum: "Living space," which Hitler demanded for the German master race he planned to create. This space was to be conquered in Eastern Europe and would be ethnically cleansed of populations already living there to make way for German settlement in the future.

M.A.D.: Acronym for "mutually assured destruction," the premise of nuclear deterrence that a nuclear exchange would leave no victors.

Memorial: An organization based in Russia today that seeks to commemorate and keep alive the memory of the victims of Stalinism and to resist historical amnesia on the subject.

Mukhabarat: The secret police and security forces of Saddam Hussein's regime in Iraq.

Nazism: "National Socialism," the ideology of Hitler's movement, which ruled Germany from 1933–1945. Its core ideas were racism, anti-Semitism, militarism, a total state, the cult of the leader, and the *Volksgemeinschaft*. Historians debate whether it was a subvariety of Fascism or in a category all its own.

Nazi-Soviet Pact: Treaty of friendship signed between Stalin and Hitler in 1939, enabling Hitler to begin the Second World War with his attack on Poland. Secret clauses carved up Eastern Europe into spheres of influence. The treaty seemed an impossibility because of the ideological hatred between the new friends.

N.E.P.: Lenin introduced the New Economic Policy in 1921, backtracking in ideological terms to revive the economy by allowing limited free enterprise. Stalin eliminated NEP in the late 1920s.

Nomenklatura: Privileged elite classes of party members and specialists arising in Communist countries, contrary to the egalitarian ideology of the state, enjoying special privileges.

Perestroika: The "restructuring" program announced by Gorbachev in 1985 to reform the Communist economic system, coupled with *Glasnost'*. The process quickly escaped Gorbachev's control.

Propaganda: Originally a religious term, it has come to signify the deliberate spreading of ideological ideas and interpretations to win the hearts and minds of a population, even if through lies.

Punkt: The radio of Stalin's Soviet Union, pre-tuned to a government channel. Similar radios are found in many other ideological regimes, such as in North Korea today.

Red Guards: Mao's special units in China's Cultural Revolution in 1966–1976. They terrorized Chinese society to cleanse it of allegedly counter-revolutionary tendencies and to break with the past.

Red Terror: The systematic use of violence by Lenin and the Bolsheviks against their opponents, ordered in 1918, to consolidate their revolution and hold on Russia.

S.A.: The *Sturmabteilungen*, or "storm troopers," were units of Nazi thugs on the model of Mussolini's Blackshirts who terrorized the opponents of the Nazis. Once in power, Hitler purged their leaders in 1934.

Social Darwinism: The belief, building on Darwin's evolutionary theories, that societies should pursue policies that benefit the strong and should allow the weak to fail, because these were considered natural processes. A constituent part of modern biological racism.

Socialism: An ideology organized around the principle of communal ownership in economics and social cooperation. It has been called one of the most important ideas of human history.

Socialist Realism: In 1932, this became the formal artistic doctrine in the Soviet Union, whereby artists were to portray reality as it was in the process of becoming, not in its contemporary state. Art was subservient to propaganda, with predictable aesthetic results.

SS: The *Schutzstaffel*, or "protective unit," Hitler's personal bodyguard, which grew into a racial elite and empire-within-an-empire under Heinrich Himmler's leadership. The SS was charged with the Nazis' racial programs, including genocide against the Jews.

Stakhanovites: "Hero workers" of Soviet industrialization and the Five-Year Plans, held up as propaganda models for others in stage-managed feats of overproduction. They were often hated by fellow workers.

Stasi Staatssicherheit: "State Security," the remarkably extensive secret police of the East German state.

Storm troopers: Elite trenchfighters of the First World War (called *Sturmtruppen* in Germany, *Arditi* in Italy) who believed they had invented a new form of desperate heroism and enjoyed the war as an adventure.

Taylorism: "Scientific management" theories of American Frederick Winslow Taylor, adopted by Henry Ford's factories in 1914, which promised rational planning of economic progress. They won worldwide enthusiasm.

Terror: The deliberate and organized use of violence, intimidation, and fear to achieve political ends. It includes the targeting of civilians and ordinary citizens. The term originates with the Reign of Terror of 1793–1794 in the French Revolution.

Terror Famine: In 1932–1933, Stalin's collectivization led to resistance and famine in Ukraine. Estimates are that five to seven million died. The Soviet authorities shut off the region and kept news of the famine secret.

Total war: Term used in the aftermath of World War I to describe the all-consuming nature of modern industrial war, mobilizing entire populations, societies, and economies. In total war, the boundaries between soldiers and civilians would be blurred and civilians would increasingly be the targets of violence.

Totalitarianism: A term first used in the 1920s by anti-Fascists to describe their foes and taken up by the Fascists themselves. The term signifies the ambitions for total control of the subject populations by dynamic ideological regimes. Hannah Arendt's work theoretically explored totalitarianism as a modern form of rule.

Treaty of Lausanne: The 1923 Treaty of Lausanne between Greece and Turkey ended their war with agreements for "population transfers" of ethnic minority populations. Masses of people were uprooted on either side in a brutal process of ethnic cleansing, but ironically, this action was often held up as a positive precedent for solving ethnic conflict.

Turbo-Folk: Electronic pop-music with folk-song style in Serbia of the 1990s, propagating the messages of Greater Serbia.

Tutsi: The minority group of pastoralists, traditionally dominant in Rwanda, targeted in the 1994 Rwandan genocide.

United Nations: Established in 1945, this organization was to work for collective security, peace, and progress. Cold War tensions hampered its operation, but even after the Cold War's end, its future role remains uncertain and its effectiveness in preventing genocide, dubious.

Utopia: A term invented in Thomas More's book of the same name in 1516, meaning "No-place." Utopia describes an imagined perfect society in which all contradictions have been overcome.

Volksgemeinschaft: The "people's community" promised by the Nazis was to be a classless, racially pure society, cleansed of outsiders and those the Nazis considered inferior.

Biographical Notes

Arendt, Hannah (1906–1975). A German-Jewish refugee from Nazi Germany, she came to the United States and became a noted political philosopher on the faculty of the University of Chicago. Her classic work, *The Origins of Totalitarianism* (1951), is of lasting significance and likely to be read many centuries hence. She remains a controversial figure because of her relationship with German philosopher Martin Heidegger, who had supported the Nazis, and because of her *Eichmann in Jerusalem* (1963), which popularized the notion of the "banality of evil."

Berlin, Sir Isaiah (1909–1997). Born in Riga, Latvia, Berlin's family emigrated to Britain. After study at Oxford, he became a noted historian and writer on political philosophy. His works in the history of ideas are classics, as are his meditations on the challenges of liberalism. He was knighted in 1957.

Bin Laden, Osama (b. 1957). Born in Saudi Arabia into a wealthy family, bin Laden was drawn to Islamist radicalism and became the leader of the al Qaeda terrorist group, with worldwide networks of activists, which launched the attacks against the United States on September 11, 2001. He is currently in hiding, probably somewhere in Central Asia.

Canetti, Elias (1905–1994). A remarkable polymath intellectual, novelist, playwright, and philosopher, who was born in Bulgaria and grew up in Vienna. His works are written in German and include the 1960 study *Crowds and Power*, an extended and sparkling examination of crowd psychology and the dynamics of masses. His interest in the topic was awoken by personal observation of the interwar turmoil in Germany and Austria. He was awarded the 1981 Nobel Prize in literature.

Gorbachev, Mikhail Sergeyevich (b. 1931). Born into a peasant family in Stavropol, Gorbachev studied law at Moscow University and rose through the ranks of the Komsomol youth league and the party. In 1985, he was appointed General Secretary of the Party to reform the Soviet Union. A true believer, often misunderstood in the West, Gorbachev planned to use the programs of *Perestroika* and *Glasnost* to put the Soviet system on a firm, efficient footing. The programs and the expectations they had raised throughout the Soviet Union and in satellite states in Eastern Europe soon escaped his control. He vacillated between liberalization and repression of the sort seen in Vilnius, Lithuania, in 1991. In the summer of 1991, his hardliner allies attempted a coup that collapsed almost immediately, leading to the breakup of the Soviet Union. Gorbachev remains a celebrity in the West but is intensely unpopular in Russia today.

Havel, Vaclav (b. 1936). Czech playwright and human rights activist. His absurdist writings were eloquent commentary on the absurdist political regime ruling his country. He was imprisoned for his human rights activities with Charter 77. In the 1989 revolutions, he led the dissident group Civic Forum and became president of the country in the same year, later becoming president of the Czech Republic after the breakup of Czechoslovakia.

Hitler, Adolf (1889–1945). Born in the Habsburg Empire to a customs official's family, Hitler was a loner and dreamer as a youth. The Vienna Academy of Fine Arts rejected him in 1907, and he began a downward slide into the Viennese underworld. When World War I began in 1914, Hitler was exultant at having found meaning at last and volunteered for the German army, serving with distinction in the trenches of the Western Front. Germany's defeat left him shattered but also woke a determination to enter political life. In 1919, Hitler joined the small German Workers' Party and went on to become its "leader," or *Führer*, changing the name to the National Socialist German Workers' Party, or Nazis. After the failed Beer Hall *putsch* in 1923, Hitler served a minimum sentence in jail and wrote *Mein Kampf*, articulating the strategy of the "legal path to power." With the Depression came political breakthroughs for the Nazi Party. On January 30, 1933, Hitler became chancellor of Germany. The Nazi Party coordinated and controlled the country through the policies of *gleichschaltung*. Hitler consolidated his own control, purging even his own storm troopers when necessary. He pursued an aggressive foreign policy, breaking the Versailles Treaty and allying with Stalin to begin World War II with his attack on Poland. In 1941, he invaded the Soviet Union in turn to achieve *Lebensraum*, and the genocide against the Jews began in full force. Six million Jews were killed by the Nazis' machinery of death, following their racial plans. When the war turned against Nazi Germany, Hitler retreated into the unreal world of the Berlin bunker, where he committed suicide in 1945 as Soviet armies approached, leaving the Third Reich, which was to last a thousand years, in ruins.

Hussein, Saddam (b. 1937). Born near Tikrit to a peasant family, Hussein gained a reputation as a street thug and became active in the Ba'ath Party. He was wounded in a coup attempt in 1959 and fled into exile in Egypt. On returning to Iraq after the Ba'ath Party came to power, he became leader by 1979. His wars with Iran (1979–1988) and 1990 invasion of Kuwait testify to his strategic ambitions. He used chemical weapons against the Kurds, authorized brutal repression of the Iraqi population, and sought to develop weapons of mass destruction, evading UN inspections until his regime was toppled in 2003.

Huxley, Aldous (1894–1963). British writer of wide-ranging interests. In addition to many other novels, his 1932 *Brave New World* was a classic dystopia, focusing on cloning and biological conditioning. In 1958, he published *Brave New World Revisited*, in which he concluded that the state he had imagined in his fiction decades ago was now far closer than he had ever expected, an alarming prospect.

Kim Il-Sung (1912–1994). North Korean dictator, known as "Great Leader," installed by Soviet forces after World War II. He was born Kim Son Ju near Pyongyang, became an anti-Japanese guerrilla, was trained and educated in the Soviet Union, and served in the Soviet army during World War II. He launched the disastrous Korean War (1950–1953) in an attempt to rule the entire country. He crafted the ideology of *juche*, or "self-reliance," pursuing autarky and radical isolation for the nation of 22 million. An elaborate personality cult was built up around him. In 1994, Kim Il-Sung was succeeded by his son, Kim Jong-Il.

Kim Jong-Il (b. 1941). Current leader of North Korea, called "The Sun of the Twenty-first Century." He was born in Siberia and schooled in East Germany. He has a reputation for being a volatile and cruel playboy, with a fanatical enthusiasm for film (leading to the kidnapping of movie actors). His style of leadership intensified the personality cult that surrounded his father and, in foreign policy, has been expressed in aggressive brinksmanship and production of arms, including a nuclear weapons program.

Lenin, Vladimir Ilyich (1870–1924). Born Vladimir Ilyich Ulianov in Simbirsk, the son of a school inspector. After the example of his brother, Lenin became active in revolutionary politics, was arrested, and was exiled to Siberia. After 1900, he lived in exile in Western

Europe. In 1903, he led the Bolsheviks in a split with the Russian Social Democrats and organized a party of committed professional revolutionaries. In 1917, while World War I raged, German generals facilitated his return to Russia to undermine the war effort there. Lenin's Bolsheviks seized power in November 1917 and consolidated their control. After winning the Civil War, Lenin instituted the NEP to speed economic recovery. He enabled the rise of Stalin within the party and state. After a stroke in 1922, Lenin died in 1924. The city of Petrograd was renamed Leningrad, and his body was mummified and displayed outside the Kremlin.

Mao Zedong (1893–1976). Born in Hunan province to a farmer family, Mao was attracted by Marxist ideas and cofounded the Chinese Communist Party in 1921. Fighting as a guerrilla, he argued for the revolutionary potential of the peasantry. In 1934, the Long March of encircled Communist guerrillas to northern China launched a myth of Mao's genius for leadership. After World War II, civil war continued between Chinese Nationalists and the Communists, with the latter victorious by 1949. Mao forged ahead with the revolutionary transformation of China with the 1958 Great Leap Forward, which left massive economic dislocation and famine in its wake. Mao again sought to radically overhaul the system in the Cultural Revolution of 1966, which devastated Chinese society and institutions, until his death in 1976.

Milosevic, Slobodan (b. 1941). Born in Serbia to Montenegrin parents, he joined the Communist Party at 18 and rose quickly through its ranks, becoming part of the leadership elite of Yugoslavia. By 1987, as Communist ideology was eroding as a legitimation for rule, Milosevic discovered the power of revived aggressive Nationalism at the ancient battlefield of Kosovo. When Croatia, Slovenia, and Bosnia moved to break away from Yugoslavia in the early 1990s, Milosevic mobilized paramilitaries and the Yugoslav army to block their independence. Bosnia was subjected to ferocious ethnic cleansing before NATO intervention in 1995. In 1999, Milosevic moved against ethnic Albanians in Kosovo province in Serbia, but his project of demographically transforming the area through expulsions was reversed by another NATO attack. Milosevic is now on trial at The Hague for war crimes.

Mussolini, Benito (1883–1945). Born in the Romagna region of Italy, this son of a Socialist had an unruly youth and entered into

Socialist politics. During the First World War, his convictions changed, because the military mobilization of the nation appealed to him. After serving in the war, he founded the Fascist movement in 1919, organized squads of Blackshirts, and after the stage-managed March on Rome of 1922, became the dictator of Italy. Increasingly, Mussolini's regime, unable to live up to its ambitions, moved closer to Nazi Germany, an earlier rival. In 1943, Mussolini was forced to resign but afterwards presided over a small Fascist province. In 1945, he was caught by partisans while trying to flee and was killed and hung upside down in Milan.

Orwell, George (1903–1950). Born Eric Arthur Blair in India, where his father was part of the British civil service, Orwell's journalism and writing showed a passionate commitment to Socialist ideas. *Homage to Catalonia* (1938) summed up his outrage with the Communist purges of their own allies in the Spanish Civil War, which he participated in on the Republican side. His *Animal Farm* (1945) was a parable condemning totalitarianism, while the classic dystopian novel *1984* (1949) warned of trends that Orwell believed were already well advanced in the modern world.

Pol Pot (1925–1998). Born Saloth Sar to a Cambodian peasant family, he apparently spent some time in a Buddhist monastery before studying in Phnom Penh, where he joined the Communists. From 1949, he studied in Paris but neglected his education and was forced to return to Cambodia. By the late 1960s, he was the mysterious leader of the Khmer Rouge, who came to power in 1975. Under his leadership, policies of ruralization, radical social revolution, and mass murder in the killing fields caused the deaths of some two million. Vietnam's invasion overthrew the government, but Pol Pot and his followers withdrew into the jungles, where he died many years later, without being brought to trial.

Solzhenitsyn, Aleksandr Isayevich (b. 1918). Born in Rostov-on-Don, Solzhenitsyn studied mathematics and served as an artillery officer in the Soviet army in World War II. In 1945, he was arrested for criticizing Stalin and was sent to the Gulag. He described his personal experiences there in the 1962 novel *One Day in the Life of Ivan Denisovich* and related the history of the Gulag in the 1973 study *The Gulag Archipelago*. In 1970, he was awarded the Nobel prize in literature but was then arrested and deported from the Soviet Union in 1974 for his criticism of the state and party. In exile in

Switzerland and the United States, Solzhenitsyn continued to write and, after the collapse of the Soviet Union, returned to Russia. He was among the severest critics of the Soviet system but also sternly warned the West of what he saw as *its* failings.

Stalin, Josef (1879–1953). Born Josef Vissarionovich Dzhugashvili in Georgia, Stalin attended and was expelled from seminary studies in Tiflis. Turning to revolutionary politics, he acquired distinction as a bank robber "expropriating" capital for the movement. Stalin's role in the 1917 Bolshevik seizure of power was not major, but he was active in the Civil War and rose through the party ranks, occupying important bureaucratic positions that gave him leverage in the struggle for succession after Lenin's death in 1924. Stalin beat out Trotsky and other rivals by 1927 and later had them murdered. He launched a drive to industrialize the country with the Five-Year Plans and collectivization, which resulted in the Terror Famine in Ukraine and elsewhere, costing millions of lives. In the 1930s, Stalin purged the party, army, and society repeatedly, with show trials dramatizing his power and infallibility. In 1939, Stalin and Hitler pledged friendship in the Nazi-Soviet Pact. Stalin seized his share of Eastern Europe, the Baltic States, and parts of Poland. When Hitler attacked the Soviet Union in 1941, Stalin was caught unawares. After initial panic, he rallied the population with implicit promises of liberalization after the war. Once the war was won, he betrayed those promises with further violence, including the deportation of entire peoples and liberated Soviet prisoners of war. Just before his death in 1953, in circumstances that are still unclear and disputed today, Stalin (who was already responsible for the death of millions) was perhaps planning an even larger round of renewed purges.

Trotsky, Leon (1879–1940). Russian revolutionary. Born (as Lev Bronstein) in Yelisavetgrad, Trotsky became active as a Menshevik Socialist in Russia and in exile. In the 1905 Revolution, Trotsky led the St. Petersburg Soviet. In 1917, he switched his allegiance to Lenin's Bolsheviks and was instrumental in their coming to power. As commissar for foreign affairs and architect of the Red Army during the Russian Civil War, Trotsky was one of the most prominent Old Bolsheviks and seemed a natural successor to Lenin, but he was pushed aside by Stalin in 1927, exiled, and finally assassinated in Mexico by an agent of Stalin.

Zamyatin, Yevgeny Ivanovich (1884–1937). Russian writer, novelist, and playwright, born in Tambov province and educated in the capital, St. Petersburg, as a naval engineer. His writing was experimental and satirical. Zamyatin supported the Bolsheviks before the revolution but turned against them after 1917, because he intuited the growing repressive nature of the regime and expressed his fear for the future of Russian literature. In his novel *We*, written in 1920 (published in Russia only in 1988), he created the modern dystopia, which anticipated full Stalinism in many ways. Remarkably, he was allowed to leave the Soviet Union in 1931 and died in exile in Paris.

Bibliography

Essential Reading

Arendt, Hannah. *The Origins of Totalitarianism.* New York: Harcourt, Brace, 1951. Classic political philosophy with theoretical explanations for total states. Likely to be read centuries from now to understand the age.

Becker, Elizabeth. *When the War Was Over: Cambodia and the Khmer Rouge Revolution.* New York: Simon and Schuster, 1986. Harrowing overview of Pol Pot's regime.

Benjamin, Daniel, and Steven Simon. *The Age of Sacred Terror.* New York: Random House, 2002. A new analysis of radical Islamists and terrorism after September 11, 2001.

Berlin, Isaiah. *The Crooked Timber of Humanity: Chapters in the History of Ideas.* London: John Murray, 1990. Humane and eloquent discussions of the utopian tradition.

Bessel, Richard. *Germany after the First World War.* New York: Oxford University Press, 1993. Fascinating, deeply textured history of postwar Germany.

Brendon, Piers. *The Dark Valley: A Panorama of the 1930s.* New York: Knopf, 2000. Compelling vignettes of a troubled decade.

Burleigh, Michael, and Wolfgang Wippermann. *The Racial State: Germany, 1933–1945.* New York: Cambridge University Press, 1991. Dissection of Nazi racial utopian aims.

Canetti, Elias. *Crowds and Power.* New York: Viking Press, 1962. The 1981 Nobel laureate meditates on crowd psychology. An incredible range of allusions and bursting with insight.

Conquest, Robert. *Stalin: Breaker of Nations.* New York: Viking Press, 1991. Unsparing biography of a violent political career by a pathbreaking historian of Stalinism.

Eksteins, Modris. *Rites of Spring: The Great War and the Birth of the Modern Age.* Boston: Houghton Mifflin, 1989. An insightful, provocative study of the cultural impact of the war. Reviewers either loved or hated it.

Fritzsche, Peter. *Germans into Nazis*. Cambridge, MA: Harvard University Press, 1998. Forceful, evocative argument that Germans became Nazis "because they wanted to become Nazis," drawn by effective social appeals.

Gay, Peter. *Schnitzler's Century: The Making of Middle-Class Culture, 1815–1914*. New York: W.W. Norton, 2002. Keen and well-written examination of what came before the 20th century's disruptions.

Glover, Jonathan. *Humanity: A Moral History of the Twentieth Century*. London: Jonathan Cape, 1999. Evocative meditations on the century's record.

Graham, Loren R. *The Ghost of the Executed Engineer: Technology and the Fall of the Soviet Union*. Cambridge, MA: Harvard University Press, 1993. Not only a classic in the history of science, but this elegant, brief book is also a gripping human story of an engineer who fell victim to Stalin.

Hamann, Brigitte. *Hitler's Vienna: A Dictator's Apprenticeship*. New York: Oxford University Press, 1999. A fine study of the influence of Vienna on the young Hitler.

Honig, Jan Willem, and Norbert Both. *Srebrenica: Record of a War Crime*. New York: Penguin Books, 1997. Detailed examination of a recent atrocity and reasons for international abdication.

Huxley, Aldous. *Brave New World*. New York: Harper, 1946. Classic dystopia of cloning and conditioning.

Judah, Tim. *The Serbs: History, Myth and the Destruction of Yugoslavia*. New Haven: Yale University Press, 1997. Deeper historical perspective on the war in the Balkans.

Keegan, John. *The First World War*. New York: Knopf, 1999. Authoritative study of World War I.

———. *The Second World War*. London: Hutchinson, 1989. Excellent overview of World War II.

Kershaw, Ian. *Hitler*. New York: Longman, 1991. A shorter examination by the author of the now-standard two-volume biography.

Koehler, John O. *Stasi: The Untold Story of the East German Secret Police*. Boulder, CO: Westview Press, 1999. Dramatic narrative of the workings of the East German security forces.

Laqueur, Walter. *A History of Terrorism*. New York: Little Brown, 1977 (reissued New Brunswick, NJ: Transaction, 2001). Wide-ranging erudite overview of terrorism and explanations for the phenomenon.

―――. *Fascism: Past, Present, and Future*. New York: Oxford University Press, 1996. Survey of Fascism's varieties and the debates still ongoing on its essential identity and nature.

Mack Smith, Denis. *Mussolini*. London: Weidenfield and Nicolson, 1981. Considered one of the best political biographies ever written, a detailed summary of the man and his political trajectory.

Mackey, Sandra. *The Reckoning: Iraq and the Legacy of Saddam Hussein*. New York: Norton, 2002. Timely survey of Iraq's history and the Ba'athist regime.

Malia, Martin. *The Soviet Tragedy: A History of Socialism in Russia, 1917–1991*. New York: Free Press, 1994. A synthesis of a scholarly career, in which Malia discusses not only the historical record and inner logic of the Bolshevik project, but also historiography.

Marrus, Michael. *The Holocaust in History*. Hanover, NH: Brandeis University Press, 1987. Summary of decades of scholarship on the Holocaust, concisely presenting different specialized themes.

Marx, Karl, and Friedrich Engels, *The Communist Manifesto*. Originally published 1848. A booklet of scant pages that affected the lives of billions.

Mosse, George L. *The Crisis of German Ideology: Intellectual Origins of the Third Reich*. New York: Grosset and Dunlap, 1964. An enduring classic of cultural history examining the deeper roots of Nazi ideas in German culture.

―――. *Towards the Final Solution: A History of European Racism*. New York: Howard Fertig, 1978. Mosse usefully places German racism in the wider European context of evolving *biological racism*.

Moynahan, Brian. *The Russian Century: A History of the Last Hundred Years*. New York: Random House, 1994. Wonderfully written scenes and waystations of Russia's violent century.

Muravchik, Joshua. *Heaven on Earth: The Rise and Fall of Socialism*. San Francisco: Encounter Books, 2002. Sweeping popular overview of one of the most important ideas of mankind.

Naimark, Norman. *Fires of Hatred: Ethnic Cleansing in Twentieth-Century Europe*. Cambridge, MA: Harvard University Press, 2001.

Sophisticated examination of cases of ethnic cleansing in Europe, weighing similarities and contrasts.

Orwell, George. *1984*. Originally published 1949. The classic dystopian novel of future despotism under Big Brother.

Pinker, Steven. *The Blank Slate: The Modern Denial of Human Nature*. New York: Viking Press, 2002. Weighing the current state of scientific debate on questions of human nature, Pinker argues for acceptance of its reality.

Pipes, Daniel. *Militant Islam Reaches America*. New York: W.W. Norton, 2002. Articles on different aspects of radical Islamist ideology.

Pipes, Richard. *Communism: A History*. New York: Modern Library, 2001. Vigorously argued brief summary of the internal logic and historical record of Communism by an esteemed historian of Russia.

Power, Samantha. *"A Problem from Hell": America and the Age of Genocide*. New York: Basic Books, 2002. Both reasoned and impassioned, this study examines attempts to proscribe genocide and criticizes America's record in preventing genocides. Essential reading for an understanding of fundamental issues of human rights.

Schaer, Ronald, Gregory Claeys, and Lyman Tower Sargent, eds., *Utopia: The Search for the Ideal Society in the Western World*. New York: Oxford University Press, 2001. Dense and wonderfully illustrated catalog of an exhibition on utopias, from ancient times to the present.

Spence, Jonathan. *Mao Zedong*. New York: Viking, 1999. A brief and elegant biography.

Zamyatin, Yevgeny. *We*. New York: Penguin Books, 1993. Dystopian novel of the future, a model for Orwell's *1984*, and uncannily foreshadowing full-blown Stalinism.

Supplementary Reading

Becker, Jasper. *Hungry Ghosts: Mao's Secret Famine*. New York: Free Press, 1996. A journalist's harrowing study of Chinese famine, including oral history testimony.

Chang, Iris. *The Rape of Nanking*. New York: Basic Books, 1997. Unsparing recounting of Japanese atrocities in Nanking.

Chol-Hwan, Kang, and Pierre Rigoulot. *The Aquariums of Pyongyang: Ten Years in the North Korean Gulag*. New York: Basic Books, 2002. The first memoir of a survivor of North Korean prison camps.

Coughlin, Con. *Saddam: King of Terror*. New York: Harper Collins, 2002. Topical biography of Iraq's ruler.

Dolot, Miron. *Execution by Hunger*. New York: W.W. Norton, 1985. A memoir of the Terror Famine in Ukraine written simply and with great immediacy.

Fulbrook, Mary. *Anatomy of a Dictatorship: Inside the GDR, 1949–1989*. New York: Oxford University Press, 1995. Social history of East Germany, emphasizing different phases in its development.

Gleason, Abbott. *Totalitarianism: The Inner History of the Cold War*. New York: Oxford University Press, 1995. A critical examination of the genealogy and uses of the totalitarian concept.

Gourevitch, Philip. *We Wish to Inform You That Tomorrow We Will Be Killed with Our Families: Stories from Rwanda*. New York: Farrar, Straus, and Giroux, 1998. Chilling accounts of the unfolding of the Rwandan genocide.

Griffin, Roger. *The Nature of Fascism*. New York : St. Martin's Press, 1991. Griffin proposes a general definition of Fascism as seeking a utopia of a regenerated national community.

Hochschild, Adam. *King Leopold's Ghost: A Story of Greed, Terror, and Heroism in Colonial Africa*. Boston: Houghton Mifflin, 1998. An accessible narrative of the brutalities of colonial rule in Belgian Congo.

Hoffer, Eric. *The True Believer: Thoughts on the Nature of Mass Movements*. New York: Harper and Row, 1951. Provocative and deliberately absolute theses on the psychology of political faith.

Horne, John, and Alan Kramer. *German Atrocities 1914: A History of Denial*. New Haven: Yale University Press, 2001. A study of the atrocities committed in Belgium and France and their subsequent denial. Admirable detective work.

Hovannisian, Richard G. *The Armenian Genocide in Perspective.* New Brunswick: Transaction Publishers, 1986. Approaches the debate concerning the Armenian massacres in terms of history, psychiatry, religion, and other interpretive modes.

Hukanovic, Rezak. *The Tenth Circle of Hell: A Memoir of Life in the Death Camps of Bosnia.* New York: Basic Books, 1996. Personal testimony of recent inhumanity from the Balkan wars.

Jünger, Ernst. *The Storm of Steel.* New York: Howard Fertig, 1996. The diary of a German storm troop officer on the Western Front, first published in 1919. Disturbing but gripping reading.

Kershaw, Ian. *The "Hitler Myth": Image and Reality in the Third Reich.* New York: Oxford University Press, 1987. Fascinating study of the mechanics and contradictions of the leader cult.

King, David. *The Commissar Vanishes: The Falsification of Photographs and Art in Stalin's Russia.* New York: Metropolitan Books, 1997. Striking illustrated record of retouched and manipulated images. An absolutely amazing series of images.

Klemperer, Victor. *The Language of the Third Reich: lti—Lingua Tertii Imperii: A Philologist's Notebook.* New Brunswick, NJ: Athlone Press, 2000. A stunning dissection of Nazi distortion of the German language, at last available in English translation.

Kotkin, Stephen. *Magnetic Mountain: Stalinism as a Civilization.* Berkeley: University of California Press, 1995. A detailed study of Stalin's city of Magnitogorsk.

Laqueur, Walter. *The New Terrorism: Fanaticism and the Arms of Mass Destruction.* New York: Oxford University Press, 1999. A sober assessment of how terrorism is evolving today.

Levi, Primo. *Survival in Auschwitz: The Nazi Assault on Humanity.* New York: Collier, 1961. Tragic observations from Levi's personal experience on the concentration camp universe constructed by the Nazis to make their racial theories into self-fulfilling prophecies.

Lincoln, W. Bruce. *Red Victory: A History of the Russian Civil War.* New York: Simon and Schuster, 1989. A masterly survey of the entire sweep of Russia's civil war in all its complexity.

Lindqvist, Sven. *"Exterminate the Brutes": One Man's Odyssey into the Heart of Darkness and the Origins of European Genocide.* New

York: New Press, 1996. Impressionistic reflections on connections between imperialism and extermination.

Nisbet, Robert. *History of the Idea of Progress.* New York: Basic Books, 1980. Classic intellectual history of a crucial but ambiguous concept in Western civilization.

Orwell, George. *Homage to Catalonia.* New York: Harcourt, Brace, 1952. A classic text of modern political disillusionment, relating Orwell's experiences in the Spanish Civil War.

Payne, Stanley. *A History of Fascism, 1914–1945.* Madison: University of Wisconsin Press, 1995. A complete survey of Fascism and other authoritarian movements imitating its style and forms by a leading historian of Spain.

Pipes, Richard, ed. *The Unknown Lenin: From the Secret Archive.* New Haven: Yale University Press, 1996. New archival documents reveal Lenin's role and orders.

Proctor, Robert N. *Racial Hygiene: Medicine under the Nazis.* Cambridge, MA: Harvard University Press, 1988. History and prehistory of Nazi eugenics.

Reed, John. *Ten Days That Shook the World.* New York: International Publishers, 1919. An evocative eyewitness account of the October Revolution by an American journalist sympathetic to the Bolsheviks.

Rothstein, Edward, Herbert Muschamp, and Martin E. Marty. *Visions of Utopia.* New York: Oxford University Press, 2003. Collection of three lively essays on the status of utopian thinking.

Rummel, R. J. *Death by Government.* New Brunswick, NJ: Transaction Publishers, 1994. A collection of statistics on the century's toll on human life, chilling in cumulative effect.

Solzhenitsyn, Aleksandr. *One Day in the Life of Ivan Denisovich.* New York: Dutton, 1963. The working day of a denizen of the Gulag presented with the immediacy of the author's own experience.

Wheen, Francis. *Karl Marx: A Life.* New York: Norton, 2000. A new and elegant biography of Marx in accessible form.

Yourcenar, Marguerite. *Coup de Grace.* New York: The Noonday Press, 1981. A 1939 novel about the nihilistic *Freikorps*.

Internet Resources

Illinois State University maintains a Web site devoted to documents concerning recent terrorism and responses to it: http://www.mlb.ilstu.edu/crsres/terrorism/home.htm.

The organization Memorial, headquartered in Russia, seeks to keep alive the memory of Stalin's victims. Its Web site also includes visual materials and texts in English: http://www.memo.ru/eng/index.htm.

To observe an ongoing propaganda exercise with bizarre rhetorical bombast, see the English-language Web site posting North Korean News Agency items: "Korean News. News From KOREAN CENTRAL NEWS AGENCY of DPRK (Democratic People's Republic of Korea)": http://www.kcna.co.jp/.